ISBN 978-1-331-34733-0
PIBN 10177425

CF THE **REIGNS** OF

RICHARD II., HENRY IV., HENRY V., AND HENRY VI.

WRITTEN BEFORE THE YEAR 1471;

WITH

AN APPENDIX,

CONTAINING THE 18TH AND 19TH YEARS OF RICHARD II. AND THE
PARLIAMENT AT BURY ST. EDMUND'S, 25TH HENRY VI.

AND

SUPPLEMENTARY ADDITIONS FROM THE COTTON. MS. CHRONICLE
CALLED "EULOGIUM."

EDITED BY

THE REV. JOHN SILVESTER DAVIES, M.A.

OF PEMBROKE COLLEGE, OXFORD.

PRINTED FOR THE CAMDEN SOCIETY.

M.DCCC.LVI.

LONDON:

J. B. NICHOLS AND SONS, PRINTERS,

PARLIAMENT-STREET.

COUNCIL OF THE CAMDEN SOCIETY

FOR THE YEAR 1855-6.

PREFACE.

THE Early English manuscript Chronicle, from which the following pages are printed, is a version of the English Chronicle called the Brute. Attention was first invited to it through the medium of Notes and Queries, and by the courtesy of William J. Thoms, esq. the editor of that publication, an opinion was obtained from sir Frederick Madden, which resulted in the issue of the present volume by the Camden Society. The manuscript itself is still deposited in a private library, as it has been for more than two hundred years, and therefore cannot be generally accessible.*

Sir Frederick Madden found that the writer of the Chronicle had followed the prose English Chronicle called the Brute, as far as the end of Edward III. without introducing any important variation from the received text, with the exception of a new story relative to bishop Grostete's difference with pope Innocent IV. But from the beginning of the reign of Richard II. the matter was found more valuable; large and curious additions occur, though the text of the Brute remains as before the thread of the narrative. It is this portion of the history which is now for the first time printed.

Sir Frederick Madden discovered in the margins of the manuscript, particularly towards the close, several notes in the hand-writing of Stowe, who has freely used this history in his Annals, though without specifying it. Perhaps, therefore, our manuscript was one of

* It is in the possession of John Speed Davies, esq. the Editor's father, to whom it has descended through the Speeds, from its last user John Speed the chronologer.

those "dangerous books of superstition," the fame of which brought upon Stowe a commission of inquiry in 1568.*

At Stowe's death, in April 1605, his valuable library was dispersed, and the manuscript of the following Chronicle no doubt at that time fell into the hands of John Speed the chronologer, already for some few years known to the literary world, under the patronage of sir Fulk Greville afterwards lord Brooke, fortified too with the friendship of Camden, Cotton, Spelman, and others, his immediate contemporaries, and with the countenance of John Stowe. Speed's Theatre of Great Britain had appeared in 1596; the first edition of his History was issued in 1614.

Speed has used this Chronicle in the earlier part of his History, apparently contented with Stowe's copious extracts in the latter part. Occasionally he has quoted the language, and has also left some marginal notes in his handwriting, as appears by comparing them with " David's harp tuned unto Teares," a manuscript of the historian's, presented, as a note on the fly-leaf states, to his son John Speed the anatomist, of St. John's College, Oxford, on April 19th, 1628.

Unfortunately neither Stowe nor Speed help us to discover who the writer of the Chronicle was, or where it was written. Stowe, while transcribing pages, has never acknowledged his obligation; Speed was ignorant of its history, and quotes it as " Antiq. MS.," " an old MS.," " an ancient MS.," " a namelesse old MS." No internal evidence enables us to assign it to any particular monastery: perhaps the ballad set upon the gates of Canterbury (see p. 91–94) is most like an indication of the locality of the writer.

The date however of this compilation is determined by an expres-

* Life of Stowe, iv. xiv. ; Strype's Stowe's Survey, vol. i.

sion in the text (see p. 99, l. 30), where the writer alludes to
Henry VI. as king, or at least as still alive. This will confine it
between the limits, March 4th, 1461, the accession of Edward IV.
(see p. 110), and May 22nd, 1471, the death of Henry VI.
Henry regained the royal power and assumed the royal style on
Oct. 9th, 1470, and at the battle of Barnet, April 14th, 1471, was
finally driven from the throne.

Much has been lost from the reign of Richard II. The leaves
of the MS. at this part appear to have been designedly cut; but
I have been fortunate enough to discover the source from which the
compiler borrowed the matter he has introduced into the reigns of
Richard II. and Henry IV., and have therefore been able to restore
in the Appendix the greater part of what has been destroyed. The
continuation of the history called Eulogium, Cott. MS. Galba,
E. VII, is the basis of the new matter in the first two reigns of the
English text. From this valuable history our compiler translated
very largely; frequently, it will be seen, changing the arrangement of the history, and occasionally making corrections and
additions. For instance (pp. 16, 17) he has altered the locality of
Richard's resignation, before the duke of Lancaster and archbishop
Arundel, from *Conway* to *Flint;* and (p. 23) has added, in common
with the Brute Chronicles, the fact of the marriage of lord Grey of
Ruthyn with one of the daughters of Owen Glyndwr.

Besides filling up what has been lost from the English text, I
have added sections omitted by the compiler of the Chronicle, on
account of their interrupting the course of the narrative (see Sup-
plem. Add. XVIII. p. 140), with one or two other additions which
appeared interesting. I by no means pretend, however, to have
exhausted all that is useful from this portion of the valuable

Eulogium. I felt that I ought to place a limit on my extracts, and trust I may not even now be thought to have extended this volume to too great a length. Probably this apology may be more needed for the notes, which seemed to accumulate even while I was endeavouring to repress them, and I feel that they do not possess that air of novelty which I could have wished for them. Indeed this volume is offered to the Society with considerable diffidence, yet with the hope that it may not have been a useless labour.

With regard to the history of the Chronicle called the Brute, I cannot do better than refer the reader to an interesting article by sir Frederick Madden on that compilation, which will be found in Notes and Queries, new series, vol. i. p. 1–4. The copy in question begins with the heading, *"How this land was first called Albion, and of whom it hadde that name, and how the geauntez were ygote ye shal here as foloweth afterward.* Capitulum primum. In the yeer fro the begynnyng of the worlde M¹· M¹· M¹· ixc. lxxxx. ther was in the noble lond of Grece a worthi kyng and a my3ti and a man of gret renoun that was callid Dioclician," &c. It may be useful to note its variation from the common text in the first three reigns here published.

The MSS. used for this purpose are the following Oxford MSS. —Bodleian, Rawl. B. 190, 4to. vellum, imperfect at beginning, which is supplied, as a note in his hand states, by the hand of Thomas Baker,* the non-juror, of St. John's College, from a MS. in the public library at Cambridge. The MS. ends in the usual way with the siege of Rouen, " rewle and governaunce," 6 Hen. V. It has been much used by Hearne, who has supplied many leaves

* I am indebted for this information to the Rev. W. D. Macray, M.A. of New College, Oxford.

which had been lost, and we learn from a note at the end of the
volume, that his sources were MSS. Ashmole, 791, 793.

Rawl. B. 173, small folio, vellum. Heading illegible. Text
begins, "In the noble londe of Surre ther was a noble kynge of
myght," &c. This Chronicle goes down to the Armagnac alliance
with England, 13 Hen. IV. and resumes after the marriage of
Henry V., giving an account of the coronation banquet, rather different from that of Fabyan. After the death of Henry V. follows a
list of mayors and sheriffs for a few years in Henry VI.

Rawl. B. 196, folio, paper. Heading, "*Here may a man here
how Engelonde was first called Albyone, and afterwarde whanne hit
had first name*" (*sic.*) "In the noble lond of Surrye," &c. It ends
"rewle and governaunce," 6 Hen. V.

Rawl. B. 216, folio, vellum, in double columns. Imperfect in
the beginning: immediately after "rewle and governaunce,"
6 Hen. V., follows, "And aftir this folowith the appointmentȝ,
treteȝ, and accordementȝ of pees perpetuelle bytwene kyng Charles
... and Henry V.... and of the marriage of Katerine the doughter
of the said kyng Charles, in manner and forme," &c., occupying
two leaves and one column. In the same volume, by the same
scribe, is "the bocke of Johan Maundeville, knyght, (which)
techith the weyes to Jerusalem," &c.

Rawl. B. 205, folio, vellum. Heading, "*Here men may hiren
how Englonde first was called Albione, and thrughe whome it hadde the
name.*" ' In the noble lande of Sirrie ther was a noble kyng and
myghti, and a man of gret renoun," &c. It ends with the "great
parliament," 21 Ric. II. Hearne considered this a good MS.; on
the fly-leaf he has written, "See MS. Ashmole 791, but chiefly 793."

Ashmole MS. 793, folio, paper and vellum. "Here begynnethe

a booke in Englishe tong, callid Brute of Englond, or the Cronycles of Englond, compilyng and tretyng of the seid land." "*How it was firste a wildrenesse, and alle for lette, and no thyng therynne, but wylde bestes and fowles.*" It ends at the siege of Rouen (6 Hen. V.), with the words, " and atte every gate ij. or iij. M^{l.} of goode mennys bodies armed : and manfully countred withe our Englishe men. Heere endethe the Booke of Cronycules."

Ashmole, 791, vellum and paper, imperfect at beginning and end. It ends with the death of James I. of Scotland (1436), with the words "a legate of the poopys beynge that tyme in Scotteland, as it was seyde, bare the kyngys scherte wyth hym, and schewed it to the poope." The reigns of Richard II. and Henry IV. are very meagre in this copy. A note on the first page of this Chronicle attributes it to William de Regibus.

The new matter of the present volume will be found to be the following sections :—

P. 1, l. 12, " And they," *to* p. 3, l. 22, " was gouerned." P. 4, l. 20, " be counsel," *to* p. 5, l. 20, " hoom agayne." L. 31, " And this parlement," *to* p. 6, l. 18, " take vp and brent." P. 7, l. 12, " also relece," *to* l. 25, " to silence." P. 8, l. 10, " The archebisshop," *to* l. 13, " deliuerid." L. 18, " so evir," *to* last line, " executid it not." P. 10, l. 3, " I have do," *to* l. 22, " evirmore." P. 11, l. 11, " Thanne the king," *to* p. 12, l. 2, " Cauntirbury." L. 12, " Ferthirmore," *to* last line, " so they dede." P. 13, l. 31, " and therto thay," *to* p. 14, l. 29, " that saw it." P. 16, l. 1, " and saide," *to* p. 17, l. 2, " ynoughe." L. 6, "And aftirward," *to* p. 18, last line, " comyng," &c. P. 19, l. 9, " and was anoynted," *to* l. 13, " king Richarde." L. 15, " and deliuerid," *to* l. 19, " parlement." " L. 21, " and made sir Roger," *to* p. 20, l. 2, " not void." L. 11, "The kyng also," to l. 26, "Reigate." L. 29, "And on of," to p. 21, l. 2, "money." L. 11, "and meny," to l. 13, "housej." L. 25, "Whanne kyng Richard," to l. 26, "his counsel." P. 22, l. 9, "breek the trewej," to l. 20, "be him." L. 22, "broughte," to l. 25, "ayen." P. 23, l. 12, "Also a womman," to l. 16, "the mater." L. 21, "And about this tyme," to p. 29, l. 24, "he was alive." P. 31, l. 11, "And the cause," to p. 34, l. 2, "was cesid." P. 35, l. 1, "And this," to l. 9, "mensoun," &c. P. 36, l. 14, "And this same," to l. 17, "newe thyngis." P. 37, l. 16, "This same yeer," to l. 24, "vnclej wiff." L. 27, "And this same yeer," to last line "in no wise."

Thus far our compiler has drawn from the Eulogium: deviations under Henry V. are,—

P. 43, l. 4, "And whilis," to l. 26, "our lady." P. 44, l. 6, "And anon aftir, to l. 18, "Vernulle." P. 46, l. 4, "And this same tyme," to l. 5, "manne."

The whole of the reign of Henry VI. is quite different from that in the printed text of Caxton, though agreeing in *matter* as far as page 78, with the exception of the following variations:—P. 54, l. 28, "And this," to last line, "peple." P. 56, l. 25, "And among," to p. 60, l. 25, "not longe aftir." The particulars on p. 61. P. 64, l. 1, "And this," to l. 22, "it was said." P. 70, l. 21, "whoos godfadres," to l. 25, "baptized." Last line, "The xxxiij yere," to p. 77, l. 8, "he dyed." P. 78, l. 7, "One of the causes," to l. 25, "for theyme." From the last line of this page to the end, it is an exception when there is any agreement in matter between the two chronicles.

The Eulogium is the larger of two chronicles which fill a folio volume, on vellum, of 206 leaves, which has been partially injured

by the fire of 1731. The shorter chronicle embraces from the Nativity
of our Lord to the year 1364, ending with the colophon, " Corpus
scribentis benedicat lingua legentis." It commences on the 4th
leaf, and is preceded by an alphabetical table of contents or index
to the Eulogium. That history begins on the 16th leaf with an
interesting introduction, in which the writer apologises for his want
of learning,* and pleads that the persuasion of the prior of his
house not less prevailed in inducing him to undertake the historian's
labour than did his own wishes.† He has divided his work into
five books. I. From the Creation of the World to the Ascension of
our Lord. II. The preaching of the Apostles, deaths of Martyrs,
Assumption of the Virgin, the Roman Popes, &c. III. First habi-
tation of Italy; building of Rome; history of the Emperors, Pagan
and Christian. IV. The Geography of the World, showing what
parts are habitable and what not, provinces, seas, rivers, &c.,
especially the geography of Britain. V. A Chronicle from Brute
to A.D. 1362,‡ continued to A.D. 1413. The author himself gave
his work the title of Eulogium.§

It may be inferred that the writer of our English Chronicle was
of the same monastery as the authors of the Eulogium, since at

* Occupatio infructuosa me multa scire impedit.

† Rogatus enim pluries a Priore meo Claustrali quod de gestis antiquorum, de partibus
propinquis ac remotis, de mirabilibus, de bellis, de gestis antiquis Christianorum et paga-
norum, modo chronico, aliquid actitarem, ita ut tetra otia, omninò infructuosa, leviùs
evacuarem.

‡ "Terminatum est hoc opusculum in anno Domini 1362, sub rege Edwardo a Con-
questu tertio." By a misreading of the figures this Chronicle has been described as ending
in 1367 in a MS. note on the fly-leaf, and the mistake has been frequently copied. No
change in the hand occurs till 1364, where the writer who finished the volume commences.

§ Quia ex laboribus antiquorum aliqua paucula medullata extraxi, hoc libellum conglo-
batum Eulogium volo nominari. Non enim sine causâ Eulogium illud assero, quia stu-
dentibus et orantibus maximam præstabit recreationem cum voluerint a labore quiescere.

the time of the compilation of the English text that history probably had not travelled beyond its convent walls. It never appears to have been multiplied, as only two copies are known to exist, that in the Cottonian collection, and another in the library of Trinity College, Cambridge. (R. vii. 2.)

A controversy exists, however, as to the locality of the Eulogium. Leland in his Collectanea (vol. i. pt. ii. p. 302-314), at the head of several extracts from it, some of which the reader will recognise, has placed the following heading: " Ex altero chronico *Maildulphesbiriensis* monasterii, cui titulus Eulogium historiarum, autore monacho ejusdem loci, sed incerti nominis." Leland conveys a false impression when he adds, " ex prologo apparet scriptum fuisse hoc chronicon, flagitante Priore *Maildulphesbiriensi*." No house is mentioned. He is also wrong in the date, " Terminatum est hoc opusculum, anno Domini, 1361 ;" but has given the right date (1362) in his second volume. Leland, it appears from the heading to his second body of extracts (vol. ii. pt. i. p. 395-398), judged only from certain internal evidence—" quibusdam *conjecturis* ducor." These conjectures were no doubt founded on the fact that there is much relating to the foundation of Malmesbury abbey in the second book, and several notices of that abbey are dispersed throughout the work. Bishop Tanner has followed Leland in opposition to the Cottonian Catalogue. In that catalogue the work is attributed to Ninian, a monk of Canterbury, on the authority of the writer of a long note, opposite the introduction to the Eulogium, who has made this statement from Caius, "De antiquitate Cantabrigiensis Academiæ," 1568 ;*

* P. 67 : "*Ninianus* quoque in Eulogio Historiarum has easdem urbes recenset ; et *Nennius* in catalogo urbium." P. 273 : " Eulogii enim libro quinto (quem monachus *Cantuariensis*, non Maildunensis, ut Lelandus ait, scripsit), ubi de Arvirago sermo est, sic scribitur, " Vespasianus mare sulcans," &c. (Comp. Eul. f. 127.)

adding, as another argument for the locality of Canterbury, that the author calls saint Thomas the archbishop his patron.*

Mr. Macray has suggested that this work may have been confounded with *Nennius's* Eulogium Britanniæ. This appears to have been the case with the writer of the note alluded to, who refers us in Bale to Nennius, the old British writer, or to Ninian, the apostle to the Picts.† But Caius does not appear to have been so misled, and in his list of writers has astonished the writer of the note by quoting " *Nennii, Elwodugi discipuli, Eulogium,*" " Ninianus," and " *Eulogium historiarum,*" as different works. It does not appear why he has separated the two last.

The Cottonian copy of the Eulogium formerly belonged to Dr. Dee, the philosopher of Mortlake, as his note on the first page of the index states: " Jões Dee, 1574; September 25. Of the gift of Mr. Dyckenson at Popular by Mr. John Stow the cronicler   (three words illegible) Lōdon." From the Diary of Dr. Dee, and Catalogue of his library, published by the Camden Society in 1842, we find among his books, " Eulogium temporis a condito orbe in annum Christi 1367,‡ monachi cujusdam Niniani . . . . pergamento, fo." Dr. Dee therefore agreed in the opinion of Caius on the authorship of this book.

Such is the controversy. It is much to be regretted that we are not able to assign this English Chronicle either to Canterbury or to Malmesbury with any certainty.

---

* " Inter cetera mirabilia, unum licet enarrare de sancto Thomâ meo patrono Cantuar. Metropol., accidit enim ipso exulante primo exilii sui anno." (Compare also p. 14 of this volume.)

† " Pro his Nenniis et Ninianis vide Bale, De Scriptoribus Angliæ, centur. 14, fol. 192; centur. 10, fol. 27; centur. 1, fol. 60, et 72, et 14."

‡ See note on page xii.

The reader is indebted, with me, to sir Frederic Madden, for the two interesting chapters which are placed at the commencement of the Appendix (p. 111-118). The chapter on the death of the duke of Gloucester appears to be especially valuable. I extract the following remarks from sir Frederick Madden's description of the MS. from which the transcripts are taken:—

The Manuscript is a folio on vellum and paper, in the library of the duke of Bedford at Woburn, and was written in 1448 by Richard Fox, of St. Alban's, as appears by a note on the 5th leaf from the end, and the name in several other places. It begins with a table of contents filling 6 folios, at the end of which are the names of the kings of England from William the Conqueror to Henry VI. in three hexameter lines. Immediately below which the name of the writer occurs.

On folio 7 the Chronicle commences thus : " *Alfrede was the fyrst kynge that euer was anoynt in this londe.* After Elfrede regned his brother Alfryde, a noble man and wyse," &c. The manuscript proceeds regularly through the series of kings, compiled from several authorities, until the end of the reign of Edward I. This part is totally different from the Brute, and much fuller, particularly after the Conquest; but from the accession of Edward II. until the close (6 Hen. V.), it is the same as the Brute, yet occasionally has passages not in the common copies; as, for instance, the account of the 18th and 19th years of Richard II. (See Appendix, p. 111-115.) The Chronicle ends like the usual version of the Brute, " restede hym in the castelle tyl the towne was sette in rewle and governaunce." (6 Hen. V.)

After this follow the deposition articles of Richard II. and the coronation of Henry IV., chiefly translated from the Rolls of Parlia-

ment, but containing additions of great interest. At the end is
written, " And thus enduth the Deposynge of kyng Richarde the
secounde aftre the Conqueste.

Quod Rychard Fox

Off seynt Albones.

Anᵒ Dn̄i M¹ cccc xl. viijo."

Next comes the interesting tract relative to the death of the duke
of Gloucester. (See Appendix, p. 116-118.) Then the Acts of the
parliament at Winchester (27 Hen. VI.), five lines of verse on the
deposing of Richard II., and some orders of the common council of
London relative to the fellowship of cooks and butlers, about fees
and customs at the lord mayor's feast.

The nature of my obligation to sir Frederick Madden I have
already stated, and I desire to offer him my thanks.   I am indebted
also to John Gough Nichols, Esq. for some kind suggestions while
the work was at press, owing to which it is more perfect than it
would have been; and to my friend the Rev. William Dunn Macray,
M.A. of New College, Oxford, and of the Bodleian Library, for the
kind assistance he has often given, and always been ready to give
me; and for having compared the pages of the Chronicle as they
passed through the press with the manuscript, by which revision
some mistakes were avoided.

April, 1856.

REIGNS OF RICHARD II., HENRY IV., HENRY V., AND HENRY VI.

RICHARD II.

Of Kyng Richard the secunde aftir the Conquest, the sone of Prince Capitulum cxlij.
Edwarde; and of the risyng tyme; and of meny othir notable Folio 145 b.
thyngis.

AFTIR King Edward the iij^{de}, that was bore at Wyndesore,   A. D. 1377.
regned Richard the secunde, the sone of prince Edwarde, that [Reign began June 22nd.]
was bore at Burdeux, and crouned at Westmynstre in the xj. yeer
of his age.

And the ij^{de} yeer of his regne began a debaat betuene the lord   Anno ij.
Latymer and ser Raaff fferers knyghte, and Johan Hawle and
Richard Shakele squyers, for the erl of Dene, that was take prisoner
in the bataille of Spayne,* be the said squiers; the whiche prisoner
the lord Latymer and the said ser Raaf wolde haue had. And thay
of Spayne sente to the king for delyueraunce of the said erl; but the

---

* The battle of Navaretta, fought between Najarra and Navaretta, in which Peter the
Cruel, aided by the Black Prince, obtained a victory over his brother Henry and the
French, and regained the Crown of Castile, A. D. 1367. The Earl of Denia, in Valen-
cia, was among the prisoners.

CAMD. SOC.   B

ij. squiers dredyng* that thay sholde lese the raunsoun of thair
prisoner, and wolde not brynge him forth atte kyngis commaundement. Wherfore the kyng was wroth, and saide that thay hadde
maad a prison in thair owen house withynne his reme ayens his
wille and commaundement: and therfore he sente thaym to the tour
of Londoun; and thay brak out therof and fledde to Westmynstre.
And the constable of the tour and the said lord Latymer and ser
Raaff fferrers wente to Westmynstre, and wolde haue brought
thaym agayne, but thay made defens, and Hawle was slayn in the
chirche atte gospel of the high masse, and anon the monke3 cesid of
diuine serui3e; and meny sundaie3 aftirward, the said persone3
were denounced acursid, as brekers and defoulers of thair privilegis;
and wolde not halow ne reconsile agayn thair chirche. The king
sente meny tyme3 be his writtes to the Abbot of Westmynstre, forto
appere befor him, and forto cece of his cursyng, and that he sholde
halowe agayn his chirche, and serve God therynne aftir the fundacion
therof, and alle the mater sholde be bro3t to a good ende. But the
abbot wolde not appere, ne cece of the castyng of the cen-
suris of the chirche, for he saide that the chirche of Westmynstre was
halowed be saint Petir be myrakille, and therfore it nedid not to be
halowed of non othir manne, and shewde and broughte forth the cro-
nicle how saint Petir halowed it, as folowethe . . . .

* * * *

endowed with meny possessiouns and privilegis. And whanne the
tyme was come that the chirche sholde be halowed, and alle thyng
was redy that was necessary to the solennite therof, Mellit, Bisshop
of Londoun, lay in his tentis the ny3t before the dedicacioun, and
there was greet concours and multitude of peple, not onli for deuo-
cion but also forto se the newe and unkid solennite. And the same
nyghte, on the ferthir side of the Thamyse, saint Petir, in liknesse
and in the habit of a pilgryme apperid to a fissher, and behighte

---

* See note at the end of the volume.

him for his trauail, to sette him ouer the watir ; and whanne he was come ouer, he wente into the chirche, and anon sodenli the chirche was ful of heuenli lighte that made the nyghte as light and as cleer as the day. And with saint Petir . . . . .

* * * *

Reme, and paide for hir xxij. m^l marc. Ther was offrid vuto him the erlis dou3ter of fflaundris, with whom he sholde haue had alle fflaundris, but he refusid hir, and aftirward the duke of Burgoyne weddid hir, and be hir he was erl of fflaundris.

The vij. yeer of king Richard, the ffrenshemen and the Scottis were confederid to gedir, and ordeyned iij. grete ostis forto haue come in to Engelond, and the Scottis sholde haue come yn in the north, and the other ij. ostis in the est and west partie3. The king heryng this, be avise of his counsel, gadrid an huge ost and wente in to Scotland; but the Scottis durste not fi3te with him, his power was so greet : the othir ij. ostis of the Frenshemenne cam not, for thay lay longe tyme in the hauene of Scluys, abidyng wynd and wedir, but the wynde wolde nevir serue thaym but alwey was ayens thayme. Thanne the king brende the toun of Edinburgh, and cam in to Englond ayenne.

And this same tyme, king Richard made the erlle of Oxenforde and ser Michael de la Pole, and othir flaterers, chief of his counsel ; and be thaym was gouerned.

The viij. yeer of King Richard, ser Edmund of Langley, erl of Cambrigge, the kingis uncle, wente in to Portugale, with a faire companie of menne of arme3 and archiers, to helpe and strengthe the king of Portugale ayens the king of Spayne ; and there the king of Portugale badde the victory, thorough help of Englishmenne ; and aftir this journey the erl cam hoom agayne.

This same yeer king Richarde held his Cristemasse at Eltham ; and thider cam to him the king of Ermonie,* that was drive out of

---

* Leo, King of Armenia.—See note.

A.D. 1384-5. his lond be the Turkis, to axe of him help and socour: and the kinge yaf him grete yiftis, and so he retourned hoom ayeene.

Anno ix°. The ix. yeer of king Richard, he held a parlement at West-mynstre, and there he made ij. dukis, a markeys, and v. erlis. Ffirst, he made ser Edmund of Langley, erl of Cambrige, his vncle, duke of York ; and his othir vncle, ser Thomas of Wodestoke, that was erl of Bukynghame, he made duke of Gloucestre; and the erlle of Oxenforde he made markeys of Dyuelyn, and commaunded that he sholde be callid duke of Yrlonde; ser Harri of Bolyngbroke, the dukeȝ sone of Lancastre, he made erl of Derby; ser Edward, the dukis sone of York, he made erl of Roteland; ser John Holond, the erlis brothir of Kent, he made erl of Huntyngdoun; ser Thomas Mowbray, erl of Notyngham, he made erl marchal of Engelond ; and ser Michael de la Pole, knyghte, he made erl of Suffolk and Chaun-celler of Engelonde.

And at this same parlement, the erl of March, in the playn parlement among alle the lordis and comuneȝ, was proclamed heir parent, and next to the croune aftir king Richard: the which erl sone aftir was slayn in Yrlond with the wilde Yrishmenne . . . .

Fragment B.
[Anno xj°] be counsel of a Burgeis of Londoun, cam to Westmynstre, wenyng to haue discomfited thaym with helpe of men of Londoun. The Archebisshop of Canterbury besoughte the king that he wolde admitte thaym to his presence pesibly, withoute eny greuaunce, for to trete of peeȝ, and the kyng it graunted vnder his feith, and so the archebis-shoppe wente and broughte thaym befor the king, sitting in West-mynstre halle, and thair ost abood withoute. Thanne saide the kyng, " Who made you so hardy forto arise and arme you ayens the pees of me, and of my reme?" The duke of Glovcestre

*   *   *   *

A. b. same place forto refourme peeȝ betuene thaym, and the kyng it

grauntid. But in the morow, he chaunged his purpos, and wente to A.D. 1387-8.
the tour of Londoun : and the lordis cam with thair power in to
saint Johannes feld, ar d sente for the mair of Londoun, and he ladde
thaym in to Guyldehalle, and alle the Cite was vnto thaym frendly
and wellwil id. Thamme sente the kyng for the lordis to come and
speke with him in the tour, and thay saide the place was not sure, (
but out of the tour thay were redy to speke withe him. Tho
comaunded the kyng the mair of Londoun, forto reise and arme the Folio 147.
Cite agayns thayme. " Sire," saide the mair, " God it forbede! thay
bith your trew lige men, and frendis to the reme." The kyng was
wrothe, and sente the duke of Yrlond with his lettris patenti3, and
with his baner displaid, in to Chestreshire, forto brynge a power of
Chesshiremen and othir. And the v. lordis beforsaide mette with
him beside Oxenforde, with the kyngi3 baner displaid ; and anon as
the duke wiste what thay were, he fledde, and rood ouer the
Thamyse in to the yle of Shepeye, and fro thenne3 he wente ouer se
in to Almayne, and nevir cam agayne. And the lordis beheddid the ,
chief knygat that was with the duke, and took fro thayme the kynge3
baner, and folde it gedir, and bettyn the Chesshiremen, and droof
thaym hoom agayne, and seue   .   .   .   .   .
maister Alisaunder Nevile, Archebisshoppe of York, fledde also ouer ,
se, as befor ys saide, and cam neuer agayne.

Thanne thise v. lordis ordeyned a parlement at Westmynstre ;
and there, ser Robert Tresilian, a justice ; Nicholl Brembre, knyghte
and cite3evn of Londoun ; ser Johan Salisbury, a knyghte of the
kynge3 hous ; and ser Simon of Beverley, a worthi knyghte of the
garter, for whom the queue knelid befor the v. lordis to haue saued
his lif, but she myght not be herd ; ser John Beauchampe, kny3t,
stiward of the kyngis hous ; ser Jame3 Berners, and othir, were Folio 147 b.
iugid to be drawe and hanged : and ser Simon of Beuerley was beheddid atte Tour hil. And this parlement endurid fro Candelmasse
to midsomer.

And tho v. lordis were quyt before the justice3 of alle thyng that

A.D. 1387.8. was put ayens thaym, and made a lawe and an ordenaunce, that yf /
the parlement appelid or enpechid eny man of eny cryme, he sholde
be dampned withoute ansuer, for with the parlement he my3te not
fi3te ; and made the parlement appele meny men of meny thyngis
that thay were not gilti of, and exilid for euermore the forsaid duke ⟩
of Yrlond, ser Michael de la Pole, and maister Alisaunder Nevile, ⟩
archbishop of York, and dyvers othir. And thay made alle men of
the parlement swere to obserue and kepe alle the ordenaunce3 and
statutis that were ymaad in the saide parlement ; and made also
the kyng swere agayne forto kepe his lawe3, and that he shold
folowe the counsel of his trewe lorde3, and not of suche flaterers as
were aboute him; and that he sholde nevir hurte ne enpeche eny of
thaym for that thay hadde do in the said parlement; and of this   ⟍
the kyng, though he baar it hevili, graunted unto thaym a chartre
of pardoun.

Fragment C.   And this yeer deide maister John Wiclif, and was buried at
Lutterworthe, where he was parsoun ; but aftirward, be sentence of
the chirche, his bones were take vp and brent.

Anno xij°.   The xij. yeer of king Richard, duryng this same parlement, he
leet crie and ordeyne general justis at Londoun, in Smythfeld, for
alle maner straungers, and othir that thider wolde come: and thay
of the kyngis side were alle in on sute, thair cotearmuri3, sheldis,
hors-trappuris, and alle, was white bertis, with cronne3 aboute
thair neckis, and cheynes of gold hangyng ther upon, and the cronne
hangyng lowe befor the hertis bodye, the whiche hert was the kyngis
liverey, that he gaf to knyghtis and squiers and othir.

And atte firste comyng to thair justis, xxiiij. ladie3 ladde xxiiij.
kny3tis of the gartir, with cheyne3 of gold, and alle in the same
sute her (sic) of bertis as before is said, fro the tour of Londoun,
on horsbak, thorou3 the cite of Londoun in to Smythfeld . . . .

        *   *   *   *

C. b
[Anno xiv°.]   thorough alle Spayne, that the duke badde sente in to Engelond for
a grettir ost ; and the kyng of Spayne wenyng it hadde be trewe,

and began to trete with the duke, and so thay were acordid in this manere: that the king of Spayne sholde wedde the eldir doughtir of the duke of Lancastre, that was righte heir to Spayne, and sholde yeue unto the duke an huge summe of money in hand, and euery yeer aftir, duryng the livis of the duke and of the duchesse his wif, x mˡ marc. of gold, the whiche gold thay of Spayne, atte thair owen auenture and cost, sholde brynge yeerli vnto Baione, to the dukeȝ assigneeȝ: and herof the king of Spayne made to the duke good surete.

And the same tyme the duke maried anothir of his douȝtris to the kyng of Portugale. And in that viage me . . . .

*　　　　*　　　　*

also relece the remenaunt of kyng Johannes raunsoun that was unpaied; and the duke said, forto bere the armes of Ffraunce it was non availle ne profit, and Caleis greued more Engelond and dede more hurt therto than profit, for the grete expensis aboute the keping therof; but the duke of Gloucestre and the erlis of Warwic and of Arundelle garnsaide it, and wolde not assente therto.

In this parlement, the duke of Lancastre axed and desirid that his sone shold be the parlement haue be declarid and demyd as next heir to the crovne; but the erl of March withsaide it, and saide, he was come of ser Leonel the secunde sone of king Edward: and the duke saide, that kyng Harri the iijᵈᵉ. badde ij. soneȝ, Edmund and Edward, the whiche Edmund hadde a crokid bak and was a mys-shape and an vnlik

*　　　　*

thaym to silence.

The xv. yeer of king Richard, he held his Cristemasse in the maner of Wodestoke; and there the erlle of Penbroke, a yong lord and tendir of age, wolde haue lerned to juste with a knyghte callid ser John Saint Johan, and thay riden togedir in the park of Wodestoke, and there the erl of Penbroke was slayn with that

A.). 1391-2.   othir knyghtis speer, as he cast it from him whanne thay hadde coupid.

Anno xvj°   The xvj. yeer of king Richard, Johan Hende, beyng that tyme mair of Londoun, and John Walworth and Harri Vanner shirevis of Londoun that same year, a bakeris man of Londoun baar a basket ful of horsbred in to ffleetstrete toward an ostrie hous, and there cam a yoman of the bisshoppis of Salesbury, callid Romayn, and took an horsloof out of the basket; and the baker axed him whi he dede so, and this

Fragment E.   The Archebisshop abood there vnto nyghte, wenyng to haue had
[Anno xx°.]   delyueraunce agayn of his brothir, and whanne he saw it wolde not be, he wente hoom vnto Lambhithe fule of sorou.   And on the morow the king deliuerid the said erlle of Arundelle to on that was his enemy, and he put him in prison in the yle of Wyghte, and anon alle the erlis godis were eschetid in to the kyngis hand.

The king also arested the erlle of Warwic in his owen court, and sente him to the tour of Londoun.

And anon aftir the king rood with an huge company in to Essex, to Plasshe, where the duke of Gloucestre lay; and to him he saide, " Thou wilt not come to me, and therfor I come to the, and I areste

Dux Glouces- the."   The duke answerde to the king, and saide, " Sire, I truste
triæ captus est.   your grace and that . . . . . .

        *   *   *   *

E. b.   ffrensshemenne forto helpe him, and thay cam ridyng thorouȝ the reme with thair speirs bore uprighte.   And thanne the king sente to eueri bisshope, abbotis, gentilmen, and marchauntis, and vnder colour of borowyng he badde of thaym an huge summe of money neuer to be paid agayne; so that a symple gentilman paide xl. ti.

Thanne the erl of Rutland, the erl of Huntingdoun, the erl of Salisbury, the erl of Notynghame, and othir, appelid the duke of

Gloucestre, the erl of Arundell, and the erlle of Warwic of treson A.D. 1396-7. doon ayens the king the x. and xj. yeer of his regne, and the kyng sente a justice to the said duke of Gloucestre, forto axe and enquire of him, how he wolde excuse him of such thyngis and appelis as were put and laid ayens him ; and the duke wroot

*   *

In the xxj. yeer of king Richard, he ordeyned and held a parle- A.D. 1397-8. ment at Westmynstre, that was callid the grete parlement, and this Ca^m. clxv. parlement was maad onli forto sle the erlle of Arundelle and othir, Fragment F. as thaym likid at that tyme.   And for thair jugement, the kyng leet Anno xxj° make a long and large hous of tymber in the paleis at Westmynstre, that was callid an Hale; couered with tiles, and open on bothe sides and atte endis, that alle men myghte se thorough ; and the king commaundid eueri lord, knyghte, and squier, forto bryng with thaym thair retenues, and come to the parlement as strong as thay myghte. And the king him self sente in to Chestreshire for a gret multitude of yomenn and archiers, and thaym he held in his hous, and thaym most loued and cherisshed aboue alle othir, the whiche

*   *   *   *

so evir procurid, and orlabourid (*sic*), to the graunt of eny suche com· F. b. missioun, he sholde be holde for a traitour.   Also he reuoked alle the statutis that were maad in the parlement holden the x. and xj. yeer of his regne, and also alle the chartris of pardoun, and nameli the pardoun that he grauntid frely to the erlle of Arundelle ; for, as he saide, that was grauntid in preiudice of him and of his cronne. Also atte supplicacion of the parlement, he pardoned to the erlle of Derby and the erlle of Notynghame the ridyng that thay rood with the duke of Gloucestre ayens the duke of Yrlond ; and thay put thaym in the kingis grace : and also he pardoned thaym that were put in the commission before rehersid, and executid it not.   And

*   *   *

I haue do eny thing amys, I haue therof the kingis pardon." "That pardon," saide the duke, " is reuoked be the parlement, for it was grauntid whanne thou were kyng." The erl saide, " Yf that pardon may not serue, I haue anothir pardoun that the king grauntid me frely v. yeer gone of his owen mocioun." " And that pardoun," saide the duke, " is also reuoked be ordenaunce of the parlement." " fforsoth," saide the erl, " the king may be his prerogatif graunte his chartre of pardoun to whom it likith him, for alle maner of trespas ; and yf ye haue ordeyned that he may not or shal not do so, ye haue do more ayens his prerogatif thanne evir dede I ; and yf thou, John duke of Lancastre, were wel examned, thou hast do more ayens the kyng than I." Thanne the erlle was counselid to put him in the kyngis grace, and he saide, " I put me in the grace of the high kyng of heuene, and for the lawez and comune profit of Englond I am redy to dye." And anon the duke yaf on him iugement and saide, " The kyng pardoneth the thy drawyng and hankyng, but thyn hed shalle be smyte of atte tourhille, in the same place where ser Simon of Beuerley was beheddid, and thi childryn shall be disheritid, and excludid fro the parlement and the kyngis counsel for evirmore."

Thanne on Saint Matthewez day, apostel and euangelist, the erl was lad fro the place of his jugement, and his handis bounde behynde him, thorough the cite of Londoun unto the Tourhille, and there his hed was smyte of. And vj. of the lordis that sat on his iugement, riden with him with greete strengthe of men of armes and archiers to se thexecucion done aftir thair jugement, for thay dradde that the erl sholde haue be rescued be thaym of Londoun : and thus deide the gode erl and is buried atte ffrere Austynes, in Londoun.

And on the morow ser Richard erl of Warwic was broughte in

to the parlement, in to the saide hale, and badde the same iugement A.D. 1397. as the erl of Arundel badde, and, as his counsel bad him, he confessid and saide, that alle that he hadde do, he dede be the counsel and stiryng of the duke of Gloucestre and of the erl of Arundelle, trustyng also in the holynes and wisdoum of the Abbot of Saint Albonez, and of the Recluse of Westmynstre, that saide it was lawfulle that he dede, " notwithstondyng," he saide, " if I haue do amys, I put me in the kyngis grace;" and so be instaunce of lordis, because he was of gret age his deth was relesid, and was dampned to perpetuel prison in the Yle of Mann.

Thanne the king made thaym of the parlement forto acuse maister Thomas Arundelle, archebisshoppe of Cauntirbury, because he procurid and labourid forto be in the forsaid commissioun, and it excutid and selid whanne he was chauncellere ; and the speker of the parlement began to purpose ayens him, and the king bad him holde Folio 149. his peez and say no more ayens his cosin, and bad the Archebisshope go his way safli. And whanne he was go the kyng sente to him a messager and commaunded him come no more in the parlement, Nota duplici- and thanne he was exilid for euer, and that he sholde be privid of tatem Regis
Ricardi. alle his godis .

And the Monday next aftir, the lord Cobhame of Kent, and ser Johan Cheyne, knyztis, were brought in to the parlement in to the same hale, and there thay were iugid to be drawe and hangid, but thoroughe praier and instaunce of the lordis, thair iugement was foryeue thaym and relesid to perpetuel prisoun.

Thanne said the Archebisshoppe Arundelle, " I wille not go out of this lond, here I was bore, and here I wille die." The king and the duke of Lancastre wente to him, and the king saide unto him in this wise, "Fader, be not sory for to go out of this lond, for I ensure you be my trouthe, that ye shal come agayn withynne short tyme, and ther shal be non othir Archebisshoppe of Cauntirbury whilez ye and I live." Thanne the Archebisshoppe took his leve, and on Mighelmasse eve at Donor he wente ouer se to Rome.

A D. 1397-8.

And whanne he was go, the king made ser **Rogere Walden, a** clerck of his owen, archebisshoppe of Cauntirbury. And he made also at this parlement v. dukeȝ, a markeis, and iiij. erlis. First, he made the erl of Derby, sir Henri of Bolyngbroke, duke of Hereforde; the erlle of Rutland he made duke of Avmarle; the erlle of Kent

Folio 149 b.

he made duke of Surreie; the erl of Huntyngdoun he made duke of Excestre; the erl of Notyngham he made duke of Norfolk; the erl of Somerset he made markeis of Dorset; the lord Spenser he made erlle of Glovcestre; the lord Nevile of Raby he made erl of Westmerland; ser Thomas Percy he made erlle of Worcestre; and ser William Scroope he made erl of Wilshire and Tresourer of England. fferthirmore the kyng made alle the men of this parlement coumpromitte in to xij. diners personeȝ, continuyng the said parlement, that where and whanne it likid thayme thay'myghte make statutis aftir thair owen ordenaunce; and made alle the lordis swere vpon saint Edwardis shryne, forto kepe with al thair myghte the statutis of the same parlement; and atte request of the parlement, alle the Bisshoppis acursid at Poulis cros alle tho that dede ayens the said statutis and ordenaunces. And whanne this was ydo, the kyng wente in to the west cuntre.

Aftir this, the kyng in solenne daieȝ and grete festis, in the whiche he wered his croune and wente in his rial aray, he leet ordeyne and make in his chambir, a trone, wherynne he was wont to sitte fro aftir mete vnto euensong tyme, spekynge to no man, but ouerlokyng alle menn; and yf he loked on eny mann, what astat or degre that evir he were of, he moste knele.

Folio 150.
Nota auariciam
Regis Ricardi.

Aftirward, at Notyngham, the kyng callid his counsel togedir, and saide, that he myghte not ride sureli in his Reme, for drede of men of Londoun, and of xvij. shiris lyying aboute; and therfore he wolde gadre a greet ost forto destroie thaym, lasse than thay wolde fynde him surete. Wherfore thay ordeyned, that Londoun and euerich of tho shiris sholde gadre a gret summe of moneye, and in token of peeȝ yeue it to the kyng; and so thay dede.

And this same yer fille a greet debaat and dissension, betuene the duke of Hereford and the duke of Norfolk, in this wise. The duke of Norfolk tolde priueli, as it hadde be vnder confessioun, and in gret counsel, to the duke of Hereforde, that the kyng hadde ordeyned to sle thaym bothe, because thay rood and aroos vith the duke of Gloucestre. The duke of Hereforde saide, "The king hath therof grauntid vs his pardoun." Thenne saide the duke of Norfolk, "The kyng is not trewe, as it hath wel apperid be the duke of Gloucestre and the erl of Arundel." The duke of Hereforde aftirward tolde this to his fader, the duke of Lancastre, and he tolde it to the king. And whanne the kyng examned the duke of Norfolk therof, he denyed it and forsook it ; and the duke of Hereford avowed it befor him, and him appelid of treson and of the deth of the duke of Gloucestre. Wherfore thay cast thair glovis and wagid bataille, and the day of thair bataille was assigned at Couentre ; at whiche day the kyng withe his lordis was there present ; and whanne bothe the dukis were redy in the place to do thair bataille, the kyng toke thair quarelle in to his handis, and exilid the duke of Hereforde for terme of x. yeer, and the duke of Norfolk for euermore : the whiche duke of Norfolk deide aftirward at Veniȝe. And the kyng grauntid to the duke of Hereforde forto haue and receyue yeerli a certayne pension of money out of Englond ; but he forbad him and made him swere, that he sholde not speke with maister Thomas Arundelle ; for the king dradde alwey his counsel and his wisdoum ; wherfore, as yt was said, the kyng so stirid and prouoked ayens him the peple of the cuntre that he sholde passe be, that unnethe he scapid with his lif.

Ferthirmore the kyng and his counsel ordeyned blanc chartris, and made lordis spirituel and temporel and othir worthi men sette to thaym thair selis ; and therto thay were most constreyned be the Bisshoppis, as it was said ; wherynne the king purposid aftirward, as men saide, to haue writen thise wordis—"Because that we befor

A.D. 1398.
Anno xxjº

Quod vis habere consilium nemini dicas.

Folio 150 b.

Nota of the blanc chartris, etc.

A.D. 1398. this tyme haue greuously offendid your mageste, we yeue unto you us and alle our godis, at your wille."

Anno xxij°.
A.D. 1398-9.

Folio 151. The xxij. yeer of king Richard, he callid his counsel and saide he wolde go in to Yrlond; but first he desirid to visite Saint Thomas of Cauntirbury, but he trust not welle in men of Londoun and of Kent; and the archebisshoppe of Cauntirbury assurid him that he myghte go saafly, and so he wente to Cauntirbury with a gret mayne of Chesshire menne, and thay wacchid aboute him day and nyghte, and ech of thaym hadde vj d. a-day; and whanne he cam to Cauntirbury, tharchebisshoppe fedde him and his men rialli; and aftir broughte him to Londoun agayne.

Thanne wente the king in to the tour of Londoun, and baar out therof alle the precious iewelx that his predecessours hadde put there Nota de aquila aurea. to be kept; and among othir thyngis, he fond there an egle of gold, and withynne the egle a violle of stoone closid, with a writyng aboute; the whiche writyng saide that our lady delyuerid that egle and the violle to Saint Thomas of Cauntirbury whileȝ he was exilid, and saide to him that with the oille that was in the violle, the gode kyngis of Englond that sholde come aftirward sholde be ennoynted; and on of tho kyngis sholde gete agayn alle the lond that his auncestris badde lost, withoute strengthe; and he sholde be grettist of alle kyngis, and he sholde bilde meny chirchis in the holi lond, and sholde driue alle the paynemes out of Babiloun, and there he shal make meny chirchis, and as ofte as he berith the said egle on his brest he shal haue the victory of his enemieȝ, and his kyngdom shall Folio 151 b. evir encrece; and this oynement shalle be founde in couenable tyme: and this egle baar king Richard alwey aboute his necke.

Thanne made the kyng his testament fulle greuous and preiudiciall to the reme, as thay saide that saw it; and made ser Edmund of Langley, duke of York, lieutenaunt of Englond; and thanne [May 31st.] wente he forth in to Yrlond.*

* He sailed from Milford Haven on the 29th of May, and landed at Waterford on the last of the month.

And whanne he hadde be there a litill tyme, ser Henri of Bolyng- A.D. 1399.
broke, erl of Derby and duke of Hereforde, whom kyng Richard Hoc anno obiit dux Lancas-
hadde exilid, heryng that his fader ser John of Gaunt, duke of Lan- triæ.*
castre, was ded, cam doun out of ffraunce vuto Caleys. And there
mette with him maister Thomas Arundelle that was archebisshoppe of
Cauntirbury, and the sone and heir of the erl of Arundelle, that was [Anno xxiijº.]
broke out of prison of the castelle of Reygate; and thay shippid at
Caleys, and cam in to Englond, and landid at Rauenesporne in the [July 4th.]
north cuntre. And there mette with thaym the erlle of Northumbirlond withe a gret power to helpe and socoure the said duke, that
cam for non othir entent, as he saide, thanne forto chalange the
duchie of Lancastre his enheritaunce.

The duke of York that was lieutenaunt of Engelond wolde haue
gon ayens thayme, but noman wolde folowe him; and ser William
Scroope, tresorer of Englond, offrid men wonder large wageȝ, but he
coude noman haue, for no money.

Thanne wroot the said duke of Hereforde to the citeȝeyns of Lon- Folio 152.
doun, and callid himself duke of Lancastre and stiward of Englond,
and saide that he wolde refourme and amende that was amys; and
anon Londoun him fauerid and supportid, and alle the kyngis castellis
were delyuerid to the duke. Ser William Scrooppe, tresorer of
Engelonde, Busshe, Bagot, and Grene, knyghtis, that were the kyngis
chief counselours, fledde in to the castel of Bristowe, and wolde
haue gon in to Yrlond, but thay were take, and thair heddis smyte
of: but Bagot ascapid in to Yrlonde and was take aftirwarde.

Whanne kyng Richarde herde telle alle this, he cam in haste out [August 13th.†]
of Yrlond in to Walis, and abood in the castell of fflynt to take counsel
what was best to dc; but no counsel cam to him, and alle his ost
landid in diuers partieȝ and wolde not folowe him. Thanne ser
Thomas Percy, stiward of the kyngis hous, brak the rod of his office

* Februarȝ 3rd.
† Richard arrived at Milford Haven on this day. See "Chronique de la traison et mort
de Ric. II.," edited by Benjamin Williams, F.S.A. (Eng. Hist. Soc.), p. 194.

A.D. 1399. in the halle befor alle men and saide, " The king wille no lenger holde householde," and anon alle the kyngis mayne forsook him, and lefte him alone.   Tho cursid the kyng the vntrouthe of Englond, and saide, " Allas ! what trust is in this fals worlde l "

Thanne wrot the duke to the stiward of the Archebisshoppe of Cauntirbury, ser Roger Waldenne, commaundyng him on peyne of his hed to kepe alle the godis of the forsaid ser Roger to the vse of Folio 152 b. maister Thomas Arundelle, and anon the said Roger remeued alle his iewelx out of the paleis of Cauntirbury, and thay were take at Rouchestre and put in to the castelle there to be kept safly.

[August19th.*]   Whanne this was ydo, the duke and maister Thomas Arundel ⁊ wente to the kyng to the castel of Flynt, and aftir a fewe wordis thay tolde him shortly he sholde no lenger regne ; and thanne maister Thomas Arundelle saide vnto him in this wise : " Thou art a fair man, but thou art falsest of alle menne.   Thou promisist and assurid me, sweryng on Goddis Body, that thou woldes, do my brothir non harm ; and whanne I badde brou3t him to thi presence, I my3te nevir se him aftir.   Thou also promisest me to calle me agayn in haste fro myn exile, and that ther sholde nevir be othir archebisshoppe of Caunterbury but I, while3 I livid ; and now thou hast maad anothir archebisshop, and also procurid my dethe.   Thou hast not rewlid thi reme and thi peple, but hast spoilid thaym be fals raisyngis of taxe3 and talage3 not to the profit of the reme, but forto fulfille and satisfie thi cursid couetise and pride.   Thou hast alwey be rewlid be fals flaterers, folowyng thair counsel and thaym avaunsyng befor alle othir trew men, refusyng the counsel of thi trew lordis ; and because thay wolde haue withstonde thi cursid malice as reson Folio 153.   wolde, thow hast thaym slayne unrightfulli, and disheritid thair heiris for evirmore, aftyr thyn ordenaunce3 and statutis ; but thay shalle not longe stonde, be Goddis'grace.   Thou hast also livid incontinentli and lecherousli, and with thi foulle and cursid ensample thou hast

* See " Chronique de la traison," p. 207.

enfectid thi court and thi reme." Thanne saide the duke, "No
more, ye haue said ynoughe." The kyng wist not what he sholde say,
but yeld him vnto the duke and saide he wolde resigne and renounce
his righte; and thanne he was lad to the tour of Londoun, and there
ykept in strong hold.

And aftirward in the vigili of saint Mighelle, were sent vuto him
bishoppis, erlis, barons, knyʒtis, and notarieʒ, forto enquire and wite
of him, if he wolde resigne as he hadde promised. First he said
Nay, and thanne thay saide unto him that he moste nedis resigne
withoute eny condicicun, and delyuerid him a cedule conteynyng
the fourme of his resignacioun ; and he redde it in presence of the
forsaid duke and of many othir lordis and a gret multitude of peple ;
wherof the tenour was this: " I, Richard kyng of Englond, renounce and resigne alle the right that I haue in the croune of Englond with thappurtenaunceʒ ; that is to say, in the remeʒ of Englond
and ffraunce, Yrlond and Scotland, and in the duchieʒ of Guyenne
and of Normandie, and in the counte of Pountif, and in Walis,
Caleis, and alle othir castellis and fortaliceʒ, that I haue now or may
haue aftirward be righte, beyonde the se and in this side, or in eny
parti of thayme, for me and myne beyris for euermore." And wit-
nessiʒ there present requirid notaries to make instrumentis vpon that
resignacioun. And thanne kyng Richard confessid how he hadde
gretly trespast ayens God and the reame, and that he was not worthi
forto regne, for he wiste welle, he saide, that he loued nevir the
peple, ne the peple him.

After this, the duke wente to Westmynstre, and there he was receyued with procession solemly of bishoppis and monkis, and there
was said a solenne masse of the Holi Gost; and aftir masse, he
wente in to the halle and the kyngis swerd was bore befor
him, and there he sat doun in his fader sete, and othir lordis
sat there also, and moche peple standyng aboute; and there
was red openli the forsaid resignacioun of king Richard, and was
acceptid of alle peple. And thanne were there red and declared

A.D. 1399.

meny notable and grete defautis that king Richard badde do ayens his oth, and the lawe3 of the reme, and how he badde exilid and slayn his lordis that were pieris of the reme, and meny othirt hyngis: wherfore he was deposid, and, in the name of alle men of Englond, proctours there assigned yeld up to hym thair homage3 ; and mais-

Folio 154.   ter Thomas Arundelle, be comune assent of alle that were there, dampned the said king Richard to perpetuelle prisoun.

Thanne aros the said duke of Lancastre and of Hereforde, and blissid him, and redde in a bille how he descendid and cam doun lynealli of kyng Harri the sone of king Johan, and was the nexte heir male of his blod, and for that cause he chalanged the croune; and alle the lordis and comune3 assentid therto.

Thanne aroo3 the Archebishoppis of Cauntirbury and of York and kiste his handis, and ladde him to the kynggis sete that was for him rialli araid ; and the Archebisshoppe of Cauntirbury, Arundelle, made there a colacion, and his theme was this: " Vir fortis dominabitur populo : " that is to say, A strong man shalle be lord ovir the peple. And aftir the colacioun, the Chaunceller of Englond theliverid the seel unto the kyng Harri, and othir officers delyuerid vp also vnto him thair selis and office3, and the kyng forthwith put thaym yn agayn. And thanne tharchebisshoppe Arundelle notified vnto the peple, that the king wolde be crovned at Westmynstre on saint Edwardis day, commaundyng alle menn to be atte parlement on the Monday next comyng, &c.

HENRY IV.

Of kyng Harri of Bolyngbroke, duke of Lancastre and of Hereforde and erl of Derby; that was the iiij^{the} Harri aftir the Conquest.

Whanne kyng Richard was deposid and putt out of his kyngdoum, the lorde; and the comune; chosen ser Harri of Bolyngbroke, duke of Lancastre and of Hereforde and erlle of Derby, sone and heir to Johan of Gaunt duke of Lancastre, to be kyng of Engelonde; and he was crouned at Westmynstre on saint Edwardes day, of maister Thomas Arundelle, archebisshoppe of Cauntirbury, and was anoynted with the oyl of the egle before rehersid : and he was the firste that was anoynted therwith, as it was said.

Thanne continued he the parlement that king Richarde badde begonne, and therynne adnullid and hadde for noughte alle the ordenaunce; and statutis that there were maad be king Richarde; and restorid the erlis sone of Arundelle to his landis, and made him erlle off Arundelle ; and delyuerid the erlle of Warwic and the lord Cobham and othir out of prisoun; and brende openli at Londoun alle the blanc chartris that kyng Richard and his counselle hadde compellid men to sele ; and disgradid alle the dukis that kyng Richarde hadde maad in his laste parlement, and restored ayenne maister Thomas Arundelle to his Archebisshopperiche of Cauntirbury ; and made ser Roger Waldenne, whom kyng Richard badde maad Archebisshoppe, bisshop of Londoun, that tyme beyng void; and made the said ser Roger forto restore alle that he hadde take of tharchebisshopriche of Cauntirbury vnto Arundelle : ffor the pope Boneface dampned and adnullid the iugement that king Richard

badde yene ayens the said Arundel be a bulle, and declarid be the
same that the chirche of Cauntirbury was not void.

This kyng Harri made Harri his eldest sone and heir Prince of
Walis, duke of Cornewaille, and erl of Chestre.

And this same yeer king Harri held his Cristemasse at Wyndesore, and on xij^{the} evyn cam thider vnto him the duke of Aumarle,
and tolde him how that he, and the duke of Surrey, the duke of
Excestre, the erlle of Salisbury, the erl of Gloucestre, and othir mo
of thair assent, were acordid to make a mommyng to the kyng on
xij^{the} day at nyghte, and in that mommyng they purposid to sle him.
The kyng was also warned therof in anothir maner. The Arche-
bisshooppe of Cauntirbury, Arundelle, aftir new yeris day, remeued fro Cauntirbury toward Wyndesore forto haue be withe
the kyng on xij. day. And in the mene tyme a man of the kyngis
hous lay alle nyghte with a comyne wommanne in Londoun, and in
the morou she saide to him, "Farwelle frende," saide she, "for
I shalle nevir se the more." "Whi so?" saide he. "Forsoth," saide

she, "for the erlle of Huntyngdoun, the erl of Salesbury, the duke of
Surrey, and meny othir, lyen in waite aboute Kyngestoun, forto sle
the kyng and the Archebisshoppe as thay come fro Wyndesore, purposing to restore king Richard ayenne to his kyngdoum." "How
knowest thou this?" saide he. "Forsoth," saide she, "on of thair
men lay with me the lattir nyght, and told me this." And he anon
in haste rood to the kyng, and tolde him as the wommanne badde said;
and the kyng warned tharchebisshoppe herof be a messager, and he
retourned ayen in to the castelle of Reigate.

Whanne the kyng was thus warned of this tresoun, he rood in
haste the same xij. nyght to Londoun, to gete him strengthe.

And on of tharchebisshoppis men rood bi Kyngestoun, and the
erl of Kent loked out at a wyndow and saw him, and commaundid
to brynge him befor him; and axed of him and saide: "Where is
thi maister?" and he said, "In the castelle of Reygate." "And
where is the kyng?" saide the erlle; and he saide, "At Londoun."
"Yf I had met with thi maister," saide the erl, "I wolde hauee shave

his croune; " and commaundid to spoile the said man of his hors A.D. 1400.
and of his money.

But as sone as the said lorde3 wiste that thair counselle was dis-
couerid and wraid, thay fledde euery man his way, and the duke of
Surrey and the erl of Salisbury with thair mayne fledde vnto the
toun of Circestre, and saide be the way that kyng Richard rood there, Folio 156.
and cam late in the euenyng to thair ynne3. The comune3 of the
toune wolde haue arestid thaym, and thay made gret defens, but atte
laste thay were discomfitid and take be the said comune3, and thay
smoot of the lordis heddis; and [they] were set on London brigge,
and thair quartris were sent to dyuers toune3 of Englond: and meny
of thair men were there ytake, and put in to prisoun, because some
of thayme put brondis of fire in to the rovis of diners menne3 house3,
wherfore aftirward meny of thaym were drawe and hanged.

At Oxenforde were take ser John Blount and ser Benet Sely, kny3tis,
and Thomas Wyntereshille squyer, and were beheddid and quartrid.

And the same yeer at Pritwelle in Essex, in a mille, ser John
Holond duke of Excestre was take be the comune3 of the cuntre,
and vnto Plasshe where as king Richard arestid ser Thomas of
Wodestoke, duke of Gloucestre ; and there thay smoot of his hed,
and yt was set on London brigge.

The same yeer at Bristowe was take the lord Spenser that was
erlle of Gloucestre, and the comune3 of the toune smot of his hed in
the market place, and it was set on London brigge.

Whanne kyng Richard herde alle this, he was utterli in despeire,
and confessid that this was do be his counsel, and for sorou and Rex Ricardus
hunger he deide in the castle of Pountfret. moritur.

And whanne that king Harri wiste verili that he was ded, he leet Folio 156 b.
close and sere him in lynne clothe alle saue the visage, and that was
left openne that men myghte se and knowe his persone from alle
othir, and so he was broughte to Londoun to Poulis, and there he
had his Dirige and masse; and the same wise at Westmynstre, and
thanne he was buried at Langley.

A.D. 1400.
And aftirward this same yeer ser Bernard Brokas, ser Johan Shelleye, knyghtis, and ser Johan Maudeleyn, a parson of king Richardis chapelle, were beheddid, and thair heddis set on Londoun brigge : and meny othir were acused of tresoun, and broughte befor the justice3, of whom none ascapid, saue onli ser Roger Waldenne.

And this same yeer, quene Ysabelle the secunde wiff of kyng Richard was put fro her dower and sente in to ffraunce with meny grete yiftis, and anon as she was come in to ffraunce, the Frenshe-menne breek the trewe3 maad betuene king Richard and thaym.

Anno ij°.
A.D. 1400.1.
The secunde yeer of his regne, he wente in to Scotland, but the Scottis wolde not mete with him ; and there the erl of Dunbar becam his manne, and the kyng yaf him the Counte of Richemunde.

This same yeer was holden a parlement at Westmynstre, and thider cam Oweyn off Glendore, a Walshman, that was sumtyme a
Folio 157.
squier of the erlis of Arundel ; complaynyng how that the lord Gray Ruthynne hadde take from him wrongfulli a part of his land ; but he my3te haue no remedy.   And the Bisshoppe of Saint Assaphe of Walis counselid the lordis of the parlement that thay sholde not mystrete the said Oweyne, lest he made the Walshmen arise ; and thay ansuerde and saide thay set nou3t be him.

This same yeer cam the emperour of Constantinople in to Englonde, to axe helpe and socour of the kyng ayens the Turkis, and broughte with him a pardon fro the Pope, be the whiche he gadrid moche money, and was longe in this lond on the kyngis cost, and thanne the kyng yaf him iiij m^l. $li.$; and so he wente hoom ayen.

Insurreccio
Walliæ.
This same yeer the Walshmenne began to rebelle ayens king Harri, and also a greet debaat began betuene the lord Gray Ruthyn and the forsaid Oweyne of Glendore : and the Walshmen destroide the kinge3 toune3 and lordshippis in Walis, and robbid and slow the kyngis peple bothe English and Walshe ; and this enduris xij. yeer.

And the king wente in to Walis with a gret power, but he my3te not take Oweyn that was chief capteyn of the Walshmenne, ne spede that he cam for ; and retourned hoom ayenne.   And the lord Gray

undertook forto kepe the cuntre, and sone aftir the said Oweyne took
the said lord Gray prisoner; and he was raunsond for prisoners of
the Marche. And atte laste Oweyn made the said lord Gray wedde
on of his doughtris, and kepte him there with his wiff, and sone aftir
he deide.

This same yeer wæs so gret derthe of corn, and so gret scarcite,
that a quarter of whete was sold for xvj. s.

And this same yeer ser Roger of Claryngdoun kny3t, the Priour
of Launde, and viij. frere menours, wherof some were maistris of
diuinite, and other to the noumbre of xij. persone3, were drawe and
hanged for treson at Tybourne.

Also a womman acusid a grey frere of Cambrigge, an old man, of
certayn wordes that he sholde haue said ayens the kyng, and his
iugement was that he sholde fi3te with the womman, and his on hand
bounde behynde him: but the Archebisshop of Cauntirbury was the
freris frend and cesid the mater.

The iij. yeer of kyng Harri, anon aftir Cristemasse, was seen and
apperid a sterre in the west, whoo3 flame3 ascendid upward, that was
callid "the blasyng sterre," and be clerckis it was callid, "stella
comata."

And aboute this tyme the peple of this land began to grucche
ayens kyng Harri, and beer him bevy, because he took thair good
and paide not therfore; and desirid to haue ayeen king Richarde.
Also lettri3 cam to certayn frendis of kyng Richard, as thay badde
be sent from hymself, and saide that he was alive; wherof moche
peple was glad and desirid to haue him kynge ayeen.

And a frere menour of the couent of Aylesbury cam to the kyng,
and acusid a frere of the same hous, a prest, and saide that he was
glad of kyng Richarde3 lif; and he was brou3t to the king, and he
saide to him:—"Thou hast herd that king Richard is alive, and art
glad therof." The frere ansuerde and saide, "I am glad as a man
is glad of the liff of his frende, for I am holden to him, and alle my
kyn, for he was our furtherar and promoter." The king saide,

" Thou hast noised and told openli that he livithe, and so thou hast excitid and stirid the peple ayens me." The frere saide, " Nay." Than saide the king to him, " Telle me trouthe as it is in thi herte; —yf thou sawest king Richard and me in the feld fighting togedir, with whom woldest thou holde?" "Forsoth," saide the frere, "with him, for I am more beholde to him." Thanne saide the king, " thou woldest that I and alle the lordis of my reme were ded?" The frere saide, " Nay." " What woldest thou do with me," saide the king, " yf thou haddist the victory ouyr me?" The frere saide, "I wolde make you duke of Lancastre." " Thou art not my frend," saide the kyng, " and therfor thou shalt lese thin hed." And thanne he was dampned befor the justice, and drawe and hanged and beheddid.

Aftir this cam anothir frere menour to the kyng, that owde no good wille to a brothir of his, axyng mercy and grace, and saide that v^c men of seculers and religious were acorded to mete togedir vpon the playn of Oxenforde on Midsomer eve, and go fro thennes to seche king Richard, " and Y and x. of my feloweȝ of the couent of Leycestre araide vs for to go with thaym : and ther is in that couent a maister of diuinite, an old manne, that spekith eville of you, and saith that king Richard shalle fiȝte ayens you, and so it is prophecied, as he saith." The viij freris and the maister of diuinite were brought bounde vnto Londoun, and the othir ij. that were acusid myȝt not be founde.

And the forsaid frere acusid meny othir freris of diuers couentis, but thay fledde away.

The king callid the archebisshop and othir lordis, and the freris were brouȝt befor thaym ; and some of thaym were yong, and some olde and sympilly lettrid : and thair acuser stood by and stedfastly acusid thayme, and thay ansuerde vnwarly. Thanne saide the king to the maister, " Thise bith lewde men, and not vnderstondyng ; thou sholdist be a wise man, saist thou that king Richard livith?" The maister ansuerde, "I say not that he

livith, but I say yf he live, he is veray king of Engelonde." The
king saide, "He resigned." The maister ansuerde, " He resigned
ayens his wil in prison, the whiche is nought in the lawe." The
kyng ansuerde, " He resigned with his good wille." " He wolde
not haue resigned," saide the maister, "yf he hadde be at his fredoum;
and a resignacion maad in prison is not fre." Thanne saide the
kyng, " He was deposid." The maister ansuerde, " Whanne he
was kyng he was take be force, and put into prisoun, and spoyled of
his reme, and ye haue vsurpid the croune." The kyng saide, "I
haue not vsurpid the cronne, but I was chosen therto be eleccioun."
The maister ansuerde, " The eleccion is noughte, livyng the trewe
and lawful possessour; and yf he be ded, he is ded be you, and yf
he be ded be you, ye haue loste alle the righte and title that ye
my3te haue to the croune." Thanne saide the kyng to him, " Be
myn hed thou shalt lese thyne hed." The maister saide to the king,
" Ye loued nevir the chirche, but alwey desclaundrid it er ye were
kyng, and now ye shall destroie it." " Thou liest," saide the king ;
and bad him voide, and he and his felowe3 were lad ayen vnto the
tour.

Thanne axed the kyng counsel, what he sholde do with thaym ;
and a kny3t that loued nevir the chirche saide, " We shal nevir cece
this clamour of kyng Richard til thise freris be destroid."

The minister of the freris wente to the kyng, and saide that he
hadde commaunded alle his bretheryne that thay sholde no thing
saw, say ne speke, in preiudice and offens of his persone, and axed
grace for thayme. The kyng saide to him, " Thay wille not be
chasti3id be the, and therfor thay shalle be chastizid be me."

Thanne were thay brou3t to Westmynstre befor the justice3, and
the justice saide unto thaym, " Ye bith enditid that ye in ipocrisie
and flateryng and fals lif, haue prechid fals sermons; wherynne ye
saide falsli that king Richard livith, and haue excited the peple to
seche him in Scotland—Also, ye in your ypocrisie and fals lif, haue
herd fals confessions, wherynne ye haue enioyned to the peple in

wey of penaunce, to seche king Richard in Walis—Also, ye with your fals flateryng and ypocrisie, haue gadrid a gret summe of money with begging, and sent it to Oweyne of Glendore, a traitour, that he sholde come and destroy Englond—Also, ye haue sent in to Scotland for v^c. men to be redy upon the playn of Oxenford on midsomer eve to seche kyng Richard. How wille ye excuse you? I counsel you to put you in the kyngis grace." The freris ansuerde, " We put vs vpon the cuntre."

And neither men of London ne of Holborne wolde dampne thaym; and thanne thay hadde an enquest of Yseldon, and thay saide "Gilti."

Thanne the justice yaf jugement and saide, " Ye shul be drawe fro the tour of Londoun vnto Tiburne, and there ye shalle be hanged, and hange an hool day, and aftirward be take doun, and your heddis smyte of and set on London brigge." And so it was don.

And the maister at Tiburne made a deuout sermon with this theme, " In manus Tuas Domine;" and swoor be his soule that he trespast not ayens king Harri, and forgaf thaym that were cause of his deth.

And another frere whanne he sholde die saide, " Yt was not our entent, as our enemie3 say, to sle the king and his sone3, but forto make him duke of Lancastre, as he sholde be."

On the morou aboute evesong tyme, on cam to the wardeyn of the freris, and saide he my3te fette away the bodie3 and burye thaym; and whanne thay came thay founden thaym caste in to dichis and heggis, and the heddis smyten of, and thay baar thaym hoom to thair couent with gret lamentacioun.

And aftirward, men of thenquest that dampned thayme, cam to the freris prayying thayme of foryifnesse, and saide, " but yf thay hadde said that the freris were gilti thay sholde haue be slayne."

And this same yeer, Oweyn of Glendore took ser Edmund Mortymer in Walis, and because he my3te not paie his raunson he wolde nevir be vnder kyng Harri, but wedded on of Oweyne3 dou3tris.

In the birthe of this Edmund fille meny wonder tokene3 ; for out

of the floor of his fader stable cam out blood, and wellid vp so hie A.D. 1402.
that it couerid the hors feet; and alle the shethis of swerdis and of Nota mirabilia portenta.
the daggaris in the hous were ful of blood, and all the axes with reed
of blood; And whanne the said Edmund lay in his cradille he my3t
not slepe, ne cece of cryynge, til he saw a swerd: and whanne he
sat in his norsis lappe he wolde not be stille til he hadde sum Folio 160 b.
instrument of warre to pleie with.

And this same yeer was the bataille of Shrewesbury on Mari [Anno iiij^{to}]
Maudeleyn eve, betuene king Harri and ser Henri Percy, the erlis A.D. 1403. [July 21st]
sone of Northumbirlord: of the whiche bataille the cause and occa-
sioun was this.

The erl of Northumbirlond praide the kyng to paie him his Nota causam belli Salopiæ
moneie due vnto him for keping of the marchis of Scotland, and
saide, "My sone and I haue spendid our good in keping of the said
marchis." The king ansuerde, "I haue no moneie, ne non thou
shalt haue." The erle saide, "Whanne ye cam in to this land ye
made promys forto be rewlid be our counsel, and ye take yeerli
moche good of the reme and paie nou3t, and so ye wrathe your
comune3: good [God?] sende you good counsel."

Thanne cam the erlis sone ser Harri Percy, that hadde weddid
the forsaid Edmunde3 sustir that was prisoner in Walis, prayyng
the kyng that he wolde suffre that the said Edmunde3 raunsoun
my3te be paid of his owene. The kyng saide, that with the money
of his reme he would not fortifie his enemie3 ayens himme. Ser
Henri Perci saide, "Shalle à man spende his good, and put him self
in perille for you and your reme, and ye wil not helpe him in his Nota ista verba inter Regem et Henr. Percy.
nede?" The king was wroth and saide to him, "Thou art a traitour!
wilt thou that I sholde socoure myn enemie3, and enemie3 of the Folio 161.
reme?" Sir Henri Percy saide, "Traitor am I none, but a trew
man, and as a trew man I speke." The king drow to him his
daggar: and ser Henri Perci saide to the kyng, "Not here, but in
the feld." And so he wente his way.

And he and his vuele ser Thomas Percy, whom king Richard

hadde maad erlle of Worcestre, gadrid a greet ost in the northcuntre, and saide thay moste fiȝte ayens the Scottis; and wente in to
Chestreshire, and took with thaym meny Chesshire men, and sente
to Oweyn of Glendore forto come and help him, but Oweyne was
aferd of treson and cam not; but meny of the Walshmen cam to
thaym: and so they cam to Lichfeld. And the said ser Henri
Percy and alle his men wered and were araid in the liverey of the
bertis, the whiche was king Richardis liverey.

And there the said ser Henri leet crie openli, and saide that he
was on of the chief causers that king Richard was deposid, and most
helper to brynge yn kyng Harri, wenyng that he wolde have
amendid the rewle of the reame ; and now kyng Harri rewlith and
gouerned worse the land than dede king Richard ; wherfor, he saide,
he wolde amende it yf he myȝte.

The kyng also gadrid anothir ost and mette with him beside
Shrowesbury, and axed of him the cause of his comyng; to whom
Percy ansuerde and saide:—" We brouȝte the yn ayens king
Richard, and now thou rewlist worse than dede he.   Thou spoilist
yeerly the reme with taxes and talageȝ, thou paest no man, thou
holdist no hous, thou art not heir of the reme; and therfore, as I
haue hurt the reme be bryngyng yn of the, I wille helpe to refourme
it." The king ansuerde and saide, " I take talageȝ for nedis of the
reme, and I am chosen kyng be comune assent of the reme, wherfor I
counsel the to put the in my grace." Percy ansuerde and saide, " I
trust not thi grace." " Now I pray God," saide the kyng, "that
thou most ansuer for alle the blood that here shalle be shed this day
and not I." And thanne saide the kyng, " Avant baner."

Thenne was there a strong and an hard bataille, and meny were
slayn on bothe sideȝ : and whanne ser Henri Percy saw his men faste
slayn he pressid in to the bataille with xxx men, and made a lane in
the myddille of the ost til he cam to the kyngis baner, and there
he slow the erl of Stafforde and ser Thomas Blount and othir; and
atte laste he was beset aboute and slayne, and anon his ost was dis-

parblid and fledde. And ser Henri Perciez hed was smyte of and A.D. 1403.
set vp at York, lest his men wolde haue saide that he badde be alive.
And ser Thomas Percy his vncle was take and beheddid at
Shrowesbury, and his hed set on London brigge.

And in this bataille the prince, kyng Harriez sone, was hurt in
the face with an arow.

And this bataille was do in the yeer of our Lord M¹. cccc. ij.* Folio 162.

After this bataille was ydo, the knyghtis and squiers of the north
cuntre that had be with ser Henri Percy, wente hoom ayen in to
Northumbirlond, and kepte thaymself in strong holdis and castellis
and wolde not truste in the kyngis grace.

And aftirward the king sente for the erlle of Northumbirlond that
was ser Henri Perciez fader; and he saide yf the kyng wolde swere
that he sholde come and go saaf til he badde excusid him in the Parlement, he wolde gladli come ; and so he cam to the parlement, and
excusid him that he was not gilty of the bataille of Shrewesbury,
and swoor vpon the cros of Cauntirbury befor the parlement, that
he sholde evir be trew to king Harri.

To this parlement cam lettris as they hadde be sent from king
Richard, semyng so euident and so trewe, that the king and all
the parlement were therof astoned, and hadde gret marvaille ; and
callid him that was his keper, and axid of hym how he wolde ansuer
to tho lettris ; and he ansuerde and saide he wolde fizte with eny
man that wolde say that he was alive.

The iiij yeer of king Harri, cam dame Johane the duchesse of Anno iiij^to
Britayne into England and landed at Falemouth in Cornewail, and
was weddid to king Harri in the abbey of saint Swithunez of Wyn- [February 7th]
chestre ; and some aftir she was crouned at Westmynstre. [February 26th]

And this same yeer, dame Blaunche kyng Harriez elder douztir Folio 162 b.
was sent vuto Coloyne with the erl of Somerset hir vncle, and
maister Richard Clifford thanne bisshop of Londoun, and othir notable

* The battle of Shrewsbury was fought in 1403, on Saturday, St. Mary Magd. eve
(Hardyng. Ed. Ellis, p. 351), July 21st. See note.

A.D. 1403. persone3, and thenne she was weddid to the duke3 sone of Beyre ; and aftir the solennite of the mariage our lordis cam in to Englond agayne.

Anno v°.   The v yeer of king Harri, the lord Thomas, his sone, wente to the A.D. 1404. se, and the erlle of Kent with him, and thay brende certain toune3 [April.] in the yle of Cagent, and took ij grete carrake3 of Jene ladenne with diuers marchaundise, because thay wold not strike their saile3 in the kyngi3 name of Engelond, and brou3te thaym in to the Camer beside Wynchilse, and there the godis were canted ; and on of the carrake3 was sodenli brent ; and so the lordis wente no ferthir at that tyme.

        And this same yeer, Johan Serle, sumtyme yoman of kyng Richarde3 robes, that was on of the principalle slears of the duke of Gloucestre, cam out of Scotland in to Englond, and saide to diuers persone3 that king Richard was alive in Scotlande ; wherfore he brou3te moche peple in gret errour and grucchyng ayens king Harri, for the peple wende feithfulli it badde be so.   But atte laste he was take in the north cuntre, and was drawe thoroughe eueri cite and burghe toun in Englond, and thanne he was brought to Londoun, Folio 163. and there at Guyldehalle he was iuged to be drawe fro the tour of Londoun thorou3 Londoun vnto Tiburne ; and there he was hanged and beheddid and quartrid, and his hed set on London brigge, October 20th.* and his quarters were sent to the iiij gode tovne3 of Englond.

        This Serle confessid that whanne king Richard was take in Walis, he staalle his signet and fledde in to Scotland, and therwith he selid meny lettris, and sente thaym to such men as were kyng Richarde3 frendis, and saide he was alive ; and so he was cause of meny menne3 dethe: and he saide also that there was a man in Scotland moche lik to king Richard, but it was not he.

Anno vj°   The vj yeer of king Harri, the erl of Marre of Scotland vnder A.D. 1405. saaf conduct cam in to Englond, forto chalange ser Edmund the [January.] erlle of Kent of certain cours of warre on horsbak, and his chalange

* Fabyan. If this is a correct date, the circumstance belongs to the 6th Henry IV.

was acceptid and grauntid, and the place take in Smythfeld; and A.D. 1405.
there they riden togedir with sharp speris dyuers cours, but the erl
of Kent badde the feld with moche worshippe.

And this same year, maister Richard Scroop archebishoppe of Insurreccio Ri-cardi Scroope Archiepiscopi Ebor. [May.]
York, and the lord Mowbray that was erl marchalle of Englond,
and a knyght callid ser William Plymptoun, gadrid a strong
power in the north contre ayens the king; and the kyng sente thider
his power and took thayme, and thay were beheddid at York: and
sone aftirward Almyȝty God shewde for the said archebisshoppe Folio 163 b.
meny grete miracleȝ.

And the cause of the said risyng was this :—The erlis sone of
Notyngham and his heir the lord Moubray compleyned to the
archebisshoppe of York, and saide that his auncestris were evir
wont of righte to be marchallis of Englond, and be that thay held
thair lond; and notwithstonding that, the king hadde yene the said
lond with the office to the erl of Westmerlond. Tharchebisshoppe
comynd of this with wise men of counsel, and aftirward he made a
sermon in the chirche of York, and exhortid and stirid the peple to
be assistent and helpyng to to the correccioun and amendement of
the myschiefs and mysgouernaunceȝ of the reme, hauyng in cousi-
deracioun the grete pouerȝe of the marchauntis in whom was wont to
be the substaunce of the richeȝ of alle the land : and also the grete
reisynges of taxeȝ, tallageȝ and custumeȝ vnder colour of borowyng :
and also, that due paiement be maad for the kingeȝ vitailleȝ : and
that the clergie and the comune peple were not vexid ne charged
with importable chargis of taxis and talagis as thay hadde longe
tyme be : and that the heiris of noble men and of lordis of the lond
myȝte be restorid to their enheritaunce hoolli, euery man aftir his
degre and birthe : and also that suche covetous men as were of the
kyngis counsel, that took away and turned to thair owen vse suche
godis as were ordeyned to the comune help of the lond, and make Folio 164.
thaym self riche withalle, be remeued and put away fro the king.

Thise articles and meney othir the archebisshoppe made be writen in English, and were set on the yatis of the cite, and sent to curatis of the tovne3 aboute, forto be prechid openli.

And the said archebishoppe and the lord Mowbray gadrid a greet ost, and wente toward the erlle of Westmerland; and the erlle cam agayns thaym with anothir ost sent fro the kyng to take thaym; and whanne they were nyghe togedir, the erl praide tharchebishoppe and the lord Mowbray, that thay my3te speke togedir and trete of pee3; and thay wente to the erlle, and the erl badde there botellis with wyne, and made thaym drynke; and while3 the said erlle fayned himself to trete, a kny3t of his rood to the archbisshoppis ost, and saide that the lordis were acordid, and in token thereof they drank togedir, " and therfore tharchebishoppe comaundeth every man forto go hoom agayne, for he shall this ny3t sowpe with the erlle."

The archbisshoppis men were aferd, for ther was a litille hill betuene tharchebisshop and thaym, so that thay my3te nowthir se him ne the erl; nothele3, thay wende it hadde be trewe that the kny3t saide, and wente tharr way and were disparblid ; and the

kny3t retourned agayn to his companie : and anon the erl and he, with thair ost, fille vpon tharchebisshoppe and lord Mowbray, and took thaym, and ladde thaym to the kyng to Pountfret.

Aftir this the king cam to York, and the citi3eynes of the cite cam out barefoot and ungirt, with haltris aboute thair neckis, and fil doun before the kyng axyng mercy and grace, because they aroo3 with tharchebisshoppe.

The archebisshoppe of Cauntirbury, Arundelle, heryng alle this, cam in haste to the kyng and to him saide, " Sire, I am your gostly fader and the secunde persone of the reme, and ye sholde accept no manne3 counsel souner than myn, yf it be good : I counsel you that if tharchebisshoppe of Yorke haue trespast so moche ayens you as it is said, reserue him to the popis iugement, and he will so ordeyne that ye shal be plesid ; and if ye wille not so, I counsel let him be reserued to the iugement of the parlement, and kepe your handis vndefoulid from his blood." The king saide, " I may

not for rumour of the peple." And tharchebisshoppe requirid a A.D. 1405.
notari to make an instrument of the kyngis ansuer, that yf nede
were it myghte be presentid vnto the pope.

Thanne were the archebisshoppe of York and the lord Mowbray
dampned vnto deth, and ser William Plympton with thaym, and [June 8th*]
were beheddid withoute the cite of York.

And whenne the archebisshoppe sholde die, he saide, "Lo! I shalle
die for the lawes and good rewle of Engelond." And thanne he Folio 165
saide vnto thayme that sholde die with him, "Lat vs suffre deth
mekely, for we shul this nyghte, be Goddis grace, be in paradis."
Thanne saide tharchebisshoppe to him that sholde smyte of his
hed, "For His loue that suffrid v woundes for alle mankynde, yene Nota ista verba
me v strokis, and I foryeve the my dethe." And so he dede: and Archepiscopi.
thus thay deide.

And anon aftir, as it was said, the king was smyte withe a lepir:
for the whiche archebisshoppe, Almyghti God sone aftirwarde
wroughte meny grete miracles.

Whanne the Pope herde of the deth of the archebisshoppe of York,
he cursid alle tho that slow him, and alle that were assentyng to his
dethe or therto yaf counselle, and commaundid tharchebisshoppe of
Cauntirbury that he sholde denounce alle thaym acursid: but
tharchebisshoppe wolde not do it alone

Thanne sente the king to the Pope, and saide that the sedicion of
the people wolde not suffre him live, and sente also vnto him the
habergeon that tharchebisshoppe was armed ynne with thise wordis:
"Pater, vide si tunica hec sit filij tui an non." And the pope
ansuerde agayn in this wise, as it was said: "Sive hec sit tunica

* This is Walsingham's date—"in crastino Pentecostis"—and probably it is correct.
In Rymer, vol. viii. p. 395 is an injunction for seizing into the king's hands the ancient
liberties, privileges, and franchises of the city of York, on account of this insurrection,
dated Pontefract Castle, June 3rd. This perhaps was issued upon the arrival of the Earl
of Westmerland with his prisoners, and the execution need not have taken place till the
date given above, even supposing the king had taken the earliest opportunity of going to
York.

CAMD. SOC. F

filij mei an non, scio quia fera pessima devoravit filium meum:"—
and sô be prive meneȝ of money the mater was cesid.

The vij yeer of king Harri, dame Luce the dukis sustir of Melane,
cam in to Englond and was weddid to ser Edmund erl of Kent, in
the priorie of saint Marieȝ in Suthwerc.

And this same yeer deide that worthi knyȝt ser Robert Knollis,
and is buried atte White Freris in Fletstrete in Londoun.

And this yeer ser Thomas Rempstoun, knyghte, lieutenaunt of the
tour of Londoun, was dround in the Thamise at Londoun brigge as he
cam fro Westmynstre.

And this same yeer, dame Philippe the yonger. douȝtir of king
Harrı was lad into Denmarc be ser Richard the dukes brothir of
York and maister Edmund Courteneve bisshoppe of Norwich, and
othir worthi men; aud there she was weddid to the king of Denmarc in a tovne callid Londoun; and aftir that our lordis cam hoom
agayne.

The viij yeer of king Harri ther was a manne callid the Walssh
clerc, and he appelid a knyghte of treson that was callid ser Perci-
valle Sowdan, and thay faughte togedir in Smythfeld, and the
knyghte ouercam the clerk and made him yelde him gilty: and
thanne he was spoilid of his armure and hanggid at Tiburne.

And this same yeer, ser Henri erlle of Northumbirlond, and the
lord Bardolf, that fledde in to Scotland for drede of king Harri,
cam agayn in to Englond forto have destroid king Harri; and the
Shireve of Yorkshire reisid peple and took thayme and smoot of

thair heddis; and the hed of the erlle and a quarter of the lord were
set on London briggee.

The ix yeer of king Harri, ser Edmund Holond, erl of Kent, was
maad Admiral of the se: and as he laide sege to the castell of
Briac, in Britaigne, he was smyte in to the hed with a quarel, and
so he deide.

And this same yeer, was a gret frost in Englond that endurid xv
wekeȝ.

And this same yeer, maister Robert Halome bisshop of Salisbury, A.D. 1409.
and othir, were sent to the general counsel to Constaunce.* Consilium Constanciense [Pisanum] ordinatum est.

The x yeer of king Harry, the erl of Dunbar that was swore
English, and whom king Harri hadde maad erl of Richemund, as
befor is said, fledde ayen in to Scotland; and saide that he fayned Anno xº.
himself an Englishmanne, forto help slee and destroie the erl of A. D. 1409.
Northumbirlond and othir that were enemie3 vnto Scotland.

And this yeer was seen blood boile out of wellis in diuers partie3 Sanguis emanavit de fontibus, etc.
of Englond; and anon aftir, meny men deide on the blody mensoun
&c.

And this same yeer the Seneschalle of Henaude, with othir worthi
menne, cam in to Englond to gete worshippe in dedis of armes ; and
he chalanged the erl of Somerset, and he delyuerid him manfulli in
alle his chalange3, and put him to the worse, and hadde the feld in
alle poyntis. The secunde day, cam in to the feld a man of the Sene-
schallis part, and ayens him cam ser Richard of Arundelle, kny3t ;
and the Henavder hadde the bettir of him in on poynt, for he brou3te
him on his kne. The iij day, cam yn anothir Henauder, and ayens Folio 166 b.
him cam ser Johan Cornewaille, knyghte, and manli quyt him, and
badde the bettir of his aduersarie3 in alle poyntes. The iiij day, cam
yn anothir Henauder, and ayens him cam ser Johan Cheyne3 sone,
and cast the Henauder in the feld, hors and manne; wherfore the
king made him kny3t. The v day, cam yn anothir Henauder, and
to him cam John Stiward, squier, and hadde the bettir. The vj
day, cam ynne anothir Henauder, and to him cam William Porter,
squier, and hadde the bettir in the feld, and the king made him
knyghte. The vij day, cam ynne anothir Henauder, and to him
came Johan Standishe, squier, and hadde the bettir in the feld,
wherfore the king made him knyghte. And that same day cam
yn anothir Henauder, and to him cam a squier of Gascoigne,
and hadde the bettir, and the king made him knyghte. The viij
day, cam in ij men of arme3 of Henaude, and to thaym cam ij

* To the Council of Pisa, not Constance, held in 1409—see note.

A.D. 1409.

soudiers of Caleis that were bretherynne ycallid the Burghes, and quyt thaym wel and manli in the feld, and hadde the bettir, and thus endid the chalangeȝ in Smythfeld, with moche worshippe.

Anno xj°.
A.D. 1409-10.

The xj yeer of kyng Harri, was a bataille do in Smythfeld betuene ij squiers, that on me [men] callid Gloucestre, that was appellaunt, and Artur, that was defendaunt; and they faught manli togedir longe

Folio 167.

tyme, and for thair manhood the king took thair quarel in to his handis, and made thaym go out of the feld both at onys, and yaf thaym grace.

Anno xij°.
A.D. 1410-1.
[December
9th.]

The xij yeer of kyng Harri, a squier of Walis called Ris ap Die, that was supporter of Oweyn of Glendore, that dede moche destruccionn to the kingis peple in Walis, was take and brought to Londoun, and drawe and hanged and quartrid.

And this same yeer, anon aftir Michelmasse, the Thamise at Londoun flowed and ebbid iij tymeȝ in a day naturelle; and ther were take therynne meny grete and straunge fissheȝ of dyuers naturis, that betokened fallyng of newe thyngis.

Anno xiij.
A.D. 1411-2.

And this same yeer, the duke of Orliaunce assemblid vnto him the duke of Barry, the duke of Burbon, the duke of Britaigne, the erl of Armynak, and othir grete men of south Fraunce; and with a gret power pursude the duke of Burgoyne, to be vengid on him

[Nov.23,1407.]

for his fader dethe whom he slow traitourly in Paris.

And the duke of Burgoyne with assistence and help of the king of Fraunce and of his sone, gadrid a gret ost of Fraunce, of Flaundris, of Almayne, of Scotland, and sente ambassiatouris to the Prince, king Harrieȝ sone, for help and socour of men of armeȝ and archiers, ayens the duke off Orliaunce. And the prince sente vnto himme the erlle of Arundelle, ser Gilbert Vmfrevile erlle of Kyme,

Folio 167 b.

[November,
A.D. 1411.]

ser Johan Oldcastelle lord Cobhame, and meny othir; and thay mette with the duke of Orliaunce at Senclowe beside Paris; and there our men him discomfited, and slow meny of his menne, and the duke fledde; and thus our men badde the victory, and cam hoom agayn with grete yiftis.

And anon folowynge, the duke of Orliaunce sente ambassiatours A. D. 1412.
to king Harri, beseching him of helpe and socour ayens his dedly [May.]
enemy the duke of Burgoyne; and thanne the king made Thomas,
his sone, duke of Clarence; and his other sone John, duke of
Bedforde; and ser Thomas Beaufort he made erl of Dorset;
and the duke of Awmarle he made duke of York; and sente
his sone Thomas, and the said erl of Dorset, and ser Johan
Cornewaille, and meny othir notable men, in to Fraunce; and they
landed at Hoggis in Normandie. And there mette with thayme at thair
landyng, the lorde Hambe, with vij M^l. men of arme3 of Frensshemenne, and all were put to fli3t, and vij C of thaym were take, and
iiij C hors, withoute tho that were slayne in the feld; and so our
lordis riden forth to Burdeux thorou3 Fraunce, for the lordis were
acordid er thay cam, and token meny prisoners be the weye; and
aftirward thay cam in to Englond agayn with the vyntage. Sir John Bew-
ford.*

This same yeer, deide ser Johan Beaufort before said erl of Dorset,
and capteyn of Caleys, and ys buried in the Abbeye of the tour hille. Folio 168.

And this same yeer, pope Johan the xxiij sent a frere menour in
to this land, the generalle of the ordre, desiryng of the king, that
he sholde sende his sone Thomas vnto Rome, forto be the popis Capteyne and rewler of his ost, ayens the king of Naplis and the Antipope Nota hic erat
scisma.
Gregore. And the same tyme the pope dispensid with the said
lord Thomas duke of Clarence, forto wedde the countesse of
Somerset, his vncle3 wiff.

The xiiij of his regne he leet make galeye3 of warre purposing Anno xiiij°.
A.D. 1412-3.
forto haue gone to Jerusalem, and there haue endid his lif.

And this same yeer it was acorded betuene the Prince, king
Harrie3 sone, and Harri bisshoppe of Wynchestre, and many othir
lordis of this lond, that certayn of thaym sholde speke to the king,
and entrete him to resigne the croune to the said Prince Harri, his
sone, because he was so gretli vexid and smyte with the seeknesse
of lepre; but he wolde in no wise.

* Marginal note in the hand-writing of Stowe.

A.D. 1413.

Rex Henricus
moritur.
[Monday,
March 20th.]
A.D. 1413.

And sone aftir he deide in the Abbeie of Westmynstre in a
chambir callid Jerusaleme, aboute the feste of saint Cutbert,
whanne he badde regned xiij yeer and a half; and is yburied in
Crichirche of Cauntirbury.

Ca^m. cxlvij.
Folio 169.

A FTIR the deth of king Harri the iiij^{the}, regned his sone king Harri the V, that was ybore at Monemouth in Walis, and crouned at Westmynstre on Passion Sunday.

A. D. 1413.
[Reign began March 21st.]
[April 9th].

And anon, the firste yeer of his regne, for the grete and tendre loue that he hadde to king Richard, he translatid his body fro Langley vuto Westmynstre, and buried him beside quene Anne his firste wiff, as his desire was.

Anno primo.

And this same yeer were ytake certayn Lollardes and hereticks, that hadde purposid thorough their fals tresoun to haue slayn the kyng and the lordis spirituel and temporel, and destroid al the clergie of the reme: but the king, as God wolde, was warned of their fals purpos and ordenaunce, and took the feld that is callid Fikettis feld, and with him maister Thomas Arundel Archebisshoppe of Cauntirbury, and leet keep the weie3 aboute Londoun. And meny of thaym were take, and drawe and hanged and brent on the galowe3 in saint Gile3 feld. And a kny3t callid ser Roger of Acton was take for Lollardrie and for treson, and drawe and hanged and brent in saint Gile3 feld.

Insurreccio Lollardorum.
[January, A. D. 1414.]

[February 10th.]

The secunde yeer of regne, he held a parlement at Westmynstre, of alle the lordis of the reme, where it was tretid and spoke of his title that he hadde to Normandie, Gascoigne, and Guyenne, that were his enheritaunce; the whiche the king of Fraunce witheld wrongfulli and vnrightfulli. And so be avise of his counsel, he

Anno ij°.
A.D. 1414.
Folio 169 b.

A.D. 1414.

In isto parlia-
mento, Rex fecit
Johannem, fra-
trem suum,
ducem Bed-
fordiæ ; et
Humfridum,
alium fratrem
suum, ducem
Gloucestriæ.

Anno iijº.
A. D. 1415.

Folio 170

[August 14th.]

sente ambassiatours to the king of Fraunce and his counsel, requiryng thayme to yelde vp vnto him his said enheritaunce, or ellis he wolde it gete be the swerd with helpe of Jhesu. The dolfyn of Fraunce ansuerde to our ambassiatours, and saide that our kyng was ouer yong and to tendre of age to be a good warriour, and not lik to make such a conquest vpon thayme. Oure ambassiatours heryng this scornful ansuer, retourned in to Englond ayen, notifying vnto the kyng and his counsel the ansuer of the dolfyn and of the counsel of Fraunce.

Thanne made the kyng redy his ordenaunce necessary forto the warre, commaundyng alle menne that sholde go with him to be redy att Suthamptoun, at Lammesse thanne next folowyng, the iij yeer of his regne. At whiche day, whan the king was redy to take his passage, it was there publisshid and openli knowe that iij lordis, that is to say, ser Richard erlle of Cambrigge brothir to the duke of York, the lord Scroope tresorer of Englond, and ser Thomas Grey, knyghte, hadde receyued an huge summe of money, that is to say, a milion of gold, forto betraie the king and his bretheryn to the Frenshemen ; wherfore thair heddis were smyte of, withoute the northgate at Suthamptoun.

Whanne this was don, the king sailled forth in to Normandie with xvC shippis, and landid at Kitcaux, in the vigily of Assumpcion of our Lady, and fro thenne; he wente to Harflieu, and it besegid be lond and be watir, and commaundyng him forto delyuer the toun, and he saide he wolde not. Wherfore the king commaundid his gonners to bete doun the wallis on euery side, and anon thay of the toune sente out to the king prayyng him of viij daie; respit in hope of rescu, and yf non wolde come, thay wolde delyver the toun : and so thay dede. And thanne the kyng made his vnele, the erl of Dorset, capteyn therof, and commaundid him to put out alle the Frensshe peple, man womman and child, and stuffe the toun with English peple.

Whanne this was don, the king wente toward Caleis be londe

forto have come in to Englond, but the Frensshemenne hadde broke alle the br ggis wher he sholde passe ouer, wherfore him moste nedis seche his way fer aboue, and so he wente ouer the watir of Swerdis, ard cam doun in to Picardie to a place ycallid Agyncourt, where alle the power of Fraunce was redy gadrid to stoppe his way, and yene him bataile.

The king seyng the grete multitude and noumbre of peple of his enemie3, praide Almy3ti God of helpe and socour, and confortid his peple, and praide euery man forto make him redy to bataille; and with such peple as he hadde, not fulli vilj M¹., he enbataillid him, and grauntid to the duke of York the vauntwarde, as his desir was. And thanne the duke commaundid every man to ordeyne him a stake of tre sharpid at bothe endis, that the stake my3te be pighte in the erthe asloope before thaym, that the Frensshemen sholde not ouerride ham; for that was fulli thair purpo3. And alle ny3t befor the bataille, the Frensshemenne made moche revelle and moche cryyng, and plaide atte dys for oure men, an archer for a blanc, as it was said.

On the morow, whanne alle was redy, the king axed what tyme it was of the day, and thay saide, "Prime." Thanne saide the kyng, "Now is good tyme, for alle Engelond praieth for vs, and therfore beth of good ebiere, and lat vs go to our iourney." And anon euery Englishe manne knelid doun, and put a litille porcion of erthe in his mouth. And thanne saide the king with an highe vois, "In the name of Almy3ti God, and of Saint George, Avaunt baner! and Saint George this day thyn helpe!" Thanne the ij bataille3 mette togecir and fou3ten sore and longe tyme, but Almy3ti God and saint George fou3ten that day for vs, and grauntid our kyng the victory: and this was on the Friday on saint Crispyne and Crispiniane3 day, in the yeer of our Lord M¹.cccc.xv. in a feld callid Agyncourt in Picardi. And there were slayn that day of the Frensshemen in the feld of Agyncourt xj. M¹. and mo: and there were noumbrid of thaym in the feld C.xx.M¹

A.D. 1415.

Thanne cam tidyngis to our kyng, that there was anothir ost of Frensshemenne ordeyned redy to fijte ayen with him; and anon he commaunded euery man to sle his prisoner, and whanne thay saw that, thay withdrow and wente thair way.

And ther were slayne in the feld on the Frensshe part, the duke of Barri, the duke of Launson, the duke of Brabanne, the erl of Narbonne, the chief constable of Fraunce, viij othir erlis, the arche-bisshoppe of Saunj, C barons and mo, and of othir worthi knyjtis and cote armuris M^l. vC. And of Englishmen were ded that day, the duke of York, the erlle of Suffolk, and of othir not passing xxvj.

And there were take prisoners of the Frensshe part, the duke of Orliaunce, the duke of Burbonne, the erl of Vandonr, the erlle of Ew, the erl of Richemund, ser Bursigaund marchalle of Fraunce, and othir worthi menne.

[November 16th.]

And aftir this, the king cam to Caleis, and so in to Englond, with alle his prisoners, and was receyued with moche iole and worshippe.

[Anno iiij^{to}.]
A. D. 1416-7.
Sigismundus, imperator, venit Angliam.
[April.*]
Folio 171 b.

This same yeer cam Sigismund, the emperour of Almayn, in to Englond forto speke with king Harri, to trete of certayn thyngij touching the pees of Englond and of Fraunce: and also for the wel-fare and vnite of alle holi chirche. And the king and his lordis mette with him at saint Thomas wateryng, withoute Suthwerk, and him receyued withe greet reuerence and worshippe, and broujte him in to Londoun, and fro thennej to Westmynstre, and there he was loggid in the paleis atte kyngis cost: and that same tyme the king yaf him the liverey of the garter.†

* After the 8th of the month. See Rymer, vol. ix. pp. 339, 340. Stowe says he landed at Dover, May 1st.

† Walsingham (p. 441) says that Sigismund was installed Knight of the Garter on the Feast of St. George, having told us that he arrived in London on May 7th. This may seem strange, as St. George's day was on April 23rd. Fabyan perhaps explains this apparent contradiction, by saying that the *celebration* of the feast had been deferred on account of the Emperor.

' And sone aftir, cam the duke of Holond in to Englond, to speke A.D. 1416.
with the emperour and with the kyng; * and he was loggid in the
bisshoppis yn of Ely, at kyngis cost.

And whilis this was in doyng in Englond, the Frenshemenne
thou3te to be vengid, and with a greet arme besegid the toun of
Harfliew bothe be watir and be lond; and badde goten and heerd [June.]
grete carrake3 of Jene, and othir smale vessellis, to ly and kepe the
movthe of the river cf Sayne, that no vitaille ne othir helpe sholde
come vppe unto the toune ; of the whiche arme the erl of Armenak
was chiefteyne.

Thanne the erl of Dorset, capteyn of Harfliew, sente messagers
to the kyng notyfying vuto him alle this doynge, and what scarcite
and penury of vitaille was withyn the toun : and anon the king
sente his brothir Johan duke of Bedforde † forto breke the sege be
watir : and he cam with a notable power and faughte with the forsaid grete carrake3, and took iiij of thaym, and meny othir Frensshe Nota capcionem
carracarum.
vessellis. And on of the grettist carrake3 of alle scapid and fledde
away ; but she was so rent and bored in the side3 in the said Folio 172.
bataille, that sone aftir it was dround. And the noble erl of
Dorset rescued the said toun be londe, and discomfitid and slow
meny of the Frenshemenne, and hadde of thaym a gracious victory.

Whanne this was don, the said duke with his prise3 and prisoners
retourned into Engelond agayne : and forasmoche as this was don in
the Vigilie of Assumpcioun of our Lady, the kyng commaunded [August 14th.]
that his chapeleyne3 sholde say euery day while3 he livid, an anteem
with the versicle and collect in remembraunce of our lady.

And whanne the emperour hadde be in this lond as longe as it [August ‡]
likid him on the kyngis cost, he took his leve of the king ; and the

* " Ante festum Ascensionis." (Wals.) Ascension day this year, 1416, was May 28th.

† He sailed after 25th of July. See Rymer, vol. ix. p. 372. His commission is
dated, Southampton, July 22nd, 1416. Id. p. 371.

‡ After the 15th of the month ; as the final treaty of mutual alliance was signed at
Canterbury on that day, 1416. See Rymer, vol. ix. pp. 377-82.

king brou3te him to Caleis, and taried there to haue ansuer fro the Frensshe party, of suche thyngis as the emperour and the king hadde sent to thaym for ; and atte laste it cam, and plesid thaym right nou3t ; and thanne the emperour past forth his way, and the king
cam in to Englond agayn.

And anon aftir, the king sente ambassiatours to the generalle counselle of Constaunce for the vnion and pees of alle holi chirche, and forto redresse and cece the scisme and strif that was thatt tyme in the chirche of Rome betuene iij popis.

And that same tyme, be assent of alle nacions it was ordeyned in this counsel, that Englond sholde be callid an nacion, and be
counted on of the v nacions that owen obedience to the pope of Rome, the whiche befor that tyme was vnder the nacion of Ducheland.

And this same yeer, the erl Douglas of Scotland cam in to Englond *, and was swore to the king for to be his trew manne ; but aftirward he brak his oth, and was slayn of Englishmenne atte
bataille of Vernulle.

How kyng Harri wente the secunde tyme in to Normandie, and of the getyng of Cane, and of the sege of Roon.

THE v yeer of his regne, he made redy his ordenaunce and his retenu forto saille in to Normandie agayne, and commanded alle menne that sholde go with him to be redy at Hamptonn, in the Witsunwike next folowyng. And thanne he made John his brothir, the duke of Bedforde, lieutenaunt of Englonde ; and thanne he saillid

† Stowe places this in the 5th Henry V.

in to Normandie with a notable power and gret ordenaunce, and A.D. 1417.
landid at Towk on Lammesse day ; and there he made xlviij knyȝtis, [August 1st.]
at his landyng.

Thanne cam tidyngis to the king that ther was a gret naueie
vpon the se of enemieȝ, that is to say, ix grete carrakis, hulkeȝ,
galeieȝ and othir shippis forto destroie his naueie : and anon, he sente
the erl of March with a suffisaunt power forto kepe the se, and he
took meny of the said naueie, and put the remenaunt to fliȝt ; and
some were dround with tempest. And on of tho carrakis droof
befor Hamptonn, and his mast was throw ouer the toun wallis : and
this was on saint Barthlmeweȝ day.   Folio 173.

Tho sente the kyng to the capteyne off Towk commaundyng him
to delyuer the toun, and so he dede. And the kyng made ser [August 9th.]
Johan Kighley capteyne thereof, and commaunded him to put out
alle the Frensshe peple.

And thanne was Loueres yoldenne to the erl marchal, and the
kyng made him capteyn therof.

And thanne the kyng held forthe his way vnto Cane, and it [August 18th.]
besegid on euery side, and sente to the capteyn forto delyuer it,
but he wolde not, wherfore thay assauted the toun ; and the duke
of Clarence bet doun the wallis with gonneȝ on his side, and first
entrid in to the tounre, and cride, " a Clarence l a Clarence l a saint
George ! " and so was the toun gote. And the kyng entrid and [September.*]
commaunded the capteyn of the castelle to delyuer it vuto him ;
and he praide him of xiiij daieȝ respit in hope of rescu, and yf
non cam, to delyuer him the castel. And vnder this composicion
was the tounne and the castel of Baions with othir touneȝ, fortaliȝ,
and villageȝ, to the nombre of xiiij. And atte xiiij daieȝ ende cam
no rescu, wherfor the castel of Cane with the othir xiiij touneȝ
were delyuerid vuto the king ; and he made the duke of Clarence
capteyn of the toun of Cane and of Baions and of the othir touneȝ

* The 4th of September or soon after. The castle of Caen held out till the 20th of
that month. Stowe's Annals.

A.D. 1417. also: and there the kyng helde saint George; feste, and made xv knyghtis of the Bathe.

Thanne the kyng gat Valeys Newelyn.

Dux Britannic venit ad Regem. Folio 173 b. And this same tyme cam the duke of Britaigne vuto kyng Harri and becam his manne.

And the kyng sente Humfrey his brothir duke of Gloucestre to Chierburghe, and Richard erl of Warwic to Dounfrount; the whiche sone aftirward were yolden vuto thayme.

In the mene tyme, the erlle of Marche, whom the kyng hadde sent to kepe the se, aftir meny storme; and grete tempestis landid at Hoggis in Normandy, and so wente forth vnto the king.

Thanne gat the kyng Argenton, Cessy, Launson, Belham, Vernul in Perche, and alle the toune; and castellis and strengthis vuto Pountlarge, and fro thenne; vnto the cite of Roon.

And this same yeer, ser Johan Oldcastelle knyghte, lord Cobham, was arestid for lollardrie, and put in to the tour of Londoun; and anon aftir he brak out therof, and fledde into Walis and there kepte him longe tyme, and atte laste the lord Powis took him, but he made gret defens and was sore wounded er he myghte be take; and Cobham suspensus est, et combustus. [December.] thanne he was brought in a horsliter to Westmynstre, and ther he was iuged to be drawe vnto saint Gilis feld, and there he was hanged and brent on the galowe; for his fals oppinions.

Anno vj. A.D. 1418-9. The vj yeer of king Harri, he sente his vncle ser Thomas Beaufort to the yates of Roon, and there he displaide the kyngis baner, and sente heroudis to the toun and bad thaym yelde it to the kyng of Englond, and thay saide shortli, thay wolde not. And thanne Folio 174. the said Beaufort took good auisement of the ground al aboute, and retourned to the king to Pountlarge: and anone aftir, thay of Roon cast down thair subbarbis that stood about the cite, that the kyng sholde there haue no socour.

[July 31st.] Rothomagus obsessa est. And the Sunday befor Lammesse day thanne next folowyng, the king with his ost besegid the cite of Roon round aboute; and dede make ouer the watir of Sayne, at Pountlarge, a strong and a my3ti cheyne of yrenne, and put it thorough grete piles of tre faste ypight in the grounde, and that wente ouer the watir of Sayne that no vessel my3to passe that way ; and aboue that cheyne the king leet make a brigge ouer the river of Sayne that man and hors and alle othir cariage my3te passe to and fro, whan nede were.

Thanne cam the erl of Warwic fro Dounfrount, and the king sente him to Caudebeek, and thay of the toun cam out and tretid with the erl to be vnder composicion and to do as Ron dede ; and it was grauntid on this condicioun, that the kyngis naueie with his ordenaunce my3te passe vpward saafli without eny let or desturbaunce ; and to this composicion thay sette thair selis. And thanne cam vp C shippis and caste there thair aneri3, and thanne was Roon besegid both be watir and le land ; and whanne this was ydo, the erl of Warwic wente ayen to the king to the sege of Roon ; and the duke of Gloucestre cam thider also fro the getyng of Chierburghe.

Thanne cam tidyrgis that the king of Fraunce, the dolfyne, the duke of Burgoyne, and al the power off Fraunce wolde come doun forto rescue the cite of Roon, and breke the sege ; but they came not.

And atte firste comyng of the kyng vnto Roon, ther were y noumbrid in the cite be heroudis, of men, wommenne, and childrynne, ccc.M[1] ; and this sege endurid xx wikis ; and evir thay of the toune hopid to haue be rescued, but it wolde not be : and meny hundreddis deide for hunger, for thay hadde etyn alle thair cattis, hors, houndis, ⅂ rattis, myse, and alle that my3te be etynne : and ofte tyme3 the men of arme3 drivenne out the poer peple atte yatis of the cite for spendyng of vitaille, and anonne our menne drof thaym yn agayne ; and yonge childrynne lay ded in the stretis, hangyng on the ded modris pappis, that pite was to se. And whanne the capteyn of the toune saw this grete myschief and hunger, he sente to the kyng, beseching him of his merci and grace, and brou3te the keye3, and delyuered him the toune, and alle the soudiers voided the toune with thair hors and harneys, and the comune3 of the toun abood stille

A.D. 1419.
Rothomagus
dedita est.
[January 19th.] in the toun payyng yeerli to the king for alle maner custumeȝ, fefermeȝ, and quatrymeȝ, xx M¹. marc. Whanne the king badde entrid the toune, and restid him in the castel til the toun were set in rewle and gouernaunce, thanne Cawdebeek and othir garisons there nyghe were yolden vndir the same appoyntement.

Folio 175. Thanne the dolfyneȝ ambassiatours, as it was before acordid, with ful power to do all thyng as he were there himself, cam to [February.] the king to Roon; and aftir meny treteeȝ had, thus it was appoynted, that at a certayn day set, the dolfyne sholde come to the toun of Dreux, and king Harri to Aueraunsshis ; and there to cheȝe a mene place, be thair bothe assent, where thay myȝte pesibli trete of the peeȝ ; to the whiche appoyntement trewli to be kept, the king and the said ambassiatours sette thair selis. Atte whiche day appoynted the king cam, but the dolfyn cam not; wherfore the peeȝ was broke at that tyme.

In the mene tyme Johan duke of Burgoyne, that hadde the rewle and gouernaunce of the kyng of Fraunce because of his seeknesse, be lettriȝ and ambassiatours souȝte king Harrieȝ grace. And the king sente ambassiatours ayen to king Charlis of Fraunce and to the said duke of Burgoyne to Prouynce, of the whiche ambas- [March.] siatours Richard erl of Warwic was chief; and in the way as he sholde go, lay a greet busshement of Frensshemenne to take him and lette his purpooȝ; but he slowȝ· and took the more part of thaym, and went forth to Provynce, and purposid his ambassiat and message.

[April.] And there it was thus accorded and appoynted, that king Harri of Englond, and Charlis of Fraunce with the quene his wif and the duke off Burgoyne, sholde come to a mene place to trete of pees : Folio 175 b. and forto do this message the erl of saint Poulle and the sone and heir of the duke of Burgoyne cam to our kyng as ambassiatours.

[Anno vijº.]
A.D. 1419-20. Thanne kyng Harri knowyng alle the ground of the mater be relacion of ambassiatours of bothe parthieȝ, appointed with his enemieȝ in this wyse : that at a certayn day he wolde come to

Maunt, and Charlis of Fraunce and the duke of Burgoyne to Pount-
toyse, to chese there a mene place forto trete of pees; the whiche
mene place for this trete sholde be Melane vp on Sayne; to the
whiche place novthir party sholde come with mo thanne M¹. M¹. v. C.
men, and in the mene tyme trewe3 sholde be on bothe partie3. The
whiche mene place was aftirward araid betuene ij village3, and [May.]
lymytid and markid betuene ij grete diche3, wherynne no man
sholde come but only suche as sholde trete of the pee3; and there
the kyngis tentis were rially pighte and arerid, and the kyngis tentis
of Fraunce also. Ard king Harri leet arere ij tentis betuene ij
diche3, wherynne bothe kyngis my3te trete apart with thair secret
counsel, and thastat of bothe kyngis obserued and kept; and a stake was
pighte in the middil of a fair playne, to the whiche, and no ferthir, ech
kyng sholde come to othir.

Atte day appoynted kyng Harri cam to Maunt, and kyng Charlis
because of his accustumed seeknesse cam not, but the queue his wiff
and the duke of Burgoyne withe othir noble princis of thair alliaunce Folio 176.
and withe M¹. M¹. v. C. men cam to Pountoyse, and aftirward to the [May 29th.]
mene place. Thanne kyng Harri first kiste the queue of Franuce,
and thanne dame Kateryne hir doughtere, for that tyme he saw hir
first; and thanne kyng Harri, the quene of Fraunce and hir dou3tir,
the duke of Burgoyne, and othir, wente into a tente, to trete of the
pee3, where thay were almost iij daie3; but it tok non ende at that tyme.

In the mene while, the dolfyn withe lettri3 and ambassiatours
stirid the duke of Burgoyne, that he ne non of his sholde assente to
the pee3. And atte v. nonas of August, whanne the said kyngis sholde
haue assemblid, the kyng of Fraunce, the quene, the duke of Burgoyne, ne non of thaym cam; wherfore it was openli knowen that the
Frensshe parte was cause that the pee3 was not endid at that tyme.

Thanne wente the kyng to Pountoyse, and gat it; and sente his
brothir the duke of Clarence with a notable power vuto Paris, and he
gat it, and retourned ayen to the kyng; and thanne gat the kyng
Bokende Villers.

CAMD. SOC.   H

And while3 this was in doyng the duke of Burgoyne, that first hadde sought kyng Harrie3 grace, wente vnder saaf conduct to the dolfyn to Motreaux; and there be the said dolfyn he was traitorly and vnmanli slayn, and cast in to a pit: and as sone as Philip his sone and his heir wiste of this, he becam kyng Harrie3 manne.

The same tyme cam certayne ambassiatours of kyng Charlis, of the duke of Burgoyne and of the cite3eyne3 of Paris, to kyng Harri to Manut, forto trete of pee3, but because kyng Harri was bisili occupied in his warris and also he supposid that the Frensshemen were not fulli enclyned to the pee3 as thanne, this trete took non ende at that tyme, but aftirward at Roon it was fulli endid.

And aftirward while3 kyng Harri held his Cristemasse in Roon, the ambassiatours of kyng Charlis and of the dukes of Burgoyne cam thider vnto him, to whom king Harri sente agayn Richard erl of Warwic, with othir wise men and a notable power of men of arme3, with fulle power and commaundement to conclude the pee3. And aftir meny wise tretee3 on bothe partie3 pee3 was concludid bi thaffinite and wedlok of king Harri and dame Katerine king Charlis dou3tir. But because certayne thyngis were necessary for the whiche the presence of bothe kyngis moste nedis be had, what for settyng to of thair selis, what for the mariage sewyng, and alsoo Charlis was so feblid with age and ofte tyme3 vexid with his custumable seeknesse; it was betuene thayme thus appoyntid, that king Harri sholde come at a day lymytid vnder trewe3 with such puyssaunce as him likid to Nogent vpon Sayne, to parfourme finally al thyng that to the pee3 was nedefulle, and yf he cam not alle thyng sholde be had as for noughte. Aftir this appoyntement thus ymaad the erl retourned to the kyng notifyng vnto him in writyng alle theffect of his ambassiat.

The king fro thenne3 went to Nogent; and there mette with him the duke of Burgoyne with a gret companie of men of arme3. And aftir meny and dyvers tretee3, the xij kalendis of Juyne, the xl yere of king Charlis regne, in the cathedralle chirche of Nogent, kyng Harri

withe the duke of Clarence his brothir and othir prince3 and noblis,
and Ysabelle queue of Fraunce with the duke of Burgoyne, beyng
there for kyng Charlis, thanne labouryng in his seeknesse forsaid,
and in thair owen name3 also, and the iij statis of Fraunce, pee3 betuene the ij remes of Englond and of Fraunce was maad, and with
certayn condicions approued. And kyng Charlis charged alle his
liegemenne on peyne of forfaiture of thair ligeaunce3 to kepe the said
pee3; and therto thay mace thair othe, and plight thair trouthe3 in
the hande3 of kyng Harri And anon quene Ysabelle of Fraunce,
and Philippe duke of Burgoyne, in the name of kyng Charlis, swoor
vpon the holy gospellis to kepe the said pee3 so concludid for thaym
and for thair heiris and successours withoute fraude and male engyne
for euermore; and this same oth made queue Ysabel, and the duke
of Burgoyne, and the iij statis of Fraunce to kyng Harri, to his
heiris and successours. And atte ix kalendis of Juyne, befor quene
Ysabel and kyng Charlis counsel, befor the parlement and the iij
statis of Fraunce, and othir English prince3 and lordis, contract of
matrimony be present wordis betuene kynge Harri and dame Katerine, kyng Charlis doughtir of Fraunce, was there maad and so-
lemny3id.

And as sone as alle this was enactid in writyng as it was acordid,
kyng Harri, kyng Charlis, the ij quenys Ysabelle and Kateryne, and
the duke of Burgoyne wente vuto Senlis and gat it ; and fro thenne3
vnto Melon and besegid it, and that sege endurid fro Juylle vnto
Nouembir in moche duresse; and atte laste for defaute of vitail, the
toun was yoldenne. Thanne the ij kyngis, the ij quenys, and the
duke of Burgoyne with thair ostis wente to Paris, and the cite3eyne3
of Paris mette with thaym in ful noble aray.

And at January next kyng Harri and dame Kateryne wente in to
Englond, and lefte at Paris Thomas duke of Excestre, gouernour,
and Thomas his brothir duke of Clarence, regent of Normandie ; the
whiche duke of Clarence was slayn there with the Scottis on Estis
evyn, while3 the kyng was in Englonde. And on the Sunday the

A.D. 1421.
Anno viij.

[Anno ix⁰.]
A.D. 1421.

Folio 178.

[Anno x⁰.]
A.D. 1422.

[May.]

Rex Henricus
obit, decus olim,
nunc dolor
orbis !

xiiij* day of Feuerer, the viij yeer of kyng Harri, dame Kateryne was crouned at Westmynstre.

At midsomer next aftir, the kyng lefte the quene in Englond, and wente ayen in to Fraunce, and took certayn garisons that were yit rebel; and besegid the toun of Meux, atte whiche sege tidyngis cam to the kyng that the quene was delyuerid; and aftir her purificacioun she wente ayen in to Fraunce.

Whanne Meux was yoldenne, kyng Harri wente to Paris, makyng ordenaunce forto besege the tovu of Cone; and thanne a sore and a feruent maladie him assaillid, and fro day to day him greuousli vexid; til he deide in the castelle of Boys Vincent, the laste day of August, whanne he hadde regned ix yeer v monethis, iij wikis, and iij daiez, and is buried at Westmynstre: on whoz soule Almyghti God haue mercy.   Amen.

* So Stowe (Annals).   The true date is 3rd Sunday in Lent, eve of St. Matthias' day, Feb. 23rd.   See Rymer, vol. x. p. 63.

HENRY VI.

Of kyng Harry the vj^e aftir the conqueste, sone of kyng Harri the
v^{the}, and of the bataille of Vernulle, &c.

A F R the noble and victorious prince kyng Harri the V, regned
his sone kyng Harri the vj^{te}, that was bore at Wyndesore, in
the feste of saynt Nicholas the confessour, and began forto regne in
the age of ix monethis and xv daie3.

And the iij^{de} yeer cf his regne *, was a gret batille don at Vernul
in Perch, betuene Johan duke of Bedforde, thanne regent of Fraunce,
and the Scottis and the Frenshemenne ; in the whiche bataille was
take the duke of Alaunsonne, and there were slayne the bastard of
Alaunsonne, the erl of Narbonne, and the erl of Marrebonne. And
on the Scottis part were slayne the erl Douglas, the erl Boghan, the
erlle of Marre, the erl of Murreye, and meny othir to the noumbre
of vij M^l. and more. And aftir the said bataille was done, ther
were y founde in the diche3 of the toun more than iiij M^l. ydround.
And thus hadde Englisshemen the victory, thanked be Almyghti
God.

The iiij yeer of his regne, on the morow aftir the feste of Simon
and Jude, aroos a gret debaat betuene Humfrey duke of Gloucestre
and master Harri Beaufort his vncle bisshoppe of Wynchestre,
being that tyme Chaunceller of Englond ; so that alle the cite of
Londoun was mevid ayens the bisshoppe, and wolde haue destroid him

---

* The 2nd of Henry VI. The battle was on August 16th, 1424.

in his yn in Suthwerk ; but the yatis of Londoun brigge were so sureli kept that no man myȝte passe out, and the Thamise was also kept that no man myȝt passe ouer.   And the said bisshoppe hadde a gret company of men of armeȝ and archiers withynne his place, to haue maad defens if nede hadde be.   But atte laste be mene of lordis and specialli of the prince of Portyngale, that was the same tyme in Londoun, this troubille was cesid : and aftirward the same yeer atte parlement holden at Leycestre thay were fulli accordid, but yit ther was prive wrath betuene thaym long tyme aftir.

The v yeer of this kyng Harri, the forsaid maister Harri Beaufort, bisshoppe of Wynchestre, was maad a Cardinal of Rome be pope Martyn the V, of the title of saint Euseby ; and sente his hat to Caleys, and thider he wente, and there receyued it.

The viij yere of his regne, he was crouned at Westmynstre on the Sunday in the feste of saint Leonard.

And sone aftir he wente into Fraunce, and was crouned at Paris the ix day of December, the x yeer † of his regne, thorough special
help and supportacioun of the said cardinalle there beyng present ; and cam the same yeer in to Englond agayn.

And this same yeer, whilis the kyng was in Fraunce, and Humfrey duke of Gloucestre his vncle beyng protectour and gouernour of this lond, aroos a man that named himself Jacke Sharpe, purposyng
with his fals feleshippe to haue destroid the chirche and the lordis spirituel and temporel: but he was take and dampned to the deth befor the said duke at Oxenforde, and drawe and hanged and quartrid ; and his hed and his quarters were set vp in dyuers placeȝ of Englond.

And this same yeer, on saint Katerineȝ eve, the lord Fitz Watier wolde haue come fro Normandie in to Englond, and ayens the wille and counsel of the shipmenne wente heddily to ship at Dope ; and whanne he was in the se, ther fil on him a greet tempest, and drounde him with moche othir peple.

* See Rymer, vol. x. p. 458.   † The 9th year of his reign.   1430.

The xj yeer of this kyng Harri, was the grete and general clip of the sunne on saynt Botulfis day; wherof moche peple was sore aferd.

And the next yeer aftir, the xij yeer of kyng Harri, was the grete frost that nevir eny such was seen before; and it endurid fro saint Kateryne; day vuto Sheoftide; and the Thamise and othir grete rivers were so hard frosen that hors and cariage my3te passe ovir.

And the nexte yeer aftir began the grete derthe of corn in this land, the whiche endurd ij yeer, so that a busshelle of whete was sold for xl. d., and the poer peple in dyuers partie; of the Northcuntre eet breed maad of farn rotes.

The xiij yeer of king Harri deide that noble prince Johan duke of Bedforde,* the kyngis vncle, and regent of Fraunce, and is buried at Roon.

The xiiij yeer of king Harri, Philip duke of Burgoyne, as a fals forsworn man, besegid the toun of Caleys with gret ordenaunce, and an huge noumbre of peple, that is to say CL.M[1]., as it was said. And forto breke the said sege Humfrey duke of Gloucestre with a gret retenu was sent to Caleys. But befor his goyng the erl of Morteyne and the lord Camoys were sent to Caleys with v C men for to kepe the toune, til more streng;he my3te come. And sone aftir, be counselle and manhood of ser Johan Radclyffe, that tyme lieutenaunt of Caleys, the said sege was broke; for whanne the duke of Burgoyne herde of the coming of the duke of Gloucestre with so gret a power, he lefte the sege and wente his way, levyng behynde him some of his gonne; and bombard; hid vnder the sande;.

Thanne wente the said duke of Gloucestre vnto Caleys, and fro thennys into Flaundris, destroyyng the cuntre and the corn stondyng vpon the grounde, and brende the toun of Poperyng and othir smale village;, and thanne cam in to Englond agayne aboute the feste of saint Bartilmew.

And this same yeer withynne a moneth aftir that the said duke of Burgoyne was fled from Caleis, Jame; kyng of Scottis besegid

Anno xj°. fuit generalis eclipsis solis, &c.

A.D. 1433.

Anno xij°.
A.D. 1433-4.

Anno xiij°.
A.D. 1434-5.
Caristia bladi.

Anno xiii[j].
A.D. 1435-6.

Anno xiiij.
[July.]
Folio 180.

[August.]

* The duke of Bedford died September 16th, 1435; consequently in the 14th of Henry VI.

A.D. 1436.

the castel of Rokesburgh in Northumbirlond with CXL.M¹. men as it was said : but thay withynne the castel kept it with iiij^{xx} menne of arme3 ayens the king of Scottis, and and all his ost. And whanne

[August.]
Folio 180 b.

the said kynge herde telle that certayn lordis of the Northcuntre wolde come and breke the sege, he fledde in Scotland ayenne.

[Anno xv°.]
A.D. 1437.
Rex Scotorum
interficitur.

And aftirward aboute the moneth of Marche be excitacion and stiryng of the erl of Atholle and othir, the said kyng of Scottis, as he was goyng toward his bed, hauyng no more vn him but onli his shirte, cruelli and vritmanli was slayne ; and as it was said he hadde on him xxx woundis, wherof vij were dedly.

Anno xix
[xviij.*]
A.D. 1440.

The xix yeer of kyng Harri, the Friday before midsomer, a prest callid ser Richard Wyche, that was a vicary in Estsexe, was brend on the Tourhille for heresie, for whoo3 deth was gret murmur and troubil among the peple, for some said he was a good man and an holy, and put to deth be malice; and some saiden the contrary ; and so dyuers men hadde of him dyuers oppinions. And so fer forth the comune peple was brought in such errour, that meny menne and wommen wente be nyghte to the place where he was brend, and offrid there money and ymage3 of wax, and made thair praiers knel-yng as thay wolde haue don to a saynt, and kiste the ground and baar away with thaym the asshis of his body as for relique3 ; and this endurid viij daie3, til the mair and aldermenne ordeyned men of arme3 forto restreyne and lette the lewd peple fro that fals ydolatrie, and meny were therfore take and lad to prisoun.

Folio 181.

And among othir was take the vicary of Berkyngchirche beside the tour of Londoun, in who3 parishe alle this was done, that receyued the offeryng of the symple peple. And for to excite and stire thaym to offre the more feruently, and to fulfille and satisfie his fals couetise, he took asshis and medlid thaym with powder of spice3 and strowed thaym in the place where the said heretic was brend ; and so the symple peple was deceyued, wenyng that the swete flauour hadde comme of the asshis of the ded

* Correction by the hand of Stowe.

heretic: for this the said vicari of Berkyngchirche confessid aftir- A.D. 1440.
ward in prisoun. And the said heretic cesid nevir vnto the laste
breth forto blaspheme and desclaundre the iiij ordris of freris, the
whiche was no token of perfeccion ne of charite.

And this same yeer in the moneth of Juylle, maister Roger Bol- [Anno] xix.*
tyngbroke that was a gret and a konnyng man in astronomye, and A.D. 1441.
Hoc anno
maister Thomas Suthwelle a chanon of saint Stevenes chapel magister Jo-
hannes Kemp,
wythynne Westmynstre, were take as conspiratours of the kyngis archiepiscopus
deth ; for it was said that the said maister Roger sholde laboure to Ebor. factus
fuit cardinalis ;
consume the kyngis persone be wey of nygromancie, and that the Feb. 1440.†
said maister Thomas sholde say massis in forboden and inconuenient
places, that is to say, in the logghe of Harnesey Park beside London,
vpon certayn instrumentis with the whiche the said maister Roger
sholde and (sic) vse his said craft of nygromancie ayens the feith
and good bleue, and was assentyng to the said Roger in alle his
workis. And the Sunday the xxv day of the same moneth, the
forsaid maister Roger with all his instrumentis of nygromancie—that Folio 181 b.
is to say a chaier ypeynted, wherynne he was wont to sitte whanne
he wroughte his craft, and on the iiij corners of the chaier stood
iiij swerdis, and vpon euery swerd hanggyng an ymage of copir—and
with meny othir instrumentis accordyng to his said craft, stood in
a high stage aboue alle mennes heddis in Powlis chircheyerd befor
the cros whiles the sermon endurid, holdyng a suerd in his right
hand and a septre in his lift hand, araid in a marvaillous aray
whereynne he was wont to sitte whanne he wroujte his nygromancie. And aftir the sermon was don, he abiurid alle maner
articles longyng in eny wise to the said craft of nigromancie, or
mys sownyng to the Cristen feith.

And the Tywisday next folowyng dame Alienore Cobham, Hic incipit pro-
cessus contra
duchesse of Gloucestre, fledde be nyjte in to the sayntewary at Alienoram Cob-
Westmynstre; wherfore she was holde suspect of certayn articles ham.
of tresoun.

A.D. 1441.

In the mene tyme, the forsaid maister Roger was examned before the kyngis counsel; where he confessid and saide that he wroughte the said nygromancie atte stiryng of the forsaid dame Alienore, to knowe what sholde falle of hir and to what astat she sholde come. Wherfore she was citid to appere befor certayn bisshoppis of the kyngis; that is to say, befor maister Harri Chicheli, archebisshop of Cauntirbury, maister Harry Beaufort bisshoppe of Wynchestre and cardinalle, maister Johan Kemp archebisshoppe of York and cardinalle, maister William Ayscoughe bisshoppe of Salisbury, and othir, on the Monday the xxij day off Juylle next folowyng, in saint Stephene3 chapelle of Westmynstre, forto ansuere to certayn article3 of nygromancie, of wicchecraft or sorcery, of heresy and of tresoun. Atte whiche day she apperid; and the forsaid Roger was brou3t forth forto witnesse ayens hir, and saide that she was cause and first stirid himme to laboure in the said nygromancie; and thanne be commaundement of the said bisshoppis she was committid to the warde of sir Johan Stiward knyghte, and of Johan Stanley squier, and othir of the kyngis hous, forto be lad to the castelle of Ledis, there to be safli kept vnto iij wikis aftir Mighelmasse next thanne comyng. But the said dame Alienore was lothe to go out of the sayntwary and fayned her seek, and wolde haue stole away priveli be watir, but she was let of her purpos and lad forth to the castel beforsaid.

Folio 182.

[Anno xx°.]
A.D. 1441.

Anonne aftir, a commission was direct to the erl of Huntyngdoun, to the erl of Stafforde, to the erl of Suffolk, and to certayn juges of bothe benchis, to enquire of al maner tresons, sorcery, and alle othir thyngi3 that my3te in eny wise towche or concerne harmfulli the kyngis persone; befor whom the said maister Roger and maister Thomas as principalle, and the said dame Alienore as accessory, were enditid of treson, yn the Guyldehalle of Londoun.

Folio 182 b.
Nota de sortilegà de Eye.

And this same tyme was take a womman callid the wieche of Eye, whoo3 sorcerie and wicchecraft the said dame Alienore hadde longe tyme vsid; and be suche medicine3 and drynkis as the said wieche

made, the said Alienore enforced the forsaid duke of Gloucestre to A.D. 1441.
loue her and to wedde her. Wherfore, and also for cause of relaps,
the same wicche was brend in Smythfeld, in the vigily of Saint
Simon and Jude.

Ferthirmore on the Satirday the xxj day of Octobir, in the chapel
beforsaid, befor the bisshoppis of Londoun, maister Robert Gilbert,
and of Lincoln maister William Alnewik, and of Norwich maister
Thomas Brouns, to whom the said archebisshoppe of Cauntirbury,
maister Henri Chichele, badde committid his power be his commissioun because of his seeknesse to fynyshe and ende this mater, the
said Alienore apperid. And maister Adam Moleyns, thanne clerc
of the kyngis counsel, redde certayn articleȝ obiectid ayens hir of
sorcerie and nygromancie, wherof some she denyed and some she
grauntid.

Thanne was this processe proroged vnto the Monday the xxiij day
of Octobir thanne next folowyng, at whiche day the said Alienore
apperid and witnesseȝ were broughte forth and examned, and she
was convict of the said articleȝ. Thanne it was axed of hir, yf she
wolde eny say ayens the witnesseȝ, and she said Nay, but submitted
hir onli to the correccioun of the bisshoppis ; and on the Friday
next, the said Alienore abiurid before the bisshoppis the articleȝ
abouesaid. And thanne she was enioyned forto appere before the Folio 183.
said archebisshoppe of Cauntirbury or his forsaid commissioners,
the Thursday the ix day of Nouembir next folowyng, forto receyue
her penaunce. And in the mene tyme the forsaid maister Thomas
Suthwelle deide in the tour of Londoun.

The Thursday abouesaid the said dame Alienore apperid befor
tharchebisshoppe and othir in the forsaid chapelle, and receyued her
penaunce vnder this fourme ; that she sholde go the same day fro
Templebarre with a meke and a demure countenaunce vnto Poulis Nota peniten-
beryng in her hond a tapir of a pound, and offre it there atte highe ciam Alienora
auter. And the Wednesday next she sholde go fro the Swan in Cobham, sibi
Thamyse strete beryng a tapir of the same weighte vnto Crichirche iniunctam.

A.D. 1441. in Londoun, and there offre it vp. And the Friday next she shold go in lik wise fro Quenehide berying a tapir of the same weighte vnto saint Mighele; in Cornhulle, and there offre it vp. The whiche penaunce she fulfillid and dede righte mekely, so that the more part of the peple badde on hir gret compassioun.

And aftir this she was committid ayen to the warde of ser Thomas Stanley, wherynne she was al her lif aftir, hauyng yeerli C marc., assigned to hir for hir fyndyng and costis ; whoo; pride, fals couetise Folio 183 b. and lecherie were cause of her confusioun. Othir thyngis myghte be writen of this dame Alienore, the whiche atte reuerence of nature and of wommanhood shul not be reherced.

And the Satirday the xviij day of Nouembir next sewyng, maister Roger Boltyngbroke at Guyldehalle at Londoun befor the said lordis and justice; was arreymed of the forsaid article; of tresoun ayens the kyngis persone, and therof be xij men of Londoun he was founde gilty. Wherfore be the iugement of ser Johan Hody that tyme chief justice of the kyngis bench, he was drawe fro the tour of Londoun vnto Tyburne ; and there he was hanged and leet doun half alive, and his bowellis take out and brent, and his hed smyte of and set on London brigge, and his body quartrid and sent to certayn tounes of Englond, that is to saye, Oxenford, Cambrigge, York and Hereforde. And whanne the said maister Roger sholde die, he confessid that he was nevir gilty of eny treson ayens the kyngis persone; but he presumed to fer in his konnyng, as he sayde, wherof he cride God mercy; and the justice that yaf on him iugement livid not longe aftir.

Anno xxj°.
A.D. 1443. The xxj yeer of king Harri, saiut Georges feste was holde at Westmynstre, and there ser Johan Beaufort erl of Somerset was maad duke of Somerset.

Anno xxij.
A.D. 1444. The xxij yeer of kynge Harri, Johan erlle of Huntyngdoun at Wyndesore was made duke of Excestre.

And this same yeer deide the forsaid Johan Beaufort duke of Somerset, the vj kalendes of May, at Wymborne mynstre in the counte of Dorset, and there he is buried.

The xxiij [xxij] yere of kyng Harri, aboute the beginnyng of Lente,
were sente ambassiatours in to Fraunce ; that is to say, the erl of Suffolk, maister Adam Moleyns dean of Salisbury and keper of the kyngis pryve seal, and ser Robert Roos, and other, to trete of the mariage betuene kyng Harri and dame Margarete the kyngis douȝtir of Cecile. And the Sunday next befor Witsuntide the xxiiij day of May, in saint Martyneȝ chirche in the toun of Touris in Tureyne, assuraunce of mariage was maad betuene the said erlle, as in name of the kyngis persone, and the said dame Margarete, before the popis legat Petrus de Monte, that tyme beyng there. And thanne were grauntid treweȝ and abstinence of warre betuene Englond and Fraunce for terme of xviij monetheȝ,—but what treson grew vnder tho treweȝ, it was sone know aftirward be alienacion of Anges and Mayne, and wilful lesyng of al Normandy; and aftir this, our ambassiatours cam hoom agayne.

The xxiiij [xxiij] yeer of kyng Harri in the moneth of Nouembir,
the said erl of Suffolk with othir wente ayenne in to Fraunce, forto brynge and condue the said dame Margarete into Engelond: the whiche erl was made befor his goyng markeys of Suffolk; and sone aftir he was maad duke.

And this same yeer, at Witsuntid, Humfrey erl of Stafford was maad duke of Bukynghame.

And this same yeer, on the Thursday the xxv. day of Feuerer was a parlement begonne att Westmynstre, in the whiche Gye [Henry]* the yong erl of Warwic was maad duke of Warwic; and the lord Beaumond was maad vicount Beaumond.

And duryng this parlement, the forsaid dame Margarete landid at Porchestre and wente fro thenneȝ to Hamptoun be water, and restid her there in the Goddeshous; and thanne she wente in to the abbey of Tychfeld, and there she was weddid to king Harri on the Thursday the xxij. day of Aprille, and maister William Ascoghe,

* This is Stowe's correction, the word " Gye" is struck out from the text and " Henry" written in the margin.

A.D. 1445. bisshoppe of **Salisbury**, dede the solennite of the marriage and weddid thaym, and on the Sunday the **xxx.** day of May next folowyng she was crouned at Westmynstre.

This same yeer in the moneth of Juylle deide the forsaid **Gye [Henry]*** duke of Warwic withoute heir male; and so in him cessid and failid the noble lyne of the erlis of Warwic, as to heir male, and remayned in his dou3tir.

[Anno xxvº.]
A.D. 1446. The **xxv.** yeer of kyng Harri, yn the monethis of Nouembir and Decembir fille grete thundryng and lightnyng, with huge and grete wyndis.

A.D. 1447.
Nota de parlia-
mento de Bury. And in the moneth of Feuerer next aftir, the **x.** day thereof, began the parlement at saint Edmundis Bury in Suffolk; the whiche parlement was maad only for to sle the noble duke of Gloucestre, who3 deth the fals duke of Suffolk William de la Pole, and ser Jame3 Fyne3 lord Say, and othir of thair assent, hadde longe tyme conspired and ymagyned. And they seyng that thay my3t not sle him be no trewe mene3 of iusti3e ne of lawe, and enfourmed falsli the king, and sayde that he wolde reise the Walshmenne forto distresse Folio 185. him and destroie him; and ordeyned that euery lord sholde come to the said parlement in thair best aray and withe strengthe. And alle the weye3 aboute the said toun off Bury, be commaundement of the said duke of Suffolk, were kept with gret multitude of peple of the cuntre, wakyng day and nyghte; vnknowyng the said peple wherfore it was: and the wedir was so cold that some of the poer peple that there wakid, deide for cold.

And ayens the ende of the parlement, the said duke of Gloucestre was sent for, for to come and ansuer to suche poynte3 of tresoun as sholde be laid ayens him; and er he cam fully into the toun of Bury, ther were sent vnto him messagers commaundyng him on the kyngis behalfs, that he sholde go streighte to his yn, and come not nyghe the kyng til he badde othirwise in commaundement. And the secunde day aftir, while3 he sat at mete in his yn, cam a sergeaunt

* Stowe's correction.

of arme; and arestid certayn kny;tis and squyers and othir special   A.D. 1447.
seruauntis of his, and ladde thaym to dyuers prisons.

And the iij. day aftır, the lord Beaumount with othir, that is to
say, the duke of Bukynghame, the duke of Somerset, and othir, cam
to the said duke of Glouzestre and arestid him: and thanne were
certayn of the kyngis hous commaunded to waite on him. And the
iij. day aftir, he deide for sorou, as some men saide, because he   [Feb. 28th.]
myghte not come to his ansuer and excuse him of suche thyngis as
were falsli put on him; for the said duke of Suffolk and lord Say,   Folio 185 b.
and othir of thair assent, so stirid and excitid the kyng ayens the
said duke of Gloucestre that he myghte nevir come to his excuse;
for thay hadde cast among thaym a prive conclusioun, the whiche as
yit is not come to the knowlage of the commune peple, and thay
wiste welle that thay sholde nevir brynge it aboute til he were ded;
but the certaynte of his dəth is not yit openly knowe, but ther is no
thyng so prive, as the gospell saith, but atte laste it shal be openne.

And this same yẑer, on the Tiwisday in the Estirwike deide   [April 11th.]
maister Harri Beaufort, bisshoppe of Wynchestre and prest cardinalle of Rome.

And this yeer in the moneth of August, deide ser Johan Holond,
duke of Excestre and erlle of Huntyngdoun.

The xxvj. yeer of king Harri was lepe yeer, and our ladie; evyn   Anno xxvjº.
in Lente fille on Estirday.   A.D. 1448.

The xxviij. yeer of king Harri, on Simon day and Jude, and other   Anno xxviij.
daie; before and aftir, the sonne in his risyng and goyng doune   A.D. 1449.
apperid as reed as blood, as meny a man saw; wherof the peple badde
gret marvaille, and demed that it sholde betokened sum harm sone
aftirward.

And this same yeer, in the feste of saint Mighelle in Monte Tumba,   [October 16th]
Roon was lost and yolden to the Frensshemenne;* beyng therynne
that tyme the duke of Somerset and the erl of Shrowesbury.

And the next yeer aftir, alle Normandy was lost.

* Rouen was evacuated, according to treaty, November 4, 1449 (Monstrelet).

A.D. 1450.
Folio 186.

And this yeer, the Friday the ix. day of Januarye, maister Adam Moleyns, bisshoppe of Chichestre and keper of the kyngis prive seel, whom the kyng sente to Portesmouth, forto make paiement of money to certayne soudiers and shipmenne for thair wage3; and so it happid (*sic*) that with boiste3 langage, and also for abriggyng of thair wage3, he fil in variaunce with thaym, and thay fil on him, and cruelli there kilde him.

Episcopus Cicestre inter-ficitur.

[June 29th.]

And this same yer, in the feste of Saint Petir and Paule aftir Midsomer, that is to say, the Monday, the laste day of Juyn saue one, maister William Ascoghe bisshop of Salisbury was slayn of his owen parisshens and peple at Edyngdoun aftir that he hadde said masse, and was drawe fro the auter and lad vp to an hille ther beside, in his awbe, and his stole aboute his necke; and there thay slow him horribly, thair fader and thair bisshoppe, and spoillid him vnto the nakid skyn, and rente his blody shirte in to pecis and baar thaym away with thaym, and made bost of thair wickidnesse: and the day befor his deth his chariot was robbed be men of the same cuntre of an huge god and tresour, to the value of x. M^l. marc., as thay saide that knewe it. Thise ij. bisshoppis were wonder couetous men, and evil beloued among the comune peple, and holde suspect of meny defautes, and were assentyng and willyng to the deth of the duke of Gloucestre, as it was said.

Episcopus Sarum occi-ditur.

Nota de Johanne Cade, capitaneo Kanciæ.
Folio 186 b.
[May 30th.*]

And this same yeer, in the moneth of May, aroos thay of Kent and made thaym a capteyne, a ribaude, an Yrissheman, callid Johan Cade; the whiche atte begynning took on him the name of a gentilmanne, and callid himself Mortymer forto haue the more fauour of the peple; and he callid himself also John Amende-alle; for forasmuche as thanne and longe before the reme of Englond badde be rewlid be untrew counselle, wherfore the comune profit was sore hurt and decresid; so that alle the comune peple, what for

* "Septimâ in Pentecoste." W. Worcester, Pentecost this year being May 24th. See our chronicler below, who fixes the date of Cade's great popularity from the day following.

taxe3 and tallage3 and other oppressions myght not live be thair A.D. 1450.
handwork and husbondrie, wherfore thay grucchid sore ayens thaym
that badde the gouernaunce of the land.

Thanne cam the said capteyn and the Kentisshmen vuto the
Blakeheth, and there kepte the feld a moneth and more, pilyng alle
the cuntre aboute; tc whom the cite of Londoun, at that tyme, was
fulle fauorable and frendly; but it last not longe aftir. In the
mene tyme the king sente notable menne to the said capteyn and
his feleshippe, to knowe thair purpose and the cause of thair insur- [June.]
reccioun. The capteyn was a sotill man, and saide that he and his
feleship were assembld and gadrid there, forto redresse and refourme
the wrongis that were don in the reme, and to withstonde the
malice of thayme that were destroiers of the comune profit; and
forto correcte and amende the defautis of thaym that were the kyngis
chief counselours; and shewde vnto thaym the articles of his
peticions concernyng and touchyng the myschiefs and mysgouern- Folio 187.
aunce3 of the reme, wherynne was nothyng conteyned but that
that was rightful and resonable, wherof a copie was sent to the
parlement holden that tyme at Westmynstre; wherfore the said
capteyne desirid that suche grevaunce3 sholde be amendid and re-
fourmed be the parlement, and to haue ansuer therof agayne, but he
badde none.

Sone aftir the kyng remeued fro Westmynstre vuto Grenewich;
and while he was there he wolde haue sent certayn lordis with a
power forto haue distressid the Kentisshmenne, but thair men that
sholde haue gon with thaym ansuerde to thair lordis and saide, that
thay wolde not fi3te ayens thaym that labourid forto amende and
refourme the comure profit; and whanne the lordis herde this, thay
lefte thair purpo3.

Thanne cride the Kentisshmenne and othir ayens the lord Say,
the kyngis chamberlayne, that was on of the kyngis fals counselours
and holden suspect of tresoun, and the king dredyng the malice of
the peple, committid him to the tour of Londoun.

A.D. 1450.

Thanne wente the kyng ayen to Londoun, and withynne ij. daie3 aftir he wente ayens the Kentisshmenne with xv M[1]. men wel araid vuto the Blakeheth, but the said Kentisshmen heryng how the king wolde come, and fledde the ny3t befor his comyns, in to the wode cuntre to Seuenok.

Folio 187 b.

The kyng thanne retourned to Londoun, and sente out a squier callid William Stafford, and ser Humfrey Stafford, kny3t, his cosyne, forto aspie where the Kentisshmen were; and whanne they knew that thay were at Seuenok, thay rood thider hastily with a few menne, wenyng to haue gotenne a singuler worshippe and laude; but thay were withyn the daunger of thaym er thay wiste it, and [June 28th ?] were there bothe yslayne, with the more part of thair men that abood with thaym.

[June 30th ?] Whanne this was don the king dissolued the parlement, and re-meued vnto Kyllyngworth. And whanne the Kentishmen herde [July 1st.] that the kyng was gon fro Londoun, thay cam ayen in to Suthwerk, [July 3rd, Friday.] and thair capteyn was loggid atte Hert. And the Thursday* aftir be fauour of some of the men of Londoun he cam in to the cite, but sone aftir thay repentid, for thay were diuidid among thay.mself; but the keie3 of the cite were delyuerid vnto the said capteyn, and he kepte thaym ij. daie3 and ij. nyghtes. And whanne he hadde entrid the cite anon he and his men fille to roborie, and robbid certayn worthi men of the cite, and put some of thaym in to prison til thay hadde paid notable summe3 of money to saue thair livis. And the said capteyn rood aboute the cite beryng a nakid swerd in his hand, armed in a peire of brigaundyne3, weryng a peire of gilt sporis, and a gilt salat, and a gowne of blew veluet, as he hadde be a lord or a kny3t,—and yit was he but a knaue,—and hadde his Folio 188. swerd born befor him.

[July 5th, Sunday.] And the Satirday next the said capteyn commaundid that the lord Say sholde be brou3t out of the tour vnto Guyldehalle in

---

* Friday, not Thursday, July 3rd. " Die Veneris, tertio die Julii." Wm. Worcest.

Londoun, where that certayn justice3 sat that tyme; and whanne he
was ycome, the Kentisshmen wolde not suffre him forto abide the
lawe, but ladde him vnto the Standard in Chepe, and there his hed
was smyte of, and his body was drawe naked at a hors taille vpon
the pament so that the flesshe clivid to the stone3 fro Chepe in to
Suthwerk, the said capteyne3 ynne. Also a squier callid Crowmer
that was the shireue of Kent, that badde weddid the said lord Saie3
dou3tir, be commaundement of the capteyne was broughte out of
Flete, that was committid thider for certayn extorsione3 that he
badde do in his office, and lad to Mile Ende, withoute Londoun, and
there withoute eny othir iugement his hed was smyte of, and the
lord Saie3 hed and his also were bore vpon ij. long shaftis vnto
Londoun brigge, and there set vppe, and the lord Saie3 body was
quartrid.

On the Sunday next, men of London seyng the tiranny and robory
of the said cursid capteyne and of his men; and whanne it was
nyghte thay laide hand on thayme that were disparblid aboute in the
cite, and bet thaym and droof thaym out of the cite, and shit the
yatis. And whanne the capteyn that was in his yn in Suthwerk
saw this, anon he with his men made assaut to Londoun brigge, and
wolde haue come yn, and spoylid the cite; and the lord Scale3 with
his menne and menne of the cite faughte with thayme fro ix. of the
clocke in the euyn, vnto x. of the clocke in the morow; and meny
men were slayn on bothe partie3, and sore wounded; and there were
slayne, Mathew Goghe a squyer of Walis, and Johan Sutton an
alderman of Londoun. And this skyrmysh endurid til the brigge of
tre was set on fire, betuene thaym of Kent and of Londoun; and
thanne thay of Kent withdrow thaym litille and litille. And thair
capteyn put alle his pilage and the godis that he hadde robbid in to
a barge, and sente it to Rouchestre be watir, and he wente be lande
and wolde haue go in to the castel of Queneburghe with a fewe men
that were left with himme, but he was let of his purpo3. And anon
he fledde in to the wode cuntre beside Lewe3, and the shireue of

Kent him pursude, and there he was wounded vnto the dethe, and take and caried in a carte toward Londoun, and be the wey he deide.* And thanne his hed was smyte of and set on Londoun brigge, and his body quartrid and sent to dyuers tounez of Englond;

whooz tirannye endurid fro Trinite Sunday vuto Saint Thomas eve† of Caunterbury : and thus endid this capteyn of myschief.

And this same yeer, the communez arooz in dyuers partiez of

Englond, as in Sussex, Salisburye, Wilshire, and othir placez, and dede moche harm to meny personez.

And this same yeer, was the yeer of grace at Rome, and began on Neweyeris day, and lastid vnto the same day the nexte yeer folowyng.

The xxix ‡ yere of king Harri, Normandie was lost be the vntrouthe and fals couetize of Edmund duke of Somerset, beyng that tyme lieutenaunt of Normandie; for he menuzid and abatid the noumbre of the soudiers that were in the garisonz, and sente thaym in to Englond vnpaid of thair wagez, wherby the strengthe of Normandie was lost.

Also the comune vois and fame was that tyme, that the duke of Suffolk William de la Pole, and the said duke of Somerset, with othir of thair assent, hadde maad delyueraunce of Aunge and Mayn withoute assent of this lond vnto the kyng of Cicile the queuez fader; and badde also aliened and sold the duchie of Normandie to the king of Fraunce ; wherfore alle the peple of this lond and specialli the communez cride ayens the said duke of Suffolk, and said he was a traitour ; and atte instaunce and peticioun of the said communez

* A proclamation, promising a thousand markes for the head of Cade, was issued 10th of July. See Stowe's Annals, 646 ; Holinshed, iii. 635. And on the 15th of the same month an order was given to the Treasurer of the Exchequer to pay the amount to Alexander Iden, sheriff of Kent (Rymer, xi. 275). This would fix his death between the 10th and 15th July. The Rolls of Parliament seem to prove that it must have taken place after the 11th Rot. Parl. v. 224.

† Eve of *translation* of Thomas of Canterbury, July 6th.

‡ The Chronicler is still in the 28th of Henry VI.

of the parlement holden that tyme at Westmynstre, he was arestid   A.D. 1450.
and put in to the tour.   [January 28th.]

   This duke of Suffolk hadde axed befor this tyme of on that was
an astronomer, what sholde falle of him, and how he sholde ende his
lif; and whanne the said astronomer hadde labourid therfore in his
said craft, he ansuerde to the duke and said that he sholde die a   Folio. 189 b.
shameful deth, and counselid him alwey to be war of the tour;
wherfor be instaunce of lordis that were his frendis, he was sone
delyuerid out of the said tour of Londoun.

Thanne the kyng seyng that alle this lond hatid the said duke
dedly, and that he myȝt not bere ne abide the malice of the peple,   [March 17,]
and exilid him for terme of v. yeer. And the Friday the iij. day of
May,* he took his shippe at Episwich and sailed forth in to the high
see, where anothir shippe callid the Nicholas of the Tour lay in waite
for him, and took him. And thay that were wythynne grauntid
him space of a day and a nyghte to shryue him, and make him redy
to God. And thanne a knaue of Yrlond smot of his hed, vpon the
side of the boot of the said Nicholas of the Tour, notwithstondyng
his saaf conduct; and the body with the hed was cast to the lond at
Douor.

And this yeer, on Newyeris day, began the yeer of grace at Saint
Jamez.

And this same yeer† saint Georges day fille on Estirday, and   [Anno xxix°.]
Corpus Christi day fille on Midsomer day, that is to say, the viij.   A.D. 1451.
kalendes of Juylle.

The xxx. yeere of kyng Harry, aboute Shroftyde, the duke of   [Anno xxx.]
Yorke, the erle of Deuenshire, and the lord Cobham, gadered a grete   A.D. 1452.
peple in destruccioun of theire enemyes that were aboute the kyng;   [February.]
and sente by an herowde to London, prayng that they myghte

---

* He was to leave the kingdom *before* the 1st of May (Rot. Parl. v. 183.)

† The 29th Henry VI. must be here intended, although Easter day in that year was
April 25, and the fixed feast mentioned in the text (St. George's) was April 23. But the
second calculation is accurate, for Corpus Christi day, 1451, fell on the 24th of June.

A.D. 1452.
Folio 190.

passe wyth theyre peple thorough the cyte, but they cowde gete no graunte therof for asmoche as the kyng had commaunded the contrary. Wherfore thay passed ouer the Temes by Kyngstone brige, and wente forthe to the toune of Derteforde in Kent; and there, besyde the toune, ordeyned and pyghte theyre felde. And thenne the kyng with many lordes wyth the nombre of xv. M¹. men, came towarde the seyde duke of Yorke, for to dystresse hym and his peple. And when the duke sawe that the peple of Kent and of other places came nat to hym as they had promysed, and that they were nat stronge ynoughe for the kyngys parte, by entrete of diuerse bysshops they yelde theym vnto the kynges grace, and so retorned to London. And there the matier was put in a rewle betwene the kyng and the seyde duke, as for that tyme.

Anno xxxj.
A.D. 1453.
[July.]

The xxxj. yere of kyng Harry, in the moneth of May, the erle of Shrouesbury was slayne besyde Burdeux; and sir Edward Hulle, knyghte, and the lorde Lyle sone of the sayde erle, and the lorde Molyns take prysoner, and after delyuered for a grete raunsom.

Anno xxxij°.
A.D. 1453-4.

The xxxij. yere of kyng Harry, and the yere of oure Lorde M¹.iiijc.liiij.* on the Saturday the xiiij. day of Octobre, in the feste of seynt Edwarde the Confessoure, was bore at Westmynstre Edward the furst sone of kyng Harry; whoos godfadres were master Johan Kempe, archebysshoppe of Caunterbury and bysshoppe cardinal
Folio 190 b.
of Rome, and Edmunde duke of Somerset, his godmother was the duchesse of Buckynghame: and master William Wayneflete, bysshop of Wynchestre, hym baptized.

A.D. 1454.

And this same yeer, deyed the same mastre Johan Kempe archebysshop of Caunterbury on the Friday the xxij. day of Marche. After whom succeded in to the seyde archebysshopryche mastre Thomas Bouchier bisshoppe of Ely, and into the office of the chaunceler, ser Richard Nevyle erle of Salysbury.

Anno xxxiij.
A.D. 1454-5.

The xxxiij. yere of kyng Harry, the erle Douglas of Scotlonde

---

* Prince Edward was born Saturday 13th October, feast of *translation* of Edw. Conf. 1453.

fled oute of Scotlande and came into Engelond, because that the
kyng of Scottis badde vnmanly and traytourly slayne the sayde erle
hys brother vnder sauf conduct. And he became kyng Harrye;
liege man, and was swore to him and dede to him homage, and had
a place assigned to him in the parlement.

This same yere, in the moneth of Juyne [May*], the kyng wolde
haue ryde to Leycestre for to haue holde a counseylle there; and
rode by the toune of Watforde, abiding there alle nyghte, and came
on the morcw to Saynt Albonys aboute ix. of the clocke.

Thenne was there a mortalle debate and a variaunce bitwene
Richard duke of Yorke, Richard erle of Salesbury, Richard erle of
Warrewyke, and Edmund duke of Somerset, be whom at that tyme
the kyng was principally gided and gouerned, as he had be beforne
by the duk of Suthfolk. And this saide duke Edmond euer kept
hym nygh the kyng, and durste nat departe fer from his presence,
dreding alwey the power of the seyde duk of York and of the forseyde erles, and euer excited and stered the kyng ageyns thaym;
notwithstandyng that the comones of this lande hated this duk
Edmond and loued the duk of York, because he loued the communes
and preserued the commune profyte of the londe.

The seyde duke Richard and the erle abouesayde, seyng that
they myghte nat prejayle ne withstond the malice of the forseyde
duk Edmond; the whiche dayly entended and prouoked the kyng to
theyre fynal destruccioun; and gadered priuyly a power of peple
and kept thaym couertly in villages aboute the toune of Seynt
Albons; and whan the kyng was there, they beseged the toune
aboute, and sente to the kyng besechyng hym that he wolde sende
oute vuto theym theyre mortal enemy, Edmond duke of Somerset,
and enemy to alle the reame; yef he wolde nat so, they wolde haue
hym by streynghte and violence. The kyng by advyse of his
counseylle answered and seyde he wolde nat delyuer him.

* Correction in the text by the hand of Stowe.
† By the hand of Stowe.

K 4 *

Whanne the duk of York and the erles herde this aunswere, thoughe the toune were strongly barred and arrayed for defence, they and theyr peple brake doune vyolently howses and pales on the este syde of the toune, and entred in to seynt Petres strete sleyng alle tho that wythestoode theym. Thanne came the kyng oute of the abbey wyth his baner dysplayed in to the same strete, and duke Edmond wythe hym, and the duk of Bokyngham, the erle of Northumbrelonde, and the lorde Clyfforde, and the lorde Sudeley beryng the kynges baner; and there was a sore fyghte, as for the tyme, and there at laste was slayne the seyde duke Edmond, the erle of Northumbrelond, and the lorde Clyfforde; the kyng that stoode vndre his baner was hurte in the necke wythe an arowe. And when the seyde duke Edmonde and the lordes were slayne, the batayle was ceased. And thus was done the Thurseday the xxij. day of May.

Thys sayde Edmond duke of Somerset had herde a fantastyk prophecy that he shuld dy vndre a castelle; wherefore in as meche as in him was, he lete the kyng that he sholde nat come in the castelle of Wyndsore, dredyng the seyde prophecy; but at Seynt Albonys ther was an hostry hauyng the sygne of a castelle, and before that hostry he was slayne.

When this was done, the forseyde duke of York and the erles retorned to Londoun, and had the kyng with theym.

And at this bataylle were slayne lx. persones of gentilmen and of other.

And this same yeer, in the moneth of Juyne was seen *stella comata*, betwene the northe and the est, extendyng her bemes towardes the sowthe. The whiche sterre was seyenne also in the court of Rome, as they reported that came fro thens.

The xxxv. yere of kyng Harry, and the yere of oure lorde M^l.cccc.lvij.* a pylgryme that alle his dayes had be a shipmanne,

---

* Michaelmas, 1457, was in the 36th Henry VI. Holinshed places the second prodigy here mentioned under November 1456.

came fro seynt James in Spayne into Englond aboute Mighelmas, A.D. 1456. and was loged in the toune of Weymouthe, in Dorsetshyre, with a brewer, a Duchemanne, the whiche had be with hym in his seyde pylgremage. And as the sayde pylgryme laye in his bedde waking, he sawe one come in to the chambre clothed alle in whyte hauing a whyte heede, and sate doune on a fourme nat fer fro hys bed; and alle the Folio 192. chambre was as lyghte of hym as it had be clere day. The pylgryme was agaste and durst not speke, and anone the seyde spirite vanysshed awey. The secund nyghte the same spyryte came ayene in lykewyse, and wythorte eny tareyng vanysshed awey. In the morow the pyl· grym tolde alle this to his oste, and seyde he was sore afeerde, and wolde no more lye in that chambre. Hys oste counseled hym to telle this to the parysshe preeste, and shryue hym of all his synnes, demyng that he hadde be acombred with some grete dedely synne. The pylgrym sayde, " I was late shryue at seynt James, and rescued there my Lord God, and sethe that tyme, as fer as I canne remembre, I haue nat offended my conscience." Natheles he was shryuenue, and tolde alle this to the preest; and the preest seyde, " Sen thow knowest thy selfe clere in conscience, haue a goode herte and be nat agast, and yef the sayde spirite come ayene, coniure hym in the name of the Fader, and of the Sone, and of the Holy Goste, to telle the what he ys." The iij^{de} nyghte the spyryte came ayene in to the chambre as he had do before, wyth a grete lyghte; and the pylgrym, as the preest had counseled him, coniured the spyryte, and bade hym telle what he was. The spyryte answered and seyde, ⸗ " I am thyne eme, thy faderes brother." The pylgrym seyde, " How longe ys it ago sen thow deyde?" The spiryte seyde, " ix. yere." " Where ys my fader?" seyde the pylgrime. " At home in his owne hous," seyde the spiryte, " and hath another wyfe." " And where ys my moder?" " In heuene," seyde the spiryte. Thenne seyde the spiryte to the pylgryme, " Thou haste be at seynt James; trowest thou that thow hast welle done thy pylgremage?" Folio 192 b. " So I hoope," saide the pylgryme. Thanne sayde the spiryte,

A.D. 1456.

" Thow hast do to be sayde there iij. masses, one for thy fader, another for thy moder, and the iij^{de} for thy selue ; and yef thou haddest lete say a masse for me, I had be delieured of the peyne that I suffre. But thow most go ayene to seynt James, and do say a masse for me, and yeue iij^d. to iij. pore men." " O," sayde the pylgrime, "howe shulde I go ayene to seynt James? I haue no money for myne expenses, for I was robbed in the shyppe of v. nobles." " I know welle thys," sayde the spirite, " for thow shalt fynde thy purce hanging at the ende of the shyp and a stoone therynne ; but thow most go ageyne to seynt James, and begge, and lyue of almesse." And when the spyryte had thus seyde, the pylgryme saw a deuelle drawe the same spyryte by the sleue, for to haue hym thennys. Thenne saide the spyryte to the pylgryme, " I haue folewed the this ix. yere, and myghte neuer speke with the vuto now; but blessed be the bous where a spyryte may speke, and farewell, for I may no lenger abyde with the, and therfore I am sory:" and so he vanysshed awey. The pylgryme went into Portyngale, and so forthe to seynt James, as the spyryte had hym commaunded ; wherefore I counseylle euery man to worship seynt James.

Also this yere, in the moneth of Novembre, in the yle of Portlond nat fer from the forseyde toune of Weymouthe was sey a cocke commyng oute of the see, hauyng a greete creeste vppon his hede and a greete rede beerde and legges of half a yerde long, and stood in the water and crew iij. tymes; and euery tyme that he crew he

Folio 193.

turned hym rounde aboute, and bekened wyth his hede towarde the north, the southe, and the weste, and he was of the coloure of a fesaunt; and when he had crowe iij. tymes he vanysshed awey.

A.D. 1457.
[August 28th.]

And this same yere, the xxviij. day of August, on the Sunday in the morow, the Frensshemen robbed and spoyled the toune of Sandewyche in Kent, abydyng thereynne an hoole day, and at the laste a kynghte of the contre called ser Thomas Kyryel drofe theym to the see, and kylde many of theym.

The xxxvj. yere of kyng Harry, in the moneth of January, dyed
the erle of Deuynshire in the abbey of Abyndoun poysened, as men
sayde, and beyng there at that tyme with queue Margarete.

And this same yere, and the yere of oure Lorde M^1.iiijc.lvij.
master Reynold Pocock bysshop of Chichestre a seculer doctour of
dyuynyte, that had labored meny yeres for to translate Holy Scrip-
ture into Englysshe ; passing the bondes of diuinite and of Crysten
beleue, was accused of certayne articles of heresy, of the whyche he
was conuyct before the archebysshoppe of Caunterbury and other
bysshopys and clerkys ; and vtterly abiured, reuoked, and renounced the sayde articles opynly at Powles Crosse in his moder
tunge as folowethe hereafter. "In the name of the Holy Trynyte,
Fader, Sone, and Holy Gost, I Reynold Pocok bysshop of Chichestre
vnworthy, of myne owne power and wylle withoute eny maner
cohercioun or drede, confesse and knowlege that I herebefore this
tyme presumyng of myne natural wytte, and preferryng my inge-
ment and naturalle resoun before the Newe and the Olde Testament,
and the auctoryte and determinacoun of oure moder hooly churche,
haue holde, wrytenne and taughte otherwys thanne the hooly
Romane and uniuersalle churche techythe, prechethe, or obseruethe ;
and ouer thys, ayenst the trew catholyc and aposteles feythe, I haue
made, wryten, taughte and publysshed meny and diuerse perylous doctrynes, bookes, werkes and wrytyng, conteynyng heresyes and errours
contrary to the feythe catholyk and determinacoun of holy churche ;
and specially these heresyes and errours folowyng, that ys to say :

"In primis, quod non est de necessitate fidei credere quod Dominus
noster Ihesus Christus post mortem descendit ad inferos.

'Item, quod non est de necessitate salutis, credere in sanctorum
communione.

* Stowe.

† By the hand of Stowe. Pecock's final examination upon the charge of heresy before
the Archbishop and bishops had been on November 28th, when he made his private
recantation (Wood, Hist. et Antiq. Univ. Oxon. bk. i. p. 222.)

" Item, quod ecclesia vniuersalis potest errare in hiis que sunt fidei.

" Item, quod non est de necessitate salutis credere et tenere illud quod consilium generale et vniuersalis ecclesia statuit, approbat, seu determinat in fauorem fidei et ad salutem animarum, est ab vniuersis Christi fidelibus approbandum, credendum et tenendum.

" Wherefore I, myserable synner, whiche here before long tyme haue walked in derkenesse, and now by the mercy and infynyte goodnes of God reduced in to the ryghte wey and lyghte of trouthe, and consideryng myself greuously haue synned and wyckedly haue enformed and enfect the peple of God, retorne and come ayene to the vnyte of our moder holy churche ; and alle heresyes and errours wryten and conteyned in my seyde bookes, workes and wrytyng, here solemply and openly reuoke and renounce, whiche heresyes and errours, and alle other spices of heresyes, I haue before thys tyme before the moste reuerend fader in God and my good lord of Caunterbury, in dyuers and lawfulle forme iudicially abiured ; submyttyng myself, beyng thanne and also nowe at this tyme verrey contryte and penytent synner, to the correccioun of the churche and of my sayde lorde of Caunterbury,

" And ouer thys, exhortyng and requiryng in the name and vertew of Almyghtye God, in the saluacioun of youre soules and of myne, that no man hereafter yeue feythe and credence to my seyde pernycyous doctrynes, heresyes and errours, neyther my sayde bookes kepe, holde or rede in any wyse; but that they alle suche bokes, workes and wrytyng, suspect of heresyes, delyuer in alle goodly haste vnto my saide lorde of Caunterbury or to his commyssioners and deputees, in eschewyng of meny inconuenientys and grete peryles of soules, the whiche elles myghte be cause of the contrary.   And ouer this declaracioun of my conuersion and repentaunce I here openly assent, that my seyde bookes, werkes and wrytyng, for declaracioun and cause aboue rehersed be deput vn to the fyre, and openly brende in ensample and terrour of alle other," &c.

'Wythe wondrethe that reson nat telle can,
Howe a mayde ys a moder, and God ys manne,
Fle reasoure, and folow the woundre,
For beleue hathe the maystry and reasone ys vnder."

Thys made the sayde Pocock, as it was seyde.

And after thys he was pryued of his bysshopryche, hauyng a certeyne pensione assigned vn to hym for to lyne on in an abbey, and sone after he dyed.

A.D. 1457.

[A.D. 1460.?]

Afterwarde this same yere, was holde a counseylle at Westmynstre aboute Shroftyde, to the whiche came the yong lordes whoos fadres were sleyne at Seynt Albonys ; that ys to sey, the duke of Somerset, the erle of Northumberlond, and his brother lord Egremount, and the lorde Clyfforde, with a grete power, and were loged withoute the walles of Londoun aboute Templebarre and Westmynstre. The cyte wolde nat receyue theym, because they came ageyrs the pease. The duk of York and the erle of Salesbury came but onely with theyre householde men in pesyble manner, thynkyng none harme, and were loged wythynne the cytee ; for they abouesayde came forto dystroy vtterly the sayde duk of York and the erle of Salesbury, and of Warrewyk ; and the cyte was euery day armed forto withstonde the malice of tho yong lordes yef nede had be. And sone after came the erle of Warrewyk fro Caleys, wherof he was capteyne, and lay wythynne the cyte.

A.D. 1458.
[February.]

Folio 194 b.

Thanne the byshoppys and other lordes tretyd betwyxt theym of the pease and accorde, and after long trete bothe partyes submytted theym to the laude and arbytrement of the kyng and his counselle. The whiche after good deliberacione and avysement yaf this awarde and arbitrement ; that xlv.li. of yerely rente shulde be amorteysed and founded in for euermore by the sayde duk of York and the erles, in the abbey of Seynt Albons, where the forseyde lordes so slayne were buryed, for to pray for theyre soules and for the soules of alle tho that were slayne there. And ouer this the sayde duk of York and the erles shulde pay to the duke of Somerset and to hys

A.D. 1458.

moder, to the erle of Northumbrelond, to the lorde Egremont and to the lorde Clyfford, a notable summe of money, for recompens of theyre fadres dethe, and for wronges done vnto theym.

Folio 195.

Where uppon was made wrytyng and suerte ; and so was the trowble ceased, and pease and accorde made betwene theym; but hit endured nat long.

One of the causes of this trouble betwene the duk of York and the duk of Somerset was thys—Duryng the kynges sykenesse the

[April 3, 1454.]

duk of York was made protector of Englond, whereof the duk of Somerset had grete indignacioun and alwey malygned ayenst hym and stered the kyng ageyne hym; natheles meny of the lordes of the counceyl fauored more the duk of York thanne hym. Wherefore for certeyne causes and articles that were leyde ayenst the

[Nov. 1453.]

seyde duk of Somerset, he was commytted by the kynges counselle to the toure of London : but be instaunce and mediacione of his frendes he was sone delyuered, vnder this condicione, that he shulde neuer after entremete, ne have a do with the gouernaunce of the reame, and that he sholde nat come nyghe the kyng by xx. myle. And for to obserue and kepe these condicions he was swore vppon a book.

[Feb. 7, 1455.]

Whenne he was delyuered oute of the toure, he took more vppon hym thenne he dyd before, stiryng the kyng dayly and maliciously ageyns the forseyde duke of York and erles, coniectyng and ymaginyng howe he myghte dystroy theyme ; but at seynt Albonys he fylle in to the same snare that he had ordeyned for theyme.

[Anno] xxxvij.*
A.D. 1458.

The xxxvij. yere, the kyng and the quene beyng at Westmynstre, the ix. day of Nouembre fylle a grete debate betwene Richard erle of Warrewyk and theym of the kynges hous, in so moche that they wolde haue sleyne the erle; and vnnethe he escaped to his barge,

Folio 195 b.

and went anone after to Caleys for a lytel before he was made capteyne therof by auctoryte of the parlement.

[Anno xxxviij.]

Sone afterwarde the yonge duke of Somerset by steryng of theyme

* By the hand of Stowe.

that hated the erle of Warrewyk was made capteyn of Caleys, and a pryue seale directe to the erle for to dyscharge hym of the capteynshyppe; but the erle forasmeche as he was made be aucto‐ ryte of the parlement, he wolde nat obey the pryue seale, but con‐ tinued forthe in the sayde offyce meny yeres after.

A.D. 1459. [October 9th.]

The xxxviij. yere of kyng Harry, in a lytylle toune in Bedford‐ shyre, there fylle a blody rayne, whereof the rede dropys appered in shetes, the whiche a woman had honged out for to drye.

Anno xxxviij. A.D. 1459-60.

In this same tyme, the reame of Englonde was oute of alle good gouernaunce, as it had be meny dayes before, for the kyng was simple and lad by couetous counseylle, and owed more then he was worthe. His dettes encreased dayly, but payment was there none; alle the possessyons and lordeshyppes that perteyned to the croune the kyng had yeue awey, some to lordes and some to other simple per‐ sones, so that he had almoste noughte to lefe onne. And suche ymposiciones as were put to the peple, as taxes, tallages, and quynjymes, alle that came from theym was spended on vayne, for he helde no householde ne meyntened no warres. For these mys‐ gouernaunces, and for many other, the hertes of the peple were turned awey from thayme that had the londe in gouernance, and theyre blyssyng was turnyd in to cursyng.

The quene with such as were of her affynyte rewled the reame as her lyked, gaderyng ryches innumerable. The offices [sic] of the reme, and specially the erle of Wylshyre tresorere of Engelond for to enryche hymself, peled the pore peple, and disheryted ryghtefulle eyres, and dede meny wronges. The quene was defamed and desclaundered, that he that was called Prince, was nat hir sone, but a bastard goten in avoutry; wherefore she dreding that he shulde nat succede hys fadre in the crowne of England, allyed vn to her alle the knyghtes and squyers of Chestreshyre for to haue theyre benyuolence, and helde open householde among theym; and made her sone called the Prince yeue a lyuery of Swannys to alle the gentilmenne of the contre, and to many other thorought the

Folio 196.

lande; trustyng thorough thayre streynghte to make her sone kyng; makyng pryue menys to some of the lordes of Englond for to styre the kyng that he shulde resygne the croune to hyre sone: but she coude nat bryng her purpos aboute.

[Sept. 23rd.] The xxxviij. yere of kyng Harry, in the moneth of Septembre, the yere of our Lord, M^l.cccc.lix. on the Sonday in the feste of Seynt Mathew, Richard erle of Salesbury, hauyng with hym vij.M^l. of wele arayed men, dredyng the malyces of his enemyes and specially of the quene and hyre company the whiche hated hym dedly and the duk of York and the erle of Warrewyk also, tooke hys wey towarde Ludlow where the sayde duk of York lay at that tyme, to thentent that they bothe togedre wolde haue ryde to the kyng to Colshylle in Staffordshyre, for to haue excused theym of certeyne articles and fals accusaciones touchyng thaire ligeaunce layde agayns Folio 196 b. theyme maliciously by their enemyes.

Blorehethe.
[Sept. 23rd.] Whenne the kyng herde of thayre commyng, they that were aboute hym counseyled hym to gadre a power for to wythestand theym, and enformed hym that they came forto dystroy hymme. Thenne lay the quene at Eglishale, and anone by hire stiryng the kyng assembled a grete power whereof the lorde Audeley was chyef and had the ledyng of thaym, and wente forthe in to the felde called Blorehethe ; by the whyche the sayde duk of York and the erl most nedes passe. And there bothe hostes mette and countred to gedre, and fauȝt mortally. And there was the lorde Audeley sleyne, and meny of the notable knyghtes and squyers of Chesshyre that had resceued the lyuery of the swannes ; and there were take prysoners, the erlles ij. sones of Salisbury, Thomas and Johan, and ser Thomas Haryngtone, and enprysoned in the castelle of Chestre ; but sone after they were delyuered.

After this discomfiture, the erlle past forthe to duke Richard to Ludlow, and thyder came to theyme fro Caleys the erle of Warrewyk, and they iij. wrote a letter vn to kyng Harry, whereof the tenoure ys thus :—

"Most Crystyne kyng, ryghte hyghe and myghtye Prince, and oure most drad souuerayne lorde, after as humble recommendacione to youre hyghe excellence as we suffice. Oure trewe entent to the prosperyte and augmentacione of youre hyghe estate, and to the commone wele of this reaume, hath be showd vn to youre hyghenesse in suche wrytyng as we made thereof. And ouer that, an endenture sygned by oure hances in the churche Cathedralle of Worcestre comprehendyng the preef of the trouthe and dewte that, God knowethe, we bere to youre seyde estate and to the preemynence and prerogatif therof. we sent vn to youre good grace by the prior of the saide churche and diuerse other doctours, and among other, by master William Lynwode, doctour of diuinite, whyche mynistred vuto us seuerally the blessed Body of God our Lorde Jhesu ; sacred whereoponne, we and euery of vs deposyd for oure sayde trouthe and dewtee accordyng to the tenure of the seyde endenture. And syth that tyme, we haue certyfyed at large in wrytyng and by mouthe by Garter kyng of Armes, nat only to youre sayde hyghenesse, but also to the good and worthy lordes beyng aboute youre moste noble presence, the largenesse of oure sayde trouthe and dewte, and oure entent and oure disposicione to seche alle the mocions that myghte serue conuenyently to thaffirmacione therof, and to oure parfyte suertees from suche inconuenient and unreuerent geopardyes, as we haue ben put ynne diuerse tymes herebefore. Wherof we haue cause to make, and owe to make, suche exclamacione and compleynt, nat withoute reasone, as ys nat unknowen to alle the sayd worthy lordes and to alle his lande, and wolle offre vs to youre hyghe presence to the same entent, yef we myghte so do wythe oure sayde sewrte, whiche onely causethe vs to kepe aboute vs suche felyshyp as we do in oure leeffulle. And hereto we haue forborne and avoyded alle thynges that myghte serue to the effusione of Crysten blood, of the drede that we haue of God and of youre royalle mageste ; and haue also eschewed to approche your seyde moste noble presence, of the humble obeysaunce and reuerence whereon we haue

CAMD. SOC. M

and duryng oure lyfe wolle haue the same. And yet neuertheles, we here that we be proclamed and defamed in oure name vnryghtefully, vnlawfully, and sauyng youre hyghe reuerence, vntrewly, and

otherwyse, that God knowethe, then we haue yeue cause; knowyng certaynly that the blessed and noble entent of youre sayde goode grace and the ryghtwysnesse thereof ys, to take, repute, and accepte youre trew and lowly sugettys, and that it accordethe neyther with youre sayde entent, ne wythe youre wylle or pleasure, that we shuld be otherwyse take or reputed. And ouer that, oure lordshyppes and tenauntes bene of hyghe vyolence robbed and spoyled, ayenst youre peese and lawes and alle ryghtewysnesse. We therefore, as we suffice, beseche youre sayde good grace, to take, repute, and receyue thervnto oure sayde trouthe and entent, whiche to God ys know, as we shewe it by the seyde tenure of the sayde endenture, and nat apply youre sayde blessednesse ne the grete ryghtewysnesse and equite whereinne God hathe euer endowed youre hyghe nobeley, to thymportune impacience and violence of suche persones as entende of extreme malyce to procede vnder the shadow of youre hyghe myghte and presence to oure destruccione, for suche inordinate couetyse, whereof God ys nat pleased, as they haue to oure landes, offices, and goodes, not lettyng or sparyng therefore to put suche thyngys in alle lamentable and to sorowfulle geopardy, as moot in alle wyse take effect by the mystery of Goddys wille and power, nor nat hauyng regarde to theffusione of Crystyne blood, ne any tendrenesse to the noble blood of thys lond suche as serue to the tuicione and defens therof, ne nat weyng the losse of youre trew liegemenne of youre sayde reame, that God defende whiche knowethe oure entent, and that we haue avoyded therfro, as fer as we may with oure sewertees, nat of any drede that we haue of the sayde persones, but onely of the drede of God and of youre sayde hyghenesse, and nat wylle vse oure sayde defence vnto the tyme that we

be provoked of necessyte, whereof we calle henene and erthe in to wyttenesse and recorde; and therynne beseche God to be oure Juge,

and to delyuer vs accordyng to oure sayde entent, and oure sayde A.D. 1459.
trouthe and dutie to youre seyde hyghenesse, and to the sayde commone wele. Most Crysten Kyng, ryghte hyghe and myghtye Prince,
and moste drad souerayne lorde, we beseche oure blessed Lord to
preserue youre honoure and estate in ioye and felycite.

" Wretynne at Ludlow, the x. day of Octobre.

" R. York, R. Warrewyk, R. Salesbury."

After theyre excusacionne conteyned in thys letter sent to the
kyng, thay withdrowe thayme, and went in to dyuers parties of beyonde the see, for the more sewrte of theyre personnes: the duke of
York wente into Yrelond, where he was worshypfully resceued.
The erles of March, of Salesbury, and Warrewyk, nat wythoute
grete geopardy and perylle, as welle in the londe as in the see,
wente vnto Caleys ard abood there.

Thanne was a parlement holden at Couentre, and they that were [Novemb. 20th
chosenne knyghtes of the shyres, and other that had interesse in the
parlement, were nat dyfferent but chosen a denominacione of thaym
that were enemyes to the forseyde lordes so beyng oute of the reame.
In the whiche parlement, the sayde duk of York and the iij. erles
and other, whos names shalle be rehersed afterward, withoute any
answere, as traytours and rebelles to the kyng were atteynt of treson,
and theyre goodes, lordshyppys and possessyons escheted in to the
kynges hande, and they and theyre heyres dysheryted vn to the
ixthe degre. And by the kynges commissione in euery cyte, burghe,
and toune cryed opynly and proclamed as for rebelles and traytoures;
and theyre tenauntes and there men spoyled of theyre goodes,
maymed, bete, and slayne withoute eny pyte; the toune of Ludlow, Folio 198 b.
longyng thanne to the duk of York, was robbed to the bare walles,
and the noble duches of York vnmanly and cruelly was entreted
and spoyled.

In the mene tyme the erle of Warrewyk, hauyng a strong and a
myghte naueye kept the strayte see, and fau3t with the Spaynardys

and kylde many of thaym, and tooke theyre grete vesselles and a carake of Jene, and gate in theym grete rychesse.

The names of the lordes and other that were atteynt in the forseyde parlement bythe these. Richard duk of York, Edward erle of Marche his sone and heyre, Richard erle of Warwyk, Edmund erle of Rutlond, Richard erle of Salesbury, Johan lorde Clyfford, lord Clyntone, ser Thomas Haryngtone, ser Johan Wenlock, Thomas Nevyle, Johan Nevyle, sones of the erle of Salesbury, James Pykryng, Johan Conyers, Thomas Par, Wyllyam Oldhalle, and Harry Ratford, knyghtes: Johan Bowser, Thomas Cook, Johan Clay, Richard Gytone, Robert Browe, Edward Bowser, Thomas Vaughan, Johan Roger, Richard Gray, Watier Deuoros, Watier Hopton, Roger Kynderton, Wyllyam Bowes, Fook Stafford, the lorde Powys, and Alys countesse of Salesbury.

In the monethe of Octobre next folowyng, the yonge duke of Somerset, Harry lord Roos, and lorde Audeley, with a certeyne nombre of men of armes, hauyng with theym the kynges letters, wente to Caleys to thentent that the seyde duk shulde haue be capteyne of Caleys, the whyche office the kyng had yene hym,† wenyng that the Erle of Warrewyk wolde lyghtely haue yolde vp the sayde offyce to him as he was commaunded by the kynges lettres; but when he came to the londe, they of Caleys wolde haue take hym, and with muche payne he escaped and fled in to the castelle of Guynes, and there helde hym meny dayes after; the sovdyers that came with hym were stryppyd oute of theyre harneys by thayme of Caleys, and let go. The lorde Audeley was take into Caleys, and the lord Roos fledde in to Flaunders, and afterward came priuely agayne in to Engelond.

Not long afterward the lord Ryuers was sent to Sandewyche for to kepe the toun, that the erle of Warrewyk and the other lordes shulde nat londe there, for it was seyde that alle Kent fauored and supported thaym; and sothe it was: and also that the seyde lord

---

* By the hand of Stowe.   † By letters dated Oct. 9th, Rymer, xi. 436.

Ryuers shulde kepe certeyne grete forstage shyppys, that were the A.D. 1459.
erles of Warrewyk, the whiche lay at ankere there in the hanene.

And whanne the seyde erle of Warrewyk sawe a conuenient tyme, A.D. 1460.
he sent some of his men to Sandwhyche by nyghte, the whyche took [January.]
the sayde lorde Ryners and Antony [Woodvill *] his sone, in theyre
beddes, and lad theym ouer to Caleys, and took with theym alle the
grete shyppes, saue on called "Grace Dieu," the whyche myghte
nat be had awey because she was broke in the botome.

Thanne aroos a knyght of Deuenshyre, called syr Bawdewyn [April.†]
Fulford, and sayde that on payne of lesyng of his hed he wolde
destroy the erle of Warrewyk and his nauey, yef the kyng wolde
graunte hym his expensis; and he resceued therfore a M^l. marc.,
and whenne he had consumed and wasted alle that money, his vyage
was done and [he] wente home ayene.

And at laste the duk of Excestre,‡ that was Amyralle, was sent
to the see with a grete nauy for to dystresse the seyde erle of
Warrewyk and his nauey, and sayled from Sandwyche to Derte-
mouthe, and there for lack of vetayle and of money hys soudyers were Folio 199 b.
dysparbeled, and wente awey fro hym. And betwene Sandwyche
and Dertemouth he mette the erle of Warrewyk, commyng oute of
Yrelond, that had be there to speke with the duk of York, and
broughte with hym hys moder that was fled theder for drede, and
lad her to Caleys; but the duke durst nat sette opponne the erle,
ne the erle wolde nat dystresse hym because he was amyral, and of
the kynges bloode, but late hym passe by.

In the monethe of Juyne, this same yere, were gadered v. hundred June, 1460.§
men for to fette and condue the duk of Somerset from Guynes in
to Englande, abydyng wynde in the poort of Sandwyche, and thyder

* Insertion by the hand of Stowe.
† After 24th of the month, see Rymer, xi. 451.
‡ He was appointed Admiral, March 19th; but he does not seem to have sailed till after
April 26th, see Rymer, ibid.
§ By the hand of Stowe.

came sowdyers of the erles of Warrewyk and spoyled theym of theyre harness and kylde some of theym ; and theyre capteyne was slayne that was called Mounfort.

Thanne sente the forseyde lordes the articles vnder wryten to the archebysshop of Caunterbury, and at large to the Communes of Engelond, of the whych articles thys ys the tenoure:—

" Worshypfulle Syres, We, the duk of York, the erles of March, Warrewyk, and Salesbury sewde and offred to haue come vnto the kyng oure souerayn lordes most noble presens, to haue declared there afore hym, for oure dewte to God and to hys hyghenesse, and to the prosperyte and welfare of his noble estate, and to the comon wele of alle his londe, as trew lyegemen, the matiers folowyng, that ys to say :

For the furst, The grete oppressyone, extorsion, robry, murther, and other vyolencys doone to Goddys churche, and to his mynystres therof, ayens Goddys and mannes law.

Item, The pouerte and mysery that to oure grete heuynesse oure sayde souerayne lorde standeth inne, nat hauyng any lyuelode of

the croune of Englond wherof he may kepe hys honorable housholde, whyche causethe the spyllyng of his sayde lyegemenne by the takers of hys seyde howsholde, whyche lyuelode ys in theyre handes that haue be destroyers of his seyde estate, and of the seyde commone wele.

Item, Howe hys lawes been parcially and vnrightfully guyded, and that by thayme that sholde moste loue and tendre hys sayde lawes the sayde oppressyon and extorsyone as (sic) most fauored and supported, and generally, that alle rightwysnesse and justice ys exyled of the sayde lond, and that no manne dredethe to offende ayenst the sayde lawes.

Item, That it wolle please his sayde good grace to lyve upponne his owne lyuelode, whereopon hys noble progenitures haue in dayes heretofore lyued as honorably and as worthily as any Crystyn prynces; and nat to suffre the destroyers of the sayde londe and of his trewe sugettes to lyue theroponne, and therefore to lacke the sustenaunces that sholde be bylongyng to hys sayde estate, and fynde hys sayde householde opponne his pore communes withoute payment, whyche nouther accordethe wyth Goddes nor mannes lawe.

Item, Howe ofte the seyde commones haue ben gretely and merueylously charged with taxes and tallages to theyre grete enporysshyng, whereof lytelle good hathe eyther growe to the kyng or to the saide londe, and of the moste substaunce therof the kyng bathe lefte to his part nat half so moche and other lordes and persones, enemyes to the sayde commune wele, haue to theyre owne vse, suffryng alle the olde possessyons that the kyng had in Fraunce and Normandy, Angew and Meyne, Gascoyne and Guyene, wonne and goten by his fadre of moste noble memory, and othir hys noble progenitors, to be shamefully loste or sclde.

Item, How they cannat cece therewith, but nowe begynne a new charge of imposiccione and tallages vpponne the sayde peple whyche neuer afore was seen; that ys to say, euery tounshyp to fynde men for the kynges garde, takyng ensample therof of oure enemyes and aduersaryes of Fraunce: whiche imposicione and tallage yef hit be continued to theyre heyres and successours, wol be the heuyest charge and worst ensample that euer grewe in Englond, and the forseyde sugettes, and the seyde heyres and successours, in suche bandom as theyre auncetours were neuer charged with.

Item, Where the kyng hathe now no more lyfelode oute of his reame of Englond but onely the londe of Irelond and the toune of Caleys, and that no kyng crystened bathe suche a londe and a toune withoute hys reaume dyuers lordes haue caused his hyghenesse to wryte letters vnder his priuy seale vuto his Yrisshe enemyes, whyche neuer kyng of Englond dyd heretofore, wherby they may haue comfort to entre in to the conquest of the sayde londe; whiche letters the same Yrysshe enemyes sent vn to me the sayde duke of York, and merueled gretely that any suche letters shuld be to theym sent, spekyng therinne gret shame and vylony of the seyde reme.

Item, In like wyse, the kyng by excytacione and laboure of the same lordes wrote other letters to his enemyes and aduersaryes in other landes, that in no wyse thay shold shew eny favoure or good wylle to the toun of Caleys, whereby they had comfort ynowghe to procede to the wynnyng therof; considered also, that hit ys ordeyned by the laboure of the sayde lordes, that nowther vetayle ner other thyng of refresshyng or defens shulde come oute of Englond to the socoure or relyef of the sayde toune, to thentent that they wolde haue hyt lost, as yt may opynly appere.

Item, It ys demed, and oweth gretely to be douted, that after that, the same lordes wolde put the same rewle of Englond, yef they myghte haue theyre purpos and entent, in to the handes and gouernaunce of the seyde enemyes.

Item, How continuelly, syth the pytyous, shamefulle, and sorowfulle murther to alle Englond, of that noble, worthy, and Crystyn prince, Humfrey duk of Gloucestre the kynges trew vncle, at Bury, hit bathe be labored, studyed, and conspyred, to haue dystroyed and murthryd the seyde duke of York, and the yssew that it pleased God to sende me of the royalle blode; and also of vs the sayde erlys of Warrewyk and Salysbury, for none other cause but for the trew hert that God knoweth we euer haue borne, and bere, to the profyte of the kynges estate, to the commone wele of the same reame, and defens therof.

Item, How the erles of Shrouesbury and Wylshyre, and the lorde Beaumount, oure mortalle and extreme enemyes, now and of long tyme past, hauyng the guydyng aboute the most noble persone of oure sayde souuerayn lorde, whos hyghenes they haue restrayned and kept from the liberte and fredom that bylongethe to his seyde astate, and the supporters and fauorers of alle the premysses, wolde nat suffre the kynges seyde good grace to resceue and accepte [us] as he wolde haue done, yet (*sic*) he myghte haue had his owne wylle, in hys sayde presence; dredyng the charge that wolde haue be layde vpponne theym of the mysery, destruccione, and wrechednesse of the sayde reame, wherof they be causes, and nat the kyng, whiche

ys hymself a[s] noble, as vertuous, as ryghtewys, and blyssed of dys- A.D. 1460.
posicione, as any prinꝛe erthely. Folio 201 b.

Item, The erles of Wylshyre and Shrouesbury, and the lorde
Beaumount, nat satysfyed nor content with the kynges possessyouns
and hys good, stered and excyted his sayde hyghenesse to holde hys
parlement at Couentre, where an acte ys made by theyre prouoca-
cioun and laboure ayenst vs the sayde duk of York, my sones
Marche and Rutlande, and the erles of Warrewyk and Salysbury,
and the sones of the sayde erle of Salysbury, and meny other
knyghtes and esquyers, of diuerse matiers falsly and vntrewly
ymagened, as they wolle answere afore Almyghty God in the day of
Dome ; the whyche the sayde erles of Shrouesbury and Wylshyre
and the lorde Beaumount prouoked to be maad to thentent of oure
destruccione and of cure yssew, and that thay myghte haue oure
lyfelode and goodes, as they haue openly robbed and dyspoyled alle
oure places and oure tenementes, and meny other trew men ; and
now procede to hangyng and drawyng of men by tyranny, and wolle
therinne shewe the largenesse of theyre vyolence and malyce as
vengeably as they can, yef no remedy be prouyded at the kynges
hyghenesse, whos blessednes ys nother assentyng ne knowyng therof.

We therfore, seyng alle the sayde myscheues, heryng also that
the Frensshe kyng makethe in hys lande grete assemble of hys peple
whyche ys gretely to be drad for many causes, purpose yet ayene
with Goddes grace [to] offre us to come ayene to the sayde presence
of oure sayde souuerayn lorde, to opene and declare there vn to hym
the myscheues aboue declared, and in the name of the land to sew
in as reuerent and lowly wyse as we can to hys seyde good grace, Folio 202.
and to haue pyte and compassione uppon hys sayde trew sugettys,
and nat to suffre the same myscheuȝ to regne upponne theym.
Requiryng yow on Goddys behalf and prayng yow in oure oune
thereinne to assyste vs, doyng alwey the dewte of ligeaunce in oure
personnes to oure sayde souuerayne lorde, to hys estate, prerogatyf,
and preemynence, and to thasuerte of hys most noble persone, where-

CAMD. SOC. N

vuto we haue euer be and wylle be trew as any of his sugettes alyue: Whereof we call God, our Lady Saynt Mary and alle the Sayntes of heuene vn to wyttenesse and record."

In the mene tyme therlle of Wylshyre tresorer of Englond, the lorde Scales, and the lorde Hungreford, hauyng the kynges commyssyone went to the toune of Newbury, the whyche longed to the duk of York, and there made inquysycione of alle thayme that in any wyse had shewed any fauoure or benyuolence or frendshyppe to the sayde duk, or to any of hys; whereof some were found gylty and were drawe hanged and quartered, and alle other inhabitantes of the forseyde toune were spoyled of alle theyre goodes.

Whanne thys was done the erle of Wylshyre went to Southamptoun, and there vnder colore for to take the erle of Warrewyk, but specyally for to stele priuyly owte of the reame as hit preued afterwardes, he armed and vytayled v. grete carrakys of Jene that were at that tyme in the port of the sayde toune, and stuffed theym with sowdyers of Englysshemen, takyng vytayle of the kynges pryce without payment, as he sholde haue made a vyage for the kyng, Folio 202 b. and put a grete parte of his tresoure in to the sayde carrakeȝ; and sone after he past owte of the port and sayled aboute in the see, dredyng alwey the commyng of the forseyde erles of Warrewyk and Salesbury, and atte laste arryued in Ducheland, and sent hys sowdyers in to Englond ayene.

Thanne were the kynges pryue seales dyrect to alle manner of bysshops, abbotys, pryores, and to alle the grete men of the spirituelte and temporalte, for to leue the kyng money withoute delay for to wage men to kepe the see costes, that the sayde erles shuld nat arryue in no syde: and the sayde erle of Wylshyre made promys to alle suche persones as lent the kyng any money, that they shulde haue assignementes and repayment of the goodes of the forseyde duk of York and erles, whom they called oponne traytours. And the seyde erle of Wylshyre taxed the summe what euery man shuld leue, and so he made leve of many grete summes. And ouer thys,

A.D. 1460.

proclamacione was made by commaundement of the kyng, that euery
cyte, toune, and burghe, and hundredys, shuld fynde certayne
sowdyers of thayre owne coste to kepe the see costys, for drede of
landyng of the seyde erles.

Ferthermore, the commones of Kent, dredyng the malyce and the
tyranny of the forseyde erlle of Wylshyre and of other, lest he wolde
exercyse his vengeaunce vppon thaym, as he had done vppon thaym
at Newbery, and sent priuyly messagers and letters to Caleys to the
forseyde erles, besechyng thaym that they wolde in alle haste possible
come and socour thaym fro theyre enemyes, promyttyng that they
wolde assyste theym with alle thayre power.

The sayde erles wcld nat anone yeue credence to theyre wrytyng
and wordes, but send ouer in to Kent the lord Fauconbrege, to
know whether theyre promys and theyre dedes sholde accorde: and
anone the peple of Kent and of other shyres aboute resorted to the
sayde lorde Fauconbrege in grete nombre, abydyng the commyng of
the erles.

Folio 203.

Whan the erles knew the trew hertes of the peple, they dysposed
theyme dayly for to com in to thys londe. And nat longe before
theyre comnyng, thys balat that folowethe was sette vppon the
yates of the cyte of Caunterbury.

> In the day of faste and spirituelle afflixione,
>   The celestialle influence of bodyes transytory,
> Set asyde alle prophecyes, and alle commixtione
>   Of injementys sensualle to ofte in memory,
> I reduced to mynde the prophete Isay,
>   Consideryng Englond to God in greuous offence, with wepyng ye;
> This text I fonde in his story:—
>   "Omne caput languidum, et omne cor merens!"
>
> Regnum Anglorum regnum Dei est,
>   As the Aungelle to seynt Edward dede wyttenesse;
> Now regnum Sathane, it semethe, reputat best,
>   For filii scelerati haue broughte it in dystresse.

Balat set
upponne the
yates of Caun-
terbury.

D. 1460.

This preuethe fals wedlock and periury expresse,
   Fals heryres fostred, as knowethe experyence,
Vnryghtewys dysherytyng with false oppresse,
   Sic " omne caput languidum, et omne cor merens ! "

A plantâ pedis, fro the pore tylyer of the lond
   Ad verticem of spiritualle eke temperalle ennoynted crown
Grace ys withdrawe and Goddys mercyfulle hand,
   Exalted ys falsehod, trowthe ys layde adoune ;
Euery reame cryethe owte on Engelondes treson.
   O falshod with thy colored presence !
Euer shulle we syng duryng thy season,
   " Omne caput languidum, et omne cor merens ! "

   Omne regnum in se divisum," sayethe dyuyne Scrypture,
   " Shall be desolate," than folewethe translacione
lio 203 b.
Into the handes of theyre enemyes, Jewes arn figure ;
   And now ys Englond in lyk reputacione,
In wey to be conquered ; truste it for sewre !
   Jhesu, for thy mercy and thy noble reuerens,
Reforme vs to goodnesse and condicione pure,
   For, " omne caput languidum, et omne cor merens ! "

Harry oure souerayne and most Crystyne kyng
   His trew bloode hathe flemed bothe be swerde and exyle ;
What prynce by thys rewle may haue long enduryng,
   That also in moste pouert hath be long whyle ?
Tho bestys that thys wroughte to mydsomer haue but a myle—
   But euer mornethe Engelond for ham that be hens
Wythe languysshyng of herte rehersyng my style,
   " Omne caput languidum, et omne cor merens ! "

Jonathas ys ded that Dauid shuld restore
   To the presence of the kyng, vnyte to make
Murum pro domo Israel, presthode dar no more
   Put hymself forthe, his fat benefyce he shuld forsake.
Mercyfulle God ! it ys tyme thow for vs awake.
   Mercenarius fugit, ne wylle make resistence,
He ferethe the wolf that wolde hys bonys crake,
   " Omne caput languidum, et omne cor merens ! "

A.D. 1460.

Tempus ys come falshede to dystroy,
  Tempus eradicandi the wedes fro the corne,
Tempus cremandi the breres that trees noye,
  Tempus evellendi the fals hunter with his horne,
Tempus miserendi on por alle to torne,
  Tempus ponendi falsnes in perpetuelle absence,
Thoroughe whom we syngyng bothe euyne and morne,
  " Omne caput languidum, et omne cor merens ! "

Send hom, most gracious Lord Jhesu most benygne,
  Sende hoom thy trew blode vn to his propre veyne,
Richard duk of York, Job thy seruaunt insygne,
  Whom Sathan not cesethe to sette at care and dysdeyne,
But by The preserued he may nat be slayne ;
  Sette hym ut sedeat in principibus, as he dyd before,
And so to oure newe songe Lorde, thyn erys inclyne,
  Gloria, laus et honor Tibi sit Rex Christe Redemptor !

Folio 204.

Edwarde Erle of Marche, whos fame the erthe shalle sprede,
  Richard Erle of Salisbury named prudence,
Wythe that noble knyghte and floure of manhode
  Richard erle of Warrewyk sheelde of oure defence,
Also lytelle Fauconbrege, a knyghte of grete reuerence ;
  Jhesu ham restore to thayre honoure as thay had before,
And euer shalle we syng to thyn Hyghe Excellence,
  Gloria, laus et honor Tibi sit Rex Christe Redemptor !

No prynce, alle thyng consydered, wythe honoure
  In alle thyng requysyte to a kynges excellence
Better may lyue, serche ary worthy predecessoure ;
  Yet hastow souuerayne lord in these lordes absence
Of alle thaym to a kyng ryghte resonable expens ;
  Thay shalle come agayne and rekene for the scoore,
And thow shalt syng wythe vs thys verrey trew sens,
  Gloria laus et honor Tibi sit Rex Christe Redemptor !

With verray good entent,
Alle the Reame of Englond
Sone to louse from sorowes bond,
Be ryghte indifferent iugement.

To the ryghte Worshypfulle Cyte of Caunterbury.

Howe the Erles landed at Sand-wyche.

Thanne the noble erles of Marche, Warrewyk, and Salysbury, hauyng wynde and weder at thayre plesaunce, arryued graciously at Sandwyche; where met wythe thaym master Thomas Bourchier archebysshop of Caunterbury, and a grete multitude of peple wythe hym; and wythe hys crosse before hym, [he] went forthe wythe the sayde erles and theyre peple toward Londoun, and sente an herowde to the cyte to knowe howe they were dysposed, and whether they wolde stand with theyme in thayre iust quarelle, and graunte

Folio 204 b.

hem leve for to passe thoroughe the cite. They that were nat frendely to the erles, counseyled the mayre and the comynalte for to ley gunnes at the brege for to kepe thaym owte, and so a lytelle diuision there was among the citezens, but yt was sone ceased.

Than sent thay of the cyte to the sayde erles xij. worshypfulle and dyscrete aldermen, the whyche, in the name of alle the cyte, graunted thaym fre entre wythe suche seruyce as they cowde and myghte do to thayr worshyppe and honoure. Thys done, the aldermen retorned to the cyte, and the sayde herowde ageyne to the lordes.

2 of July, 1460.*

And the secund day of Juylle thay entred in to Londoun. And wythe theym came the popys legat, that nat long before had be in Englond; the whyche had auctoryte by the popes bulles for to entrete pease betwene the kyng and the erles, yt (*sic*) nede were; but, how yt were, he vsurped and toke oponne hym more power thanne he had, as it was knowenne afterward.

* By the hand of Stowe.

Thanne was a convocacione of the clergy holden at Paulys in Londoun, and theder came the sayde erles: and the erle of Warrewyk there purposed, and recyted before alle the conuocacione, and innumerable peple standyng aboute, the causes of theyre commyng in to thys lond; and mysrewle and myscheues therof; and how with grete vyolence thay had be repeled and put from the kynges presence, that they myghte nat come to hys hyghenes forto excuse thaym of suche fals accusaciones as were layde ayens thaym; and now were come ayene, by Goddys mercy, accompanyed with pople for to come to hys presens, there to declare and excuse thayre innocence, or ellys to dy in the felde; and there [they] made an open othe vpponne the cros of Caunterbury that thay had euer bore trew feythe and lygeaunce to the kynges persone, wyllyng no more hurt to hym than to thayre owen personnes; wherof they took God and hys moder and alle the sayntes of beuene to wyttenesse.

The kyng, that held a counseylle at Couentre, heryng of the commyng of the erles, went to Northamptone.

The erle of Salesbury be comyn assent of the cite was maad rewler and gouernour of Londoun, in absence of the forseyde erles. And the seyde erles of Marche and Warrewyk and other lordes, that ys to say the lorde Facombrege, lorde Clyntone, lorde Bourser, prioure of Seynt Johannes, lorde Audeley, lorde Bergevenny, lord Say, lord Scroope, tharchebysshoppe of Caunterbury, the popes legat, the bysshoppe of Excetre. the bysshops of Ely, Salesbury, and Rouchestre, dressed hem forth to the kyng to Northamptone.

The lord Scales and the lorde Hungreford that before the commyng of the erles were in the cyte of London, wolde haue had the rewle and gouernaunce therof, but they of the cyte wold nat suffre thaym, for thay sayde that they were suffysaunt for to rewle the cyte thaymself; wherof the lordes hauyng indygnacione wente in to the toure of Londoun, and meny other grete men with theym, whos names betne here vndre wretynne:—lord Vessy, lord Louelle, lord Delaware, lord Kendale a Gascoyne, ser Edmond Hampden

knyghte, Thomas Broun knyghte, shireue of Kent, Johan Bruyn
of Kent, ser Geruays Clyftone knyghte, tresorer of the kynges
hows, ser Thomas Tyrelle knyghte, the duchesse of Exetre, and
many other.   And the toure was beseged by lond and by water,
that no vytayl myghte come to thayme that were wythynne.

Whanne the erles and lordes were gone to Northamptone, thay
that were wythynne the toure caste wyld fyre in to the cyte, and \
shot in smale gonnes, and brend and hurte men and wymmen and
chyldren in the stretes.   And they of London leyde grete bom-
bardes on the ferther syde of the Thamyse agayns the toure and
crased the walles therof in diuerse places ; natheles they hoped
dayly forto haue be rescued, but alle was in veyne.

The kyng at Northamptone lay atte Freres, and had ordeyned
there a strong and a myghty feeld, in the medowys beside the
Noury, armed and arayed wythe gonnys, hauyng the ryuer at hys
back.

The erles with the nombre of lx. M¹., as it was sayd, came to
Northamptone, and sent certayne bysshops to the kyng besechyng
hym that in eschewyng of effusyone of Crysten blood he wolde
admytte and suffre the erles for to come to his presence to declare
thaym self as thay were.   The duk of Bukynghame that stode
besyde the kyng, sayde vn to thaym, " Ye come nat as bysshoppes
for to trete for pease, but as men of armes ;" because they broughte
with thaym a notable company of men of armes.   They answered
and sayde, " We come thus for suerte of oure persones, for they
that bethe aboute the kyng bythe nat oure frendes."   " Forsothe,"
sayde the' duk, " the erle of Warrewyk shalle nat come to the
kynges presence, and yef he come he shalle dye."   The messyngers
retorned agayne, and tolde thys to the erles.

Thanne the erle of Warrewyk sent an herowde of armes to the
kyng, besechyng that he myghte haue ostages of saaf goyng and
commyng, and he wolde come naked to his presence, but he myghte
nat be herde.   And the iij^{de} tyme he sente to the kyng and sayde

that at ij howres after none, he wolde speke with hym, or elles dye in the feeld

The archebysshoppe of Caunterbury sent a bysshoppe of this lond to the kyng with an instruccione, the whyche dyd nat hys message indyfferently, but exorted and coraged the kynges part for to fyȝte, as thay sayde that were there. And another tyme he was sent to the kyng by the commones, and thanne he came nat ayene, but pryuely departed awey. The bysshop of Herforde, a Whyte Frere, the kynges confessoure, ded the same: wherfore after the batayle he was commytted to the castelle of Warrewyk, where he was long in pryson.

Thanne on the Thurseday the xth day of Juylle, the yere of oure Lorde M^l.cccc.lx, at ij howres after none, the sayde erles of Marche and Warrewyk lete crye thoroughe the felde, that no man shuld laye hand vpporne the kyng ne on the commune peple, but onely on the lordes, knyghtes and squyers: thenne the trumpettes blew vp, and bothe hostes countred and faughte togedre half an oure. The lorde Gray, that was the kynges vawewarde, brake the feelde and came to the erles party, whyche caused sauacione of many a mannys lyfe: many were slayne, and many were fled, and were drouned in the ryuer.

The duk of Bukyngham, the erle of Shrouesbury, the lorde Beaumont, the lorde Egremount were slayne by the Kentysshmen besyde the kynges tent, and meny other knyghtes and squyers. The ordenaunce of the kynges gonnes avayled nat, for that day was so grete rayne, that the gonnes lay depe in the water, and so were queynt and myghte nat be shott.

Whanne the feld was do, and the erles thoroughe mercy and helpe had the vyctory, they came to the kyng in his tent, and sayde in thys wyse—

" Most Noble Prince, dysplease yow nat, thoughe it haue pleased God of His Grace to graunt vs the vyctory of oure mortalle enemyes, the whyche by theyre venymous malyce haue vntrewly stered and moued youre hyghenesse to exyle vs oute of youre londe, and wolde vs haue put to fynalle shame and confusyone. We come nat to that entent for to inquyete ne grene youre sayde hyghenesse, but for to please youre moste noble personne, desiryng most tendrely the hyghe welfare and prosperyte thereof, and of alle youre reame, and for to be youre trew lyegemen, whyle oure lyfes shalle endure."

The kyng of theyre wordes was gretely recomforted, and anone was lad in to Northamptone wythe processyone, where he rested
[July 16th.] hym iij dayes, and thanne came to Lohdon, the xvj day of the monethe abouesayde, [and] loged in the bysshop's paleys. For the whyche vyctory London yaf to Almyghtye God grete lawde and thankyng.

⌐ Nat longe before this batayle it was proclamed in Lancastreshyre and Chesshyre, that yef so were that the kyng had the vyctory of the erles, that thanne euery man shulde take what he myghte and make havok in the shyres of Kent, Essexe, Middylsexe, Surreye, Sussexe, Hamshyre and Wylshyre : bot God wolde nat suffre suche fals robbery.
[July 19th.] Furthermore the Saturday the xix day of Juylle, thay that were in the toure of Londoun for lack of vytayl yolden vp the toure, and came oute : of the whyche afterward some were drawe and
Folio 207. beheded.

The lord Scales, for as meche as men of Londoun loued hym nat, he thoughte that he myghte haue stande in the more sewrte in the saintwary of Westmynstre thanne in the toure. Late in the euyn, [he] entred a boote with iij persones rowyng toward Westmynstre, and a wommanne the whiche that knewe hym ascryed hym, and anone the boote men gadered theym togedre and folowed hym, and fylle vpponne hym, and kylde hym and caste hym on the lond, besyde seynt Mary Ouerey. And grete pyte it was, that so noble and so worshypfulle a knyghte, and so welle approued in the warrys of Normandy and Fraunce, shuld dy so myscheuously.

. Whan quene Margarete harde telle, that the kyng was dyscom-

fyted and take, she flædde with hyr sone and vɪɪɪ persones in to the A.D. 1460.
castelle of Hardlaghe in Wales, and as she went by Lancastreshyre,
there she was robbed and dyspoyled of alle her goodes, to the valew
of x.M¹. marc., as yᵗ was sayde ; and sone after she went into
Scotlonde.

Thys same yeere, in the monethe of August, the kyng of Scottes
beseged the castelle of Rokesburghe in Northumbreland, and on seynt
Laurence day in the mornyng, er he had herde masse, he wolde haue Yᵉ 10 of Aw-
gust.*
fyred a grete gonne for to have shot to the castelle, and the chambre
of the gonne brake and slowe hym.

The xxxix. yere of kyng Harry, aboute seynt Mathews day in Anno xxxix.
A.D. 1460-1.
Septembre, the duk cf Somerset came fro Guynes in to Englond. Yᵉ 21 of Sep-
tembar.*
[October 8th.]

And thys same yere the Tewesday the viij. day of Octobre, a
parlement was begonne at Westmynstre ; and thyder came Richard
duk of York, that a lytelle before was come oute of Yrlond, and was
loged in the paleys, the kyng beyng there, and brak vp the dores Folio 207 b.
of the kynges chambre. And the kyng heryng the grete noyse Kynge Harry
and rumore of the peple, yaafe hym place and took another forcid to for-
sake his cham-
bar.*
chambre.

Then the seyde duk Richard, remembryng the grete and many-
folde wrongys, exylys, and vylonyes, that he had suffred and be
put vuto by thys seyde kyng Harry, and by hys ; and also how
wrongfully and vniusiy he had be, and was, dyspleased and dyseased
of hys ryghte enheritaunce of the reaume and croune of Englond,
by violent intrusyonne of kyng Harry the iiijᵗʰᵉ, whyche vnryghtefully, wrongfully, and tyrannously vsurped the crowne after the
dethe of kyng Rychard his cosyn, verray and ryghtfulle heyre
therof, and so wrongfully holdyn from hymm, and occupyed and
holde, by the sayde kyng Harry the iiijᵗʰᵉ, the vᵗᵇᵉ, and kyng Harry
the vjᵗʰᵉ that now ys in to thys tyme ; he as ryghte heyre by lynealle
descens from the saydə kyng Richard, chalaunged and claymed the

---

* Bv the hand of Stowe.

sayd reame and croune of Englond, purposyng withoute any more
delay to haue be crouned onne Alle Halow day, thanne next folowyng : and heropon sent to the lordes and comones of the parlement
in wrytyng, hys sayde clayme, tytle and pedegre, and nat wold come
in to the parlement tylle he had aunswere therof. The whyche
tytle, clayme and pedegre, after diligent inspeccione and wyse dely-
beracione of thaym had, dyscussed and approued, by alle the seyde
parlement; peese, vnyte and concorde betwene the kyng and the
[Friday, Oct.   sayde duk Richard, the Fryday in the vygylle of Alhalow was maad,
31st.]   stabylysshed and concluded, as yt appereth plenely, and ys con-
Folio 208.   teyned in tharticles here next folowyng :—
The articles be-   " Blyssed be Jhesu, in Whos handes and bounte restethe and ys
twyxt kyng   the pease and vnyte betwyxt princes, and the weele of euery reaume
Harry and the
duk of York.   yknow, by Whos direccione aggreed hit ys, appoynted, and accorded
as folowethe, betwyxt the moste Hyghe and most Myghty Prynce,
Kyng Harry the vjth, kyng of Englond and of Fraunce and lorde of
Yrelond, on that on party, and the ryghte Hyghe and Myghty Prynce
Richard Plantagenet, Duke of York, on that other party, uppon certayne matyers of variaunce mened betwyxt thayme; and in espe-
cyalle, uppon the clayme and tytle vn to the corones of Englond and
of Fraunce, and royalle power, estate, and dygnyte apperteynyng to
the same, and lordshyppe of Yrelond, opened, shewed, and declared
by the sayde duk afore alle the lordes spyrytuelle and temporalle
beyng in thys present parliament: The sayde aggrement, appoyntement and accord, to be auctorysed by the same parlement.

    " Furst, where the sayde Richard duk of York hathe declared and
opened as aboue ys sayde tytle and clayme in the manner as
folowethe

    " That the ryghte noble and worthy prince Harry kyng of Englond
the iij^{de} had issew and lawfully gate Edward hys furst begoten sone,
borne at Westmynstre the xv. kalendis of Juylle, in the vygyl of
seynt Marc and Marcellyane, the yere_of oure Lorde M^{l}.cc.xxxix. :
and Edmonde his seconde goten sone whyche was in saynt Marcelle

day, the vere of oure Lorde M^1.cc.: The whyche Edward, after the
dethe of kyng Harry hys fader, entiteled and called kyng Edward the
furst, had yssew Edwarde, hys furst begoten sone, entitled and called
after the desese of the sayde furst Edwarde, hys fader, kyng Edward the Folio 208 b.
secunde : The whiche had yssew and lawfully gate the ryghte noble
and honorable prince Edward the thryd, trew and vndowted kyng of
Engelond and of Fraunce and lord of Yrelond : Whyche Edwarde the
iij^{de} trew and vndowted kyng of Engelond and of Fraunce and lord of
Yrelond, had yssew and lawfully gate, Edward hys furst begotenne sone,
prince of Wales; Wyllyam of Hatfyeld, secund begotenne ; Leonel,
thryd begoten, duke of Clarence ; Johan of Gaunt, fourthe begotenne,
duke of Lancastre ; Edmond Langley, fyfth begoten, duk of York;
Thomas Wodstoke, syxthe gotenne, duk of Gloucestre; and Wyllyam
Wyndsore, the seuenthe goten. The sayde Edwarde, prince of Wales,
whyche dyed in the lyf of the sayde Edward, kyng, had yssew and
lawfully gat Richard, the whyche succeded the same Edward, kyng,
hys grauntsyre, in royalle dygnyte, entyteled and called kyng
Richard the secund, and deyed withoute yssew. Wyllyam Hatfeld
the ij^{de} goten sone of the seyde Edward, kyng, dyed withoute yssew.
Leonelle, the iij^{de} goten sone of the sayde Edward, kyng, duke of
Clarence, had yssew and lawfully * gat Phylyppa, his ownely doughtre * Some have
and heyre, whyche by sacrament of matrymony cowpeled vnto Ed-   denied this.†
mond Mortymer erle of Marche, had yssew and lawfully beere Roger
Mortymer, erle of Marche, her sone and heyre. Whiche Roger
erle of Marche had yssew and lawfully begate Edmund erle of
Marche, Roger Mortymer, Anne and Alianore, whyche Edmund,
Roger and Alyanore, dyed withoute yssew. And the sayde Anne
vndre the sacrament of matrymony cowpeled vnto Richard erle of
Cambrege, the sone of the sayde Edmond Langley, the fyfthe goten Folio 209.
sone of the sayde kyng Edward, as yt ys afore specyfyed, had yssew
and bare lawfully Richard Plantagenet, comonly called duk of York.

† By the hand of Stowe.

The sayde Johan of Gaunt the iiijth goten sone of the seyde kyng Edward, and the yonger brother of the sayde Leonelle, had yssew and lawfully gat Harry Erle of Derby, whyche incontinent after the tyme that the seyde kyng Richard resygned the corone₃ of the sayde reames and the sayde lordeshyppe of Yrlond, vnryghtewysly entred vpponne the same, then be alyue Edmond Mortymer erle of Marche, sone to Roger Mortymer erle of Marche, sone and heyre of the sayde Phylyppa, doughter and heyre of the sayde ser Leonelle, the iij^{de} sone of the sayde kyng Edward the iij^{de}, to the whyche Edmond the ryghte and title of the seyde corones and lordshyp by lawe and custom belonged. To the whyche Richard duk of York, as sone to Anne, doughter to Roger Mortymer erle of Marche, sone and heyre to the sayde Phylyppa, doughter and heyre of the sayde Leonelle, the iij^{de} goten sone of the saydo kyng Edwarde the iij^{de}, the ryghte, tytle, dygnyte royalle, and estate of the corones of the reames of Englond and Fraunce, and of the lordeshyppe and the londe of Yrelond, of the ryghte lawe and custume perteynethe and belongethe, afore any yssew of the sayde Johan of Gaunt the iiij^{the} goten sone of the same kyng Edwarde.

"The sayde tytle natheles natwythestandyng, and withoute preiudice of the same, the sayde Richard duk of York, tendrely desyryng the weele, reste and prosperyte of thys laude, and to sette aparte alle that that myghte be a trouble to the same; and consideryng the possessyone of the sayd kyng Harry the vj^{the}, and that he hathe for hys tyme be named, taken and reputed kyng of Engelond and of Fraunce and lorde of Yrlond; ys content, aggreed and consentethe that he be had, reputed and taken kyng of Englond and of Fraunce, with the royalle astate, dignyte and preemynence bylongyng therto, and lorde of Yrlond, duryng hys lyfe naturalle; and for that tyme the sayde duk, withoute hurte or preiudice of hys sayde ryghte and title, shalle take, worshyp and honoure hym for his souerayne lord.

"Item, The sayde Rychard, duk of York, shalle promyt and hynde hym by hys solemne othe, in maner and forme as folowethe

"In the name of God, Amenne. I Rychard, duke of York, promytte A.D. 1460. and swere by the feythe and trowthe that I owe to Almyghty God, that I shalle neuer do, consent, procure or stere, directly or indirectly, in pryve or appert, neyther, asmoche as in me ys, shalle suffre to be do, consented, procured or stered, any thyng that may be or sowne to abrygement of the naturalle lyfe of kyng Harry vj[th], or to hurte or amenusyng of hys regne or dygnyte royalle, by vyolence or any otherwyse ayens hym (*sic*) fredom or liberte: But yef any persone or persones wold do or presume any thyng to the contrary, I shalle with alle my myghte and power withstande hyt, and make yt to be wythstonde, as fer as my power wylle streche therevnto: so helpe me God, and His holy Euangelyes.

"Item, Edward erle of Marche and Edmond erle of Rutlond, sones of the sayde Richard duk of York, shalle make lyke othe. Folio 210.

"Item, It ys accorded, appoynted, and aggreed, that the sayde Rychard duke of York shalle be called and reputed from hensfoorth verray and ryghtefulle heyre to the corounes, royalle astate, dygnyte and lordeshyp abouesayde: And after the decees of the sayde king Harry, or whenne he wolle laye from hym the sayde corounes, astate, dignite and lordshyppe, the sayde duke and hys heyres shalle immediately succede to the sayde corones, royalle astate, dygnyte and lordshyppe.

"Item, The sayde Richard, duk of York, shalle haue by auctoryte of thys present parlement, castelles, maners, loudes and tenementes, wythe the wardes, mariages, releues, seruices, fynes, amerciamentes, offyces, avousons, fees and other appurtenaunces to thaym belongyng what soeuer they be, to the yerely valew of x. M[l] marc., ouer alle charges and repryses; whereof v. M[l] marc. shalle be to his owen estate; iij. M[l] vc. marc. to Edwarde hys furst begoten sone, earle of Marche, for his astate; and M[l] ti. to Edmond, erle of Rutlond, hys secund goten sone, for his yerly sustentacione, of suche consideraciones and suche entent as shal be declared by the lordes of the kynges counselle.

" Item, Yef any persone, or persones, ymagyne or compasse the
dethe of the sayde duk, and therof prouably be atteynt of open
dede doone by folkes of other condicione, that yt be demed and
adiuged hyghe tresone.

" Item, For the more estabylysshyng of the sayde accord, it ys
appoynted and consented, that the lordes spirituelle and temporalle
beyng in thys present parliament, shalle make othys to accept, take,

worshyppe and repute, the sayde Richard duk of York, and hys
sayde eyres, as aboue ys rehersed, and kepe and obserue and
streynghte, in as moche as apparteynethe vn to thaym, alle the
thynges abouesayde, and resyste to theyre power alle thaym that
wold presume the contrary, accordyng to thayre astates and de-
grees.

" Item, The sayde Richard duk of York, erles of Marche and Rutland, shalle promyt and make othe to helpe, ayde and defend the
sayde lordes and euery of theyme, ayens alle tho that wolle quarelle
or any thyng attempt ayenst the sayde lordes, or any of thaym, by
occasyone of aggrement or consenttyng to the sayde accorde, or
assystence yeuyng to the duk and erles or any of thaym.

" Item, Hit ys aggreed and appoynted that thys accorde, and euery
article therof, be opened and notyfyed by the kynges letters patentes,
or otherwyse, at suche tymes and places and in manner as hit shal
be thoughte expedyent to the sayde Richard duk of York, with
thavyse of the lordes of the kynges counseylle.

" The kyng vnderstandethe certaynly the sayde tytle of the sayde
Richard duk of York, iust, lawfulle and sufficiant, by thauyse and
assent of the lordes spiritualle and temporalle and commones, in this
parliament assembled ; and by auctoryte of the same parlement declarethe, approuethe, ratyfyethe, confermethe and acceptethe the
sayde tytle, iust, good, lawfulle, and trew, and therevnto yeuethe his
assent and aggrement of his fre wylle and liberte. And ouer that,
by the sayde avyce and auctoryte, declarethe, entitlethe, callethe,
stabylysshethe, affermethe and reputethe the sayde Richard duk of

York, verray, trew and ryghtefulle heyre to the corones, royalle astate and dygnyte, of the reames of Englond and of Fraunce and of the lordeshyppe of Yrlond aforesayde : and that accordyng to the worshyp and reuerence that therto belongethe, he be taken, accepted and reputed in worshyppe and reuerence, by alle the states of the sayd reame of Englond, and of alle hys subiectes therof; sauyng and ordeynyng, by the same auctoryte, the kyng to haue the sayde corones, reames, royalle estate, dignyte and preemynence of the same, and the sayde lordshyppe of Yrlond, duryng his lyf naturalle. And forthermore, by the same avyse and auctoryte, wylle, consentethe and aggreethe that after hys decease, or whan hit shalle please his hyghenesse to ley from hym the seyde corones, estat, dignyte and lordshyp, or therof ceasethe ; The seyde Richard duke of York and his heyres shalle immediatly succede hym, in the seyde corones, royalle astate, dignyte and worshyppe, and thaym thanne haue and ioye, any acte of parlement, statute or ordenaunce or other thyng to the contrary maad, or interrupcion or dyscontynuance of possessyone natwythstandyng. And moreouer, by the sayde avyse and auctoryte, stabylysshethe, grauntethe, confermethe, approuethe, ratyfyethe and acceptethe the seyde accorde, and alle thyng therynne conteyned, and therevnto freely and absolutely assenteth and aggreeth.

And by the same avyse and auctoryte ordeynethe and estabylysshethe, that yef any persone or persones ymagyne or compasse the dethe of the sayde duk, and prouably be atteynt of open dede done by folkes of that condicions, that it demed and adiuged hygh treason.

And forthermore ordeyneth, puttethe and stabylysshethe, by the sayde avyse and auctoryte, that alle statutys, ordenaunces and actes of parlement, made in the tyme of the sayde kyng Harry the iiijth, by the whiche he and the heyres of his body commyng of Harry late kyng of Englond the vth, the sone and heyre of the sayde kyng Harry the iiijth, and the heyres of the body of the same kyng Harry the vth comyng, were or be enherytable to the sayde corones and reames, or to the herytage or enherytament of the same, be annulled, repeled, reuoked, dampned, cancelled, voyde, and of no force or effect. And ouer thus, the kyng by the sayde aduyse, assent and auctoryte, wylle, ordeynethe and stabylysshethe, that alle other actes and statutes, maade afore thys tyme by auctoryte of parlement, nat repeled or adnulled by lyk auctoryte, or otherwyse voyde, be in suche foorce, effect and vertew as thay were afore the makyng of these ordenaunces, and that no letters patentes royalx of record, nor actys iudycyalle, maade or done afore thys tyme, nat repeled, re-uersed ne otherwyse voyde by the lawe, be preiudyced or hurt by thys present acte."

Also it was ordeyned by the sayde parlement, that the sayde Rychard duk of York shold be called Prince of Wales, duke of Cornewayle, and erle of Chestre; and [he] was made also by the sayde parlement protectoure of Englond.

Thys same yeere, in the moneth of Decembre, the duk of Somerset and the erle of Deuenshyre went in to the Northcuntre, wythe viij.c. men: and anone after the seyde duk of York, the erle of Rutland
hys sone, and the erle of Salesbury, a lytelle before Crystynmas, wyth a fewe personnes went in to the Northe also, for to represse the malyce of the Northermenne the whyche loued nat the sayd duk of York ne the erle of Salesbury, and were loged at the castelle of Sandale and at Wakefeld.

Than the lord Nevyle, brother to the erle of Westmorland, vnder a falce colour wente to the sayde duk of York, desyryng a commys-syone of hym for to reyse a peple for to chastyse the rebelles of the cuntre; and the duk it graunted, demyng that he had be trew and on hys parte. When he had his commyssyone he reysed to the nombre of viij. M^l. men, and broute thaym to the lordes of the cuntre; that ys to say, the erle of Northumbrelond, lord Clyfford, and duke of Somerset, that were aduersaryes and enemyes to duke Richarde. And whan they sawe a conuenient tyme for to fylle

theyre cruelle entent, the laste day of Decembre they fyll oponne A.D. 1460.
the sayde duk Rychard, and hym kylde, and hys sone therlle of [December 31st.]
Rutland, and meny other knyghtes and squyers; that ys to say, the
lorde Haryngtone a yong man, Thomas Haryngtone knyght, ser
Thomas Nevyle sone to therlle of Salesbury, and ser Harry Ratford
knyghte; and of other peple to the nombre of M¹. M¹.cc. The erle
of Salesbury was take alyue, and lad by the sayde duk of Somerset
to the castel of Pountfreete, and for a grete summe of money that
he shuld haue payed had graunt of hys lyfe. But the commune
peple of the cuntre, whyche loued hym nat, tooke hym owte of the
castelle by violence and smote of his hed.

When the dethe of these lordes was knowe, greete sorow was A.D. 1461. Folio 212 b.
made for thaym ; and anone, by the kynges commaundement, wryttes
and commyssiones were sent and direct to the Shyreues and other
officers, to reyse peple for to chastyse the peple and the rebelles of
the North.* And they of the Northe heryng thys gadred pryuyly a
grete peple, and came doune sodeynly to the towne of Dunstaple,
robbyng alle the cuntre and peple as they came; and spoylyng
abbeyes and howses of relygyone and churches, and bare awey
chalyces, bookes and other ornamentes, as thay had be paynems or
Sarracenes, and no Crysten menne.

The xij. day of Feuerer, the Thurseday, kyng Harry with his [February 12th.]
lordes, that ys to say, the duk of Norfolk, and Suffolk, the erles of
Warrewyk and of Arundelle, the lorde Bonevyle and other, went
oute of Londoun, and came with thayre peple to the toune of Seynt
Albonys, nat knowyng that the peple of the North was so nyghe.
And whanne the kyng herde that they were so nyghe hym, he went
oute and took hys felde besyde a lytelle towne called Sandryge, nat The secunde batayl of Seynt Albonys.
fer fro Seynt Albonys, in a place called No-mannes land, and there
he stoode and sawe his peple slayne on bothe sydes. And at the

---

* See in Rymer a commission directed to Edward duke of York for this purpose, dated
Feb. 12 (vol. xi. p. 471.)

laste, thorow the withdrawyng of the Kentisshmen with thayre capteyne, called Lovelace, that was in the vaunt-warde,—the whych
Lovelace fauored the Northe party, for as moche as he was take by
the Northurnmen at Wakefeld whan the duk of York was slayne,
and made to theym an othe for to saue his lyfe, that he wold neuer
be agayns theym,—and also be vndysposycion of the peple of the
kynges syde, that wold nat be guyded ne gouerned by theyre cap-

teyns, kyng Harryes part loste the feeld. The lordes that were wyth
the kyng seyng thus, withdrowe theym, and went theyre wey.

Whan the kyng sawe his peple dysparbeled and the feeld broke,
he went to his queue Margarete that came wyth the Northurmen,
and hyr sone Edward; for thay of the North sayde that thay came
for to restore the kyng to the quene his wyfe, and for to delyuer
hym owte of pryson; forasmeche as seth the batayle of Northampton
he had be vnder the rewle and gouernaunce of the erles of Warrewyk and Salesbury, and of other.

The sayde erle of Warrewyk dressed hym toward the erle of
Marche, commyng toward London owte of Wales, fro the dyscomfyture of the erles of Penbroke and Wylshyre. The lorde Bonevyle that came wyth kyng Harry wolde haue withdrawe hym, as
other lordes ded, and saned hymself fro his enemyes, but the kyng
assured hym that he shuld haue no bodyly harme; natheles natwythstandyng that sewrte, at instaunce of the queue, the duk of
Exetre, and therlle of Deuonshyre, by iugement of hym that was
called the Prince, a chylde, he was beheded at Seynt Albons, and
with hym a worthy knyghte of Kent called ser Thomas Kyryelle.
Ser Johan Nevyle, kyng Harryes chamburlayne, brother to the erle
of Warrewyk, was take; but sone after he was delyuered. This

bataylle was done on Shroftwysday, the yere aboue sayde, the xvij.
day of Feuerer, in the whiche were slayne M^l.ix.c.xvj. persones.

Whan thys batayle was doon, London dredyng the manas and the
malyce of the quene and the duke of Somerset and other, leste they

wolde have spoyled the cyte,—for as moche as the queue with her

counselle had graunted and yene leve to the Northurmen for to A.D. 1461.
spoyle and robbe the sayde cyte, and also the townes of Couentre,
Bristow, and Salesbury, wyth the shyrys withynne rehersed, as for
payment and recompense of theyre sowde and wages, as the comon
noyse was among the peple at that tyme;—then ther was sent vuto
the sayde quene owte of the cyte of Londoun the duchesse of
Bukynghame, with other wytty men with her, to trete with thaym
for to be benyuolent and owe good wylle to the cyte, the whyche
was dyuyded withyn hyt self; for some of the worthy and of the
Aldremen, dredyng and weyyng the inconueniens and myscheues
that myghte folow contrary to the comone wele of the cyte, and for
to stonde in sewrte of the cyte both of bodyes and of goodes no robry
to be had, graunted and promytted a certayne some of money to the
sayde quene and duk of Somerset, and that he shulde come in to the
cyte aponne thys appoyntement with a certayne nombre of persones
wyth hym. And anon hereaponne certayn speres and men of armes
were sent by the sayde duk, for to have entred the cyte before his
commyng; whereof some were slayne, and some sore hurte, and the
remanent put to flyghte. And anone after, the comones, for the
sauacione of the cyte, toke the keyes of the yates were they shulde
have entred, and manly kept and defended hit fro theyre enemyes,
vuto the commyng of Edwarde the noble erle of Marche.

Thanne kyng Harry, with Margarete his quene and the Norther-
men, went and retorned homewarde toward the North ayene: the Folio 214.
whyche Northurnemenne as they went homwarde dyd harmes
innumerable, takyng mennys cartes, waynes, horses and bestis, and
robbed the peple and lad theyre pylage into the North contre, so
that men of the shyres that they past by, had almoste lefte no bestys
to tyle theyre londe.

This same tyme the ij bretheryn of the erle of March, George
and Richard, were sent to Phylyp duk of Burgoyne for saaf garde
of theyre persones, the whyche were of the sayde duk notably

resceyued, cherysshed and honoured; and afterwarde sende hom with meny grete yeftes vn to Englond ayene.

[February 3rd.]   The iij^{de} day of Feuerer the same yere, Edward the noble erle of Marche faught with the Walsshmen besyde Wygmore in Wales, whos capteyns were the erle of Penbrook and the erle of Wylshyre, that wolde fynally haue dystroyed the sayde erle of Marche.

[February 2nd.]   And the Monday before the daye of batayle, that ys to say, in the feest of Puryficacion of oure blessed Lady abowte x atte clocke before none, were seen iij sonnys in the fyrmament shynyng fulle) clere, whereof the peple hade grete mervayle, and therof were agast. The noble erle Edward thaym comforted and sayde, " Beethe of good comfort, and dredethe not ; thys ys a good sygne, for these iij sonys betokene the Fader, the Sone, and the Holy Gost, and therfore late vs haue a good harte, and in the name of Almyghtye God go we agayns oure enemyes." And so by His grace, he had the vyctory of his enemyes, and put the ij erles to flyghte, and slow of the Walsshemen to the nombre of iiij. M^l.

Fo o 214 b.
[February 28th.]   After thys dyscomfyture he came to Londoun, the xxviij day of the moneth abouesayde, and anone fylle vnto hym peple innumerable, redy for to go with hym in to the northe, to venge the dethe of the noble duke Richard hys fadre.

    Here endethe the reygne of kyng Harry the vj^{the} that had regned xxxix. [viij.]* yere, vj monethes and iij dayes, that ys to say vnto Twysday, the iij day of Marche; and the Wennesday next after,
[Wednesday, March 4th.] vppon the morow, Edwarde the noble erle of Marche was chosen kyng in the cyte of Londoun, and began for to reygne, &c.

* Correction by the hand of Stowe.

AN APPENDIX

CONTAINING THE 18th AND 19th YEARS OF RICHARD II. AND THE PARLIAMENT AT BURY ST. EDMUND'S, 25th HENRY VI.

BY RICHARD FOX, MONK OF ST. ALBAN'S.

---

xviij ȝere. The ȝere of our Lord M¹.ccc.iiij score and **xv**, and the regne of kyng Rycharde xviij ȝere, he hulde a parlement in Irelonde, to the wheche parlement come his lyge men of Irelonde, tho that were of the Englysche Irysche, and the kyng asked of hem a subsedy, and they ȝraunted to hym.

And in that same tyme, the viij day aftur the xij day, sire Edmund, duke of ȝork, grauntfader (*sic*) to kyng Rycharde, and leefftenant of Englonde in the kynges absence, sette a parlement at Londone, to the wheche parlement come dyuers of the Irysche lordes. And the duke of Gloucetur he expowned before alle men the kynges grete nede at that tyme in specialle, for moche of his tresour was spente in his lyyng in Irelonde. And when he hadde purposed to the clergye for a Dyme, they graunted hym. And then he purposed his mater aftur the same entent to the Comunes for an hole xv peny; they seyde by protestacyon and condicyon that hat "schalle not bynde vs by no lawe to graunt only here afturward. But as at this tyme, forasmoche as we tendre and loue our sovereyne lord the kyng, we graunte to hym the **xv** peny." And this was sped on bothe partyes spirituelle and temperalle.

And in the same ȝere, the kyng beyng in Irelonde, maystur John Wyccleef, a doctour in devenyte, and in his openyons an eretyk, this seyde mayster John, in the kynges absence, hadde asocyed to hym dyuers lordes, as sire Rycharde Sturry, sire Thomas Latymer, sire Lowys Clyfforde, sire Johan Mowntagu; the wheche setten scrowis on Powlus dore of ther false Lollardie wheche they haad begunne, concludyng by xij chapytours of eresy in destruccyon of the feyth and of the status of holy churche, the wheche mevyng and menyng begynneth as thus:—

"Nos pauperes Christi homines et thesauri appostolorumque (*sic*) snorum, denunciamus Dominis, hac (*sic*) Communibus parliamenti, certas conclusiones et veritates pro reformacione ecclesie Anglie, que fuit seca (*sic*) et leprosa multis annis per manutenenciam superbe prelacie, supportate per adulationem privatorum religionum, que multiplicantur ad magnum nocumentum et dolorosum periculum hic in Angliâ," &c.

The firste conclusion that he leyde for hym, for his truthe. He began when the churche of Englonde was appered with temperelle godus, and morteysed be apropriacyone.

The secunde conclusione was, that oure prystehode that began in Rome, yfeyned of the power of angelus and archangeles, and hyt is not the same pristehode the wheche Criste ordeyned to his apostelus· And who that lyste to loke and se more of these articules, leet hym loke on Wyccleves bokes.

And here folewyng ben the vers that were sette vpon Powles dores:—

"Plangant Anglorum gentes crimen Sodomorum !
Paulos (*sic*) fert horum sunt ydola causa malorum.
Surgunt ingrati gieʒite Semoni (*sic*) nati
Nontiui (*sic*) prelati hoc defensari (*sic*) parati.
Qui reges estis populus (*sic*) quicunque preestis,
Qualiter his gestis gladiis (*sic*) prohibere potestis ?"

Anon as tythynges come to kyng Rycharde into Irelonde, he sweere a grete oth that they scholde be hanged, and alle tho that hulde with hem, without they wolde renounce and forsake theyre openyones.

And then sire Rycharde Sturry herde of the kynges oth, and anon he renounced and forsoke alle tho poyntes and articulis of Lollardy, and therto he was sworen upon a booke, the kyng beyng present.

And in that same ȝere, ther was a squyer of Staffordeschyre beryng the kynges levere, the hert of syluer, with a felow of his of Northfolke ycleped John Colby ; the wheche too ymagened a patent vnder the kynges grete seele, that the relygious of Esex and of Northfolke, and alle the nonneryes of bothe contreyes, scholde schewe to hem ther wrytynge of ther mortysementes; the wheche seyde squyer and Colby vsed and hade vsed a grete whyle, or they were aspyed, in dyuerse places of the rewme, and gate be tho menes moche goode falsly : but at the laste bothe were taken, and brouȝt to London, but John Colby deyde in pryson, and the squyer aboode the kynges comyng home out of Irelonde.

And in this same ȝere, the kyng dede do brynge the body of sir Robert Veer into Englond, the wheche was erle off Oxford.

And in this same ȝere, there apered in Fraunce a crucifix with his blody woundes ouer the churche-steple of the towne of Landavencis, the beschope, the clergie, and mony of the comune peple beholdyng theron; and hit apered so the space of halffe an our.

In that same ȝere, a barbour, called a Moret, an hethen lorde, fauȝt aȝeyns the priour of seynt Jhones of Rodes, the wheche pryour hade at his gouernaunce and ledyng but iij. c. off Cristenmen at that tyme; but manly, by Godes helpe, they fouȝt with the Moret, and slowe of the paynemus that come with hym to batayle mo than fyfty M^1. And when the Moret syȝ that he myȝt not prevayle aȝeyne the Cristen at the batayle on the londe, he began an newe warre upon the see: but, be the helpe of God, he was put to the wurse, and withdrowe hym.

And in this same ȝere, the marchantes of Northfolke were róbbed of xx. M^1. pownde be the queenes meyne of Denmarke, the wheche was an vndoyng to mony of the marchantes of Northfolke for euermore afturwarde.

xix ȝere. Item, in anno M¹.ċcc. nonogesimo vj°, and in the regne of kyng Rychard the xix ȝere, the pope wroot downe to the kyng aȝeyne the lordes, to haue hem proclamed as traytours to holy churche; and that the kyng schold be faverable to the prelates, as beschopes, abbotus, pryours, and to alle the trewe mynystris of the churche; and tho cursed Lollardes that wolde not renounce and leue hure false openyones, the kyng to geve hem the lawe as longed to suche mysbeleuers and eretykes. Also alle tho that haad purchased off the pope or of ony of his mynystris ony fredome, as chappellanes, honoris, or any capasite, the pope annulled hem, bothe of his owne tyme and also of his prodesessous (*sic*), vnto the tyme that he were bettur avysed.

And in this same ȝere, sire John, duke of Lancastre, to whome the kyng had ȝeue the Duche of Gyene, for the wheche he spent goode innumerable to gete the goode wylle of the peple of that countrey; and, when the seyde duke stoode in gode conseyte of the peple, the kyng sent for hym to come to hym into Englonde. And he come home anon aftur Cristemasse to the maner off Langeley, wher the kyng haad holde his Cristemasse; and he was reseyued wurthyly and wyrschypeffully by countynaunce out-warde, but ther was but lytylle loue withinne forth, as hit was seyde.

And anon aftur, the duke partyd fro the kyng, and rode to Lyncolle, wher Kateryne Swynfordes abydyng was as at that tyme. And aftur the utas of xij day, the duke wedded the seyde Kateryne; the wheche weddyng caused mony a monuns wonderyng, for, as hit was seyde, he haad holde heere longe before.

     And in this same ȝere, the ambassitours of Englonde and Fraunce metten togedere, and spaken for a pees betwene Englonde and Fraunce, be the assent of bothe the kynges: and apoyntement was made that bothe the kynges schulde mete oppon a serteyne grounde beȝonde Calyce; and so they dede, and ther were pyȝt bothe ther tentes ful ryally. But or they come togedere for to trete togedere, ther was an oth taken on bothe partyes, wheche oth sueth here folewyng wreten in Lateyne. The fyrste that swere was the kyng A.D. 1396. of Fraunce as thus :—

"Nos Carolus Rex Francie juramus in verbo regali super Evangelia, pro nobis et omnibus nobis subjectis, amicis, et affinitate conjunctis, et benevolentibus, quod non faciemus nec paciemur fieri, per nos nec per supra nominatos, dampnum, inpeticionem, molestiam, arestacionem, nec disturbacionem, ullo modo per tempus nostre convencionis, nec per octo dies ante convencionem et septem dies sequentes, nostro dicto filio Regi Anglie, nec alicui de suis subjectis, amicis, affinibus, nec benevolis, ante dictum tempus. Et si casu alico, insolencia vel litigia per aliquem de nostris supradictis, quod absit, emercerit (sic), nos promittimus verbo regali et per securitatem predictam, quod faciemus hec debite emendari, et sine dilacione reformari. Et juramus ulterius, super securitate predicta, quod si aliquis vel aliqui de quolicumque (sic) statu vel condicione extiterint (sic), voluerit vel voluerint contraire dicte nostre securitati, nos erimus in auxilium nostri predicti filii, pro nostro posse, ad resistendum malicie malefactorum predictorum, et conservandum nostrum dictum filium et suos, per modum quem nos et nostri scimus, et ad tenendum omnia et prosequendum sine fraude vel malo ingenio; et ad hoc juramus et promittimus sicut supra."

Idem juramentum edidit Rychardus Rex Anglorum.

And forthwith the xxvj day of the moneth of Octobre suyng, the kyng of Englonde, Rychard the Secounde, roode fro Calyce to the castelle of Gynes warde. And with hym roode the duke of Barrye, the wheche duke was sent frome the Frensche party to Calyce, to receyue the oth of the kyng [of] Englonde, and the surete for the peple of Fraunce.

M^D off the Parlement of Berye,
Anno Domini M^l.cccc.xlvj°.

A.D. 1447.
[Feb. 10th.]
[Feb. 16th.]

Th[e] Parlement of Berye, the regne of kyng Harry the vj. the xxv ʒere. The parlement began the x day of Februarye.

And onne the xvj day of the same moneth mustered the men of the same contre on the north syde of Berye on Henow Heth to the nowmbre of xl. M^l.

And on the morewe they schewed hemself on the south-este party of the towne off Berye. And there they brak up their waache, and euerye man went to his owne dwellyng-place, somme xxxtⁱ mʒle, somme xx mʒle, x mʒle, iiij mʒle, somme more, somme lesse, and no doubte of hit was (*sic*) a fervent coolde weder and a bytynge.

[Feb. 18th.]

And on the morewe, that is to seye the xviij day of Februarye and Schrooffe-Sonedayes Even, come the duke of Gloucetre fro Lanam; and or he come by halue a mʒle or more mette with hym sir John Stourtone, treserere of the kynges howse, and sir Thomas Stanley, cownteroller of the kyngus hows, in message fro the kyng, was (*sic*), as hit was reportyd by somme of the forseyd dukes meyne:—" That forasmoche as the forseyde duke of Gloucetre hadde labered in that feruent coolde wheder, hit was the kynges wylle that he scholde take the nexte wey to his loggyng, and goo to his mete." And indede he enterid in at the Southgate about xj on the clokke affore none. And by estymacyon there come with hym to the nowmbre of iiij score hors. These forseyd messageres, when they badde do the kynges comaundement, toke leue of the duke, and retournede aʒeyn to the kyng.

And the forseyde duke roode into the horse-market, and toke the wey on his lyfte hoonde to the Northgate warde, and he enteryd into a lewde lane. And then the duke asked a pore man that dwelled in the same lane, "What calle me this lane?" The pore man answered and seyde, "Forsothe, my lord, hit is called the Dede lane." And thanne the good duke remembryd hym of an olde prophesye that he hadde radde mony a day before, and seyde, "As our Lord

wylle, be h.t alle ;" and rode forth to the North Spytylle to his mete. A.D. 1447.
And anoon as he hadde eten, come to hym by the kynges comaundement the duke of Bokyngham, the marques of Dorset, the erle of
Salysbery, the vycount Bemound, the lorde Sudeley. And the
vycount Bemound areste the seyde duke of Gloucetre; and by the
comaundement of the kyng ther waytyd upon the seyde duke to
ȝemen of the crowne and a sergeaunt of armes: Barthelemewe Halley
and Pulforde, ȝemen of the crownne, and Thomas Calbrose, sergeaunt of armes.

And that same aftrenoone, bytwene viij and ix, were areste be
the kynges offyceres sir Roger Chambreleyn and sir Harry Wogan
knyghtes, Thomas Herbert, Thomas Weryot, John Wogan, Howelle
ap Dauith Thomas, and mo other, &c.

And on the Soneday was John Hobergere comaundet to warde
ageyns even.   [Feb. 19th.]

And on the Schrof-Tewesday, in the latter ende of ther mete, in
the halle, were areste sir Robert Veere, sir John Cheyne, knyȝtes; [Feb. 21st.]
John Bokkelond, counteroller with the seyde duke, Arteys, Thomas
Wylde, Rychard Myddyltone, Wallerowne, Bassyngburne, squyers;
Rychard Nedam, Jon Swafylde, ȝemen; and mo other, to the
nowmbre of xxviij^ti. And these were sent to dyuerse plases to
prisone, scmme to the Touur of Londone, somme to Wynchester,
somme to Notyngham, and somme to North-hamtone, and to other
dyuers places, as plesyd the kyng and his councelle.

And on the Thoursday next folowyng aftre the arestyng of the
sey (sic) duke of Gloucetre, he deyde sone appon iij on the belle at [Feb. 23rd.]
aftrenone, at his owne loggynge, called Seynt Saluatoures, without
the Northgate: on whose sowle God haue mercy. Amen.

And on the Fryday next folewyng, the lordes spirituelle and tem-
porelle, also knyȝtes of the parlement, and whosoeuer wolde come, [Feb. 24th.]
saugh hym dede. And ageyne even he was bowelled and rolled in
seryd cloth, and leyde in a cheste of leede, and thenne aboue the
leede a cheste of popeler boorde.

And on the Saturday next folewynge by the morewen, he was [Feb. 25th.]

bore to the Greye Freres of Babbewede, with xx torches of his owne meynye; saue the too ʒemen of the crowne and the sergeaunt of armes, ther were no mo strangeres that went with hym.

And on the Soneday folewyng at afternone, the abbot of Seynt Albones dede his Dirige.

And on the Moneday his Masse. And on the Tewesday they bruʒt hym to the Newemarket, and bood there al nyʒt. And on the Wendesday at nyʒt they laye at Berkewey. And on the Thorsday they lay at Ware. And on the Fryday they come to Seynt Albones, and there was done his Dyryge, and on the morewe his Masse, and thanne put into a feyre vout wheche was made for hym by his lyffe, and so closed and mured vp: on whose sowle God haue mercy, and on alle Cristen sowles. Amen.

Ther come with his body to Seynt Albones, too of his owne chapeleynes, mayster Roger Burgh and sir Raaffe Bewforde, pristes, the too ʒemen of the crowne, and the sergeaunt of armes. Ther came with hym his treserere Gerveyse of Clyftone, Jan de Puis, eusscher of the chambre, his cofferer Thomas Bernarde, George Lampot, Thomas Asschelle, Rychard Nedam of Douer, John Herburiour, John Acastre, and iiij hensemen, and but fewe mo of squyers. Ther come with hym ʒemen of chambre, Rychard Nylder, John Doore, Rychard Boltone, John South, Grene, Lane, and moo other; John of the Halles, Portars (sic), and the Cookes.

These were tho that were dampned.

Sir Rorgger (sic) Chambreleyne, Arteys, Rychard Myddiltone, Thomas Herbert, Rychard Nedam: these were jugid to be drawen and hanged, and so they were. But the kyng dede hem grace, or they weren dede; for he sent hem hure charturs of pardone, the wheche sauyd hure lyffuus (sic). And alle the other that were araste, bothe gentyllemen and ʒemen, the kyng dede hem grace: relesed hem of ther prisonment, and fore the more part were restored to ther goodes.

And thus endet Vmffrey the duke of Gloucetre.

SUPPLEMENTARY ADDITIONS

FROM THE CONTINUATION OF THE EULOGIUM:

COTTON MS. GALBA E. VII.

I.

[See Page 2, line 17, &c.]

Sed **Abbas** nec adquiescere nec comparere volebat, asserens eccle- **A D.** 1378. siam **suam** dedicatam fore per **beatum** Petrum miraculosè, et **alterius** Folio 192. dedicatione non indigere; ostendans chronicam dedicationis, ut sequitur:—

Tempore quo Rex Æthelbertus qui regnavit in Cantiâ, prædicante A.D. 605. beato Augustino, fidei sacramenta susceperat, nepos quoque ejus Sebertus, qui orientalibus Anglis præfuit, fidem, eodem episcopo evangelizante, suscepit. Hic Londoniis, quæ regni sui Metropolis habebatur, intra muros ecclesiam in honorem Pauli beatissimi construens, episcopali eam sede voluit esse sublimem : cui sanctus Mellitus, quem beatus papa Gregorius cum pluribus aliis in adjutorium miserat Augustino, merito simul et honore pontificali priùs omnium præfuit. Volens autem rex utrique apostolo se gratum præstare, in occidentali parte ejusdem civitatis extra muros, in honore beati Petri, monasterium insigne fundavit; multis illud donariis ornans et citans possessionibus. Venerat autem tempus, quo ecclesia fuerat in eo dedicanda; paratisque omnibus pro loco et tempore pro monasterii dignitate, agente episcopo eâ nocte in tentoriis, dies crastina præstolabatur. Magna plebis expectatio, quæ adhuc **rudis** in fide, his solenniis interesse non solùm pro devotione sed etiam pro admiratione gaudebat. Eâdem nocte, piscatori cuidam in Thamasis fluvii, qui eidem monasterio subfluit, ulteriori ripâ, in habitu peregrini beatus Petrus apparens, promissâ mercede, transponi se ab eodem et petiit et præmeruit. Egressus autem a naviculâ, ecclesiam, piscatore cernente, ingreditur; et, eece, subitò lux cœlestis emicuit, miroque splendore collustrans omnia, noctem convertit in diem. Adfuit enim cum apostolo multitudo civium supernorum egredientium et ingredientium, et, choris hymnidicis præeuntibus, melodia cœlestis insonuit. Omnia plena lumine, omnia referta dulcedine. Aures voeis angelicæ mulcebat jocunditas: nares indicibilis odoris fragrantia perfundebat: oculos lux ætherea illustrabat. Videbantur quasi mixta terrena cœlestibus, humana conjuncta divinis, et, quasi in scalâ Jacob, angeli descendentes et ascendentes in illis sacris solenniis videbantur. Paratisque omnibus quæ ad ecclesiæ dedicationem spectant solenniis, redit ad piscium piscatorem piscator egregius hominum; quem, cùm divini luminis fulgore perterritum, alienatum pœne sensibus, reperisset, blandâ consolatione reddidit hominem propriæ rationi. Ingredientes ambo cymbam simul uterque piscator, inter loquendum apostolus hominem iisdem quibus se quondam magister suus conveniens verbis, "Nunquid," ait, "pulmentarium non habes?" Et ille " Tum," inquit, "inconsuetæ lucis perfusione stupidus, tum expectatione tui detentus, nihil cepi; sed promissam a te mercedem securus expectavi." Ad hæc apostolus, " Laxa nunc," "inquit, " retia in capturam." Paruit imperanti piscator, et mox implevit rete piscium maxima multitudo; quibus ad ripam extractis, " Hunc," inquit apostolus, " qui cæteris magnitudine et pretio præcellit, Mellito episcopo, meâ ex parte, piscem defer. Pro nauticâ vero mercede, cætera tibi tolle. Ego sum Petrus qui tecum loquor, qùi cum meis concivibus, constructam in meo nomine basilicam dedicavi, episcopalemque benedictionem meæ sanctificationis auctoritate præveni. Dic ergo pontifici quæ tu vidisti et audisti; tuo quoque sermoni signa parietibus impressa testimonium perhibebunt. Supersedeat igitur dedicationi; suppleat quod omisimus, Dominici videlicet

Corporis et Sanguinis sacrosancta mysteria, populumque erudiens A.D. 605.
sermone et benedictione confirmans, notificet omnibus hunc me locum
crebrò visitaturum, hîc me fidelium votis et precibus adfuturum." Et,
his dictis, clavicularius cœlestis disparuit. Et jam nocturnis tenebris
finem dedit aurora, cùm beato Mellito, ad futuræ dedicationis cele-
branda mysteria processuro, cum pisce piscator occurrit; quem, cùm
episcopo tradidisset omnia ei quæ ab apostolo fuerant mandata, pro-
sequitur. Stupet pontifex, reseratisque basilicæ sacræ valvis, videt
pavimentum utriusque alphabeti inscriptione signatum; parietem bis
senis in locis sanctificationis oleo linitum; tot cereorum reliquias
duodenis crucibus inhærere; et quasi recenti aspersione adhuc cuncta
madescere. Refert hæc episcopus populo, et mox una vox omnium
pulsat cœlos laudantium et Deum benedicentium toto corde.

II.

[See Page 3, line 5.]

Hoc anno (1382) Rex Annam sororem Imperatoris, regis scilicet A.D. 1382.
Bohemiæ, solutis pro eâ xxij. M¹. marcis, sine consensu regni des- Folio 194 b,
col. b.
ponsavit. Oblata sibi filia fuit comitis Flandriæ, quam si habuisset, [Jan. 14th.]
jure suo postea Flandriam habuisset. Dux autem Burgundiæ ipsam
duxit, qui nunc comitatum habet.

III.

[See Page 4, line 18.]

Qui quidem comes modico tempore post in Hiberniâ interemptus A.D. 1398.
fuit. Folio 196.

Comes Arundelliæ omnes naves regis Franciæ [et]* alias, præ- A.D. 1387,
Col. b.
paratas in Angliam, de Rupellâ revertentes bonis vinis oneratas, cepit;
et, hominibus occisis, duxit in Angliam ad portum de Winchelse.

* " Die Dominicâ, in vigiliâ Annunciationis Dominicæ, magna classis navium Flandriæ,
Galliæ, et Hispaniæ . . . . conspicitur." (Walsingham.)

A.D. 1387.
[Aug. 25th.]

Anno Domini 1387° Rex in castro de Nottinghamiâ 25° die mensis Augusti, convocatis capitalibus justiciariis et uno serviente ad legem, proposuit has quæstiones, quæ sequuntur; præcipiens eis firmiter in fide et ligeantiâ suâ, quod fideliter secundum leges Anglicas ad eas responderent.

[Here follow the questions proposed to the Justices, with their answers, as they are to be found in Knyghton, col. 2694-6. Rot. Parl. III. 233, 357-8. Stat. Realm, II. 102-4. Evesham, 86-89. Immediately following the signatures of the Justices and of the Witnesses, the MS. proceeds] :—

Folio 196 b,
col. b.

Isti autem justiciarii fuerunt de consilio dominorum in parliamento præterito: et unus eorum postquam recesserat de castro dixit, " Jam meruimus cordas quibus suspendamur, quia timore mortis hæc dicta fuerunt et non de veritate."

Rex misit pro duce Gloucestriæ, comitibus Arundelliæ et Warwici, ponens insidias in viis ad capiendum eos: ipsi vero, his per amicos auditis, cum forti comitivâ in sylvâ de Haryngay juxta Londonias convenerunt.

[Sunday, Nov. 10th.]

Rex de consilio unius burgensis Londoniensis (*Page* 4, *Fragment B.*) venit ad Wesmonasterium, sperans auxilio Londoniensium ipsos debellare.

Archiepiscopus Cantuariensis supplicabat regi quod placeret sibi eos admittere ad præsentiam suam sine nocumento, et cum eis de pace tractare. Et, accepto juramento a rege, ivit et adduxit eos coram rege sedente in magnâ aulâ: exercitus eorum forìs erat. Et

[Sunday Nov. 17th.]

ait rex, " Quâ temeritate audetis vos insurgere, et contra pacem regni mei vos armare?" Respondit dux Gloucestriæ, " Nos non insurgimus neque nos armamus nos contra pacem regni, sed ad tuitionem vitæ contra inimicos nostros et regni, in quo casu quilibet homo potest arma portare. Petimusque et vos requirimus, quod fiat parliamentum

[Feb. 3rd.]*

statim post Purificationem Beatæ Virginis, et in judicio parliamenti

* The Purification was Feb. 2nd. The "Merciless Parliament" met on the day following.

nos ponemus nos; et custodiatis inimicos nostros, vestros adulatores, A.D. 1387.
faciatisque ibidem esse presentes." Et ait rex, " Parliamentum
habebis, et eis non nocebis, et te faciam ita infimum sicut minimum
garcionem coquinæ tuæ." Tum dux, " Non me inferiorem facietis
quam filium regis;" et genuflectens se dixit, " Filius sum regis."

Archiepiscopus Cantuariensis supplicabat regi quod admitteret eos
in crastino in eodem loco, et reformationi consentiret; concessitque
rex. (*Page* 4, *Fragment B. b.*) Sed in crastino mutans propositum
transivit ad Turrim.

In crastino verò domini venerunt cum exercitu suo in campum [Dec. 26th.]*
sancti Johannis, et miserunt pro majore Londoniensi, qui duxit eos Folio 197.
ad aulam communem civitatis, et amicitiam civitatis susceperunt.
Rex verò misit pro eis ut loquerentur cum eo in Turri. Qui respon-
dentes dixerunt, locum non esse tutum, sed extra Turrim cum eo
loqui parati fuerunt. Rex jussit majorem venire, cui mandavit [Nov. 10
———17.]
armare civitatem. " Absit, domine," dixit major; " ligii et fideles
vestri sunt et amici regni." Rex eum ejecit, et misit ducem Hiberniæ
cum literis suis patentibus et vexillo suo, ut Cestrenses et cæteros
occidentales adduceret. Et domini, adjunctis sibi comite de Derby
filio ducis Lancastriæ comite de Nottingham mareschallo, et adaucto
exercitu, transeundo obviaverunt duci venienti cum vexillo regis
expanso prope Oxoniam. Quidam miles prudens exiit de exercitu
ducis Hiberniæ, ut videret qui essent; et reversus dixit duci, " Hîc
sunt constabularius et mareschallus Angliæ, et præcipui domini regni;
quomodo habuistis literas veras?" Cui ait dux, " Nonne vultis
pugnare contra eos?" Respondit miles, " Absit." Et dux urgebat
equum ultra Thamisiam cum suo confessore de ordine Minorum,
magistro in theologiâ, et fugit. Cestrenses, scissis chordis arcuum

---

* There is a confusion in the history here—see note *Page* 4, *last line.* The occasion of
this second assembly of forces on the part of the Lords was the discovery of the King's
treachery in having secretly sent Robert de Vere to collect troops in Cheshire. His
defeat at Radcote Bridge was on Dec. 20th.

et cum arcubus suis verberati turpiter, redierunt. Militem quoque principalem, ducis Hiberniæ consiliarium, decollabant; et tulerunt ab eis vexillum regis et ipsum volventes plicabant. Dux autem Hiberniæ festinavit in insulam de Shipaye, et inde ad Alemaniam fugit; et Michaelis de la Pole similiter evasit; item, Alexander Nevyle Archiepiscopus Eborum ad partes ivit transmarinas; et nunquam reversi sunt.

Et prædicti quinque domini, videlicet, dux Gloucestriæ, Ricardus comes Arundelliæ, Ricardus comes Warwici, Henricus Bolyngbrok comes Darbeiæ, et Thomas Mowbray comes Notinghamiæ, in destructionem prædictorum rebellium et aliorum cum eis venientium apud Radcolbrigge, ceperunt et interfecerunt multos et quasi omnes, ex-

ceptis fugientibus.

Et tune prædicti quinque domini statuerunt parliamentum apud Westmonasterium, ubi Robertus Tresylian justiciarius, Nicholas Brembre miles, civis Londoniensis, et alii plures morti adjudicantur, et ob prædicationem eis impositam, tracti et suspensi sunt. Et in eodem parliamento, Symon de Berle valens miles de garterio, et Johannes Beauchamp miles, seneschallus hospitii regis, Jacobus Berniers miles, et alii, capti fuerunt, et apud Turrim Londoniensem decollati.

IV.

[See Page 6, line 18.]

—— ossa sua fuerunt combusta. Eodem anno Archiepiscopus Cantuariensis in convocatione cleri Londoniis statuit, nullos sacerdotes debere prædicare nisi fuerunt per diocesanos admissi.

Anno Domini 1388, Robertus Knollis ædificavit et construi fecit pontem Rofensem.

Hoc anno juventus et hæredes nobilium Angliæ perierunt in Hispaniâ, et rex Hispaniæ statuit cum duce (Lancastriæ) præliari;

dux autem transivit in Portugaliam, et tradidit filiam suam in matri- A.D. 1388.
monio* regi Portugaliæ, divulgavitque per Hispaniam (see *page* 6,
line 31) quod ipse misisset in Angliam pro alio exercitu: rex Hispaniæ hoc credens, quibusdam intervenientibus, pro certâ summâ
pecuniæ composuit cum duce; qui statim post rediit in Angliam.   [Dec. 1389.]

Anno Domini 1389, in parliamento tento† Londoniis rex retraxit A.D. 1390.
quædam privelegia Londoniensium; et ut mercatores extrinseci pos-
sent dividere merces suas, et par partes vendere in civitate, concessit.

Post hoc, rex misit Londoniensibus ut aurum sibi accommodarent; A.D. 1392.
et ipsi se excusabant dicentes se non esse aliis mercatoribus poten-
tiores.

Tunc rex vocavit ad Wodstok majorem Londoniensem, vicecomites, et alios civitatis rectores, qui coram justiciariis statuti sunt.
Quibus sic ait, "In civitate Londoniensi, pistores in x. quarteriis
frumenti vi*s*. viii*d*. excessivè lucrantur; similiter brasiatores in x.
quarteriis hordei, vi*s*. viii*d*. excessivè lucrantur; et sic carnifices in
x. bobus. Si major et vicecomites ista negassent, duodena miserorum ipsa affirmassent; ideo secundùm consilium eis datum, po-
suerunt se in gratiâ regis." Et justiciarius dixit, "Juxta statuta
regni, non solum in civitate vestrâ, sed in aliis, rex aufert a vobis
regimen civitatis pro vestro malo regimine." Posuitque tunc rex in
civitate novos officiarios suos. Postea Londonienses magnam sum-
mam auri colligunt, ita quod quidam propter illam collectam fugerunt
de civitate. Et regem venientem cum maximâ solemnitate, tanquam angelum Dei, susceperunt, tradideruntque sibi claves civitatis, et
in auro xl. M¹. *li*. ei obtulerunt: et sic regimen civitatis receperunt.

Hoc anno Urbanus Papa moritur, et Bonefacius eligitur.

Anno Domini 1390, Bonefacius vocavit Archiepiscopum Eborum A.D. 1389.
ad cardinalatum, et omnes ditiores episcopos Angliæ transferre A.D. 1393.
                                                                Col. b.

* See note to *page* 6, *line* 32.

† This parliament met at Westminster, January 17th, 13 Ric. II. 1390, and was dissolved March 2nd. (Rot. Parl.)

A.D. 1393.

nitebatur, ut primos fructus suarum ecclesiarum perciperèt. Summæ sacerdotum Romam peregrinantium pro beneficiis acquirendis, in portu Doveriæ, et summæ pecuniæ traditæ per escambium mercatorum, ad parliamentum Wintoniæ,* deferuntur. Et ibi statutum fuit firmiter tenendum, quod papa non sinatur transferre episcopos, neque extra regnum, neque infra, sine assensu regis. Et quod nullus amodò capiat beneficium a papâ, sed ecclesiastici patroni conferant sua beneficia juxta intentionem laicorum, qui jus patronatus eis contulerunt; et super hoc omnes promiserunt regi assistentiam, sicut pro coronâ

A.D. 1390.

Hoc anno fuit in Angliâ magna pestilentia, quam quintam pestilentiam vocabant.

Anno Domini 1391° nihil hic scribitur, quòd regnum Angliæ fuit in malo statu.

A.D. 1392.

Anno Domini M° ccc° nonagesimo secundo, Rex splendidè paravit capitulum fratrum minorum apud Sarum, et comedit cum eis ibidem in refectorio, habens secum reginam Annam, episcopos et alios dominos, in festo Assumptionis Beatæ Mariæ: et ibidem utebatur regalibus et coronâ.

Quod autem actum est in regno annis Domini 1393° et 1394° non scribitur propter varietatem regni Angliæ.

A.D. 1392.
[March.]

Anno Domini 1395° dux Lancastriæ de mandato regis transiit ın Franciam, et tractavit de pace cum rege Franciæ Ambianis: et rex fecit omnes expensas, et dedit sibi et cuilibet de suâ familiâ magna donaria.

A.D. 1393.

Anno Domini 1396° factum est parliamentum Londoniis,† ad

---

* This Parliament at Winchester was in 16 Ric. II. 1393. It commenced " Lundy en les oeptaves de Seint Hiller, (Jan. 20,) l'an du regne nostre Seigneur le Roi seszisme," and terminated " Lundy le disme jour de Feverer." (Rot. Parl.)

† This again must mean the Parliament at Winchester, 16 Ric. II., 1393. From Froissart we learn that the conditions of peace were something of this kind, but they are not extant on the Rolls of Parliament.

quod rediens dux Lancastriæ, formam pacis in tractatu habitam ex- A.D.1393.
pressit; videlicet, quod rex Ricardus Angliæ, arma Franciæ, Calesiam, et omnia conquesta per Edwardum, dimitteret; et omnia quæ
Edwardi erant ante vendicationes regni Franciæ, cum residuo re-
demptionis Johannis regis Franciæ, possideret. Et dixit, quod,
" arma Franciæ portare (see *page* 7, *Fragment D.*) non prodest, et
Calesia plus nocet regno Angliæ in expensis quam prodest." Sed
dux Gloucestriæ, comites Arundelliæ et Warwici omnia contradixerunt.

In hoc parliamento* dux Lancastriæ petiit quod filius suus
Henricus judicaretur hæres regni Angliæ: cui contradixit comes Folio 198.
Marchiæ, asserens se descendisse a domino Leonello secundo filio
Edwardi regis. E contrario, dux dicebat quod rex Henricus
tertius habuit (filios) duos, Edmundum seniorem et primogenitum, et
Edwardum; qui tamen Edmundus dorsum habuit fractum, et propter hoc judicavit seipsum indignum esse ad coronam. Quare pater
eorum eos sic componere fecit, quod Edwardus regnaret et post eum
hæredes Edmundi: et dedit Edmundo comitatum Lancastriæ, et ab
eo descendit Henricus filius ejus, jure matris quæ fuit filia dicti
Edmundi. Cui respondit comes dicens hoc non esse verum, sed
Edwardus fuit primogenitus, et Edmundus vir elegantissimus erat,
et nobilis miles, prout in chronicis patenter continetur. Rex autem
imposuit eis silentium.

Item in hoc parliamento dux Lancastriæ petiit regem dare sibi
ducatum Aquitaniæ sub certâ annuâ pensione, et ipse pro posse
totum acquireret; sicut rex Franciæ dedit illum cuidam militi sub
eâdem conditione. Sed dux Gloucestriæ, comites Arundelliæ et

---

* It is not unlikely that the following events occurred in this parliament. The dukedom
of Guienne had been conferred upon Lancaster, March 2, 1390 (Rymer, vii. 659) ; but
in the July (1392) preceding this Parliament, ambassadors had arrived to remonstrate
with the king on the appointment. Some assertion of his rights on the part of Lancaster
may have been distorted in this way.

A.D. 1393. Warwici, omnino contradixerunt, dicentes pertinentia ad coronam satis esse pauea. Rex tamen concessit.

A.D. 1394. Hoc anno, Hibernici veri Anglici auxilium contra puros Hibernicos petierunt. Quibus rex dixit, se velle Hiberniam adire; et ideo exegit decimam cleri, et quintam decimam laicorum, ut in parliamento solebat; statuens quod omnes nativi de Hiberniâ in Hiberniam remearent, dicens, "paucos Hibernicos esse ibidem, quare dicti puri Hibernici prævalent ibidem." Dotati vero Hibernici in Angliâ, et ecclesiastici promoti, dato auro, ab hoc statuto sunt exempti. Et rex cum exercitu transivit in Hiberniam, ubi agente quodam fratre de ordine prædicatorum, fuit ipse in periculo adversariorum; sed frater captus missus est ad turrim Londoniensem, qui postea ad preces Provincialis, carceri sui ordinis est liberatus.

[August.]

[Sept. 29th. *]

[September.†] Hoc autem anno, dux Lancastriæ transivit in Aquitaniam, ut ducatum sibi acquireret: sed Burdegalia et aliæ civitates ipsum excluserunt, dicentes quod a tempore secundi Henrici, qui jure suæ uxoris illum ducatum possedit, semper iste ducatus tenuit de rege Angliæ, et "si Rex Angliæ nos noluit habere, tenebimus de nosmet ipsis."

Col. b.

A.D. 1395. Hoc anno Makamor et quidam alii principales purorum Hibernicorum capti fuerunt, quos rex duxit in Angliam, et honorificè satis tractavit.

[May.]

A.D. 1395.
[December.] Dux vero Lancastriæ spe frustratus rediit. Hoc etiam anno, moritur Domina Anna regina Angliæ in manerio de Shene, et apud Westmonasterium sepelitur, quod factum fuit anno xviijº regni regis Ricardi. Quâ quidem reginâ mortuâ, rex obtulit regi Franciæ treugas 30 annorum, petens filiam suam in uxorem.‡

[June 7th, 1394.]

[Monday, August 3rd.]

A.D. 1396.

* Or immediately after. (Rymer, vii. 790.)   † After the 13th. (Rymer, vii. 789.)

‡ The first document in Rymer relative to Richard's marriage with Isabella of Valois, is dated July 8, 1395. The 30 years' truce was ratified by the King of France, March 11, 1396 (Rymer, vii. 832), and finally sworn to by both kings about the end of October.

Hoc anno Archiepiscopus Cantuariensis moritur, et Thomas de A.D. 1396.
Arundelliâ a monachis Cantuariensibus postulatur. Et rex, vocato [July 31.]
duce Lancastriæ, et multis comitibus et nobilibus, installationi suæ
solemniter adfuit, æstimans quod frater suus venisset ad solemni-
tatem; quem, de facto ibidem cepisset si venisset.

Anno Domini 1397°, et anno regni regis Ricardi vicesimo, rex A.D. 1396.
transivit ad Calesiam et cum rege Franciæ extra Calesiam loquebatur, [Sept. 27th.]
et desponsavit filiam suam in Calesiâ cum magnâ gloriâ et pompâ, [Oct. 27, 28.]
[Tuesday,
in ecclesiâ sancti Nicholai ibidem; Isabellam nomine, tune novem Nov. 1st.]
annorum existentem; quam solemniter et in magnis expensis duxit [Nov. 4th]
A.D. 1397.
in Angliam, quæ fuit citò post coronata apud Westmonasterium. [Jan. 7th.]

Et post adventum suum in Angliam vocavit Archiepiscopum Cantuariensem, rogans eum ut adduceret ad se comitem Arundelliæ
fratrem suum. Cui Archiepiscopus dixit, " Facietis sibi malum si
venerit?" Cui rex hoc negans assecuravit eum, jurando sibi super
corpus Christi statim post missam Archiepiscopi. Archiepiscopus
autem, cum magnâ instantiâ, fratrem suum timenter duxit ad
præsentiam regis apud Westmonasterium. Quo viso, dixit rex
comiti de Notynghamiæ, " Curam habeas de comite isto Arundelliæ;" et statim transiit in cameram. Comes vero de Notynghamiæ duxit comitem Arundelliæ in aliam cameram, et clausit
ostium. Archiepiscopus autem expectavit usque ad vesperam (see
page 8, Fragment E.), et tristis rediit ad domum suam apud
Lambhithe.

In crastino rex tradidit comitem cuidam inimico suo, ut in
castro de Wight ipsum custodiret, et statim bona sua confiscantur.

Comitem vero Warwici cepit in curiâ suâ, quem misit in Turrim. [July 10th.]

Et statim cum turbâ magnâ transiit ad mansionem ducis Gloucestriæ, in Essex, vocatam Plasshe. Quo capto, dixit sibi rex, " Tu
non vis ad me venire pro aliquo nuncio, ego igitur ad te venio, et
te arresto" Cui ait dux, " Gratiosè agatis mecum salvando vitam Folio 198 b.
meam." Cui rex, " Illam gratiam habebis quam præstitisti Symoni

A.D. 1397.   de Burley, cùm regina pro eo coram te genuflecteret: legas ista,"—
tradens sibi schedulam accusationis suæ. Et cum dux legisset,
" Ad ista respondebimus." Et rex commisit eum comiti de Noting-
ham, capitaneo Calesiæ, ut in castro ibidem ipsum custodiret.

Et postea transiit in partes occidentales Angliæ et collegit exercitum, vocavitque Gallos in auxilium: qui cum lanceis elevatis
(*see page* 8, *Fragment E. b.*) venerunt per medium regni. Misitque
ad singulos episcopos, abbates et generosos atque mercatores, et sub
colore mutui auri ipsorum nunquam persolvendi, extorsit in tantâ
quantitate quod unus simplex generosus solvit xl *li.*

[August 5th.]   Ibi autem processerunt comites Rutlandiæ, Cantiæ, Huntingdoniæ,
Sarum, Notinghamiæ, Marchio Dubluniæ, et alii appellantes ducem
Gloucestriæ, comites Arundelliæ et Warwici de criminibus læsæ
majestatis perpetratis anno regni regis x^o et xj^o.

[Wednesday,   Et rex misit unum justiciarium ad ducem Gloucestriæ, ut ab eo
Sept. 5th*]
quæreret quomodo ad appellationes responderet. Et dux manu
[Sept. 8th.]   propriâ scribendo in Anglico respondebat, literam sigillabat, et regi
[Sunday,   mittebat. Justiciarius prudenter ita literam regi tradidit, quòd
Sept. 16th.]   habuit penes se copiam sigillo regis consignatam. Cumque responsio
ducis regi non placeret, mandavit sub pænâ mortis comiti de
Notinghamiâ quod ipsum occideret. Et ipse transiit ad Calesiam,
et ibidem famuli comitis cum lecto plumali super ducem posito,
ipsum viliter suffocabant, occultè divulgantes ipsum morte naturali
obiisse.

[Sept. 17th.]   Deinde post exaltationem sanctæ crucis venit ad parliamentum rex
equitans terribiliter per medium Londoniarum cum M^l armatorum,
quorum tamen multi ficti erant; et tenuit parliamentum cum

* A commission had been issued to Sir William Rickhill for examining the Duke of
Gloucester, on August 17th, (Rymer, viii. 13. Rot. Parl. iii. 378.) At midnight,
September 5th, he was ordered by a royal messenger to join the Earl Marshal at Dover
the following evening and accompany him to Calais, where a special commission was
handed to him. The Duke's written answer was returned on the Saturday. (Rot. Parl.
iii. 430-432.)

confederatis suis in magno tentorio (*see page* 9, *Fragment F.*) quod A.D. 1397. in pavimento Westmonasterii statuerat. Et ne episcopi, abbates et clerici intermitterent se in parliamento, fecit eos et clerum compro- mittere vices suas in dominum Thomam Percy militem, sene- schallum sui hospitii. Et in hoc parliamento non secundùm legem Angliæ sed secundùm jura civilia processerunt. Nec regis periti Angliæ se ibi intromittebant.

Et primò rex ad supplicationem et petitionem sui parliamenti revocavit commissionem ab [eo] factam anno x°; et statuit quod si quis talem commissionem procuraverit, sit ut proditor puniendus.

V.

Page 10, line 2.

Deinde adduxerunt comitem Arundelliæ, et dux Lancastriæ fuit A.D. 1397. justiciarius ibidem, qui sibi exposuit appellationem dominorum et Folio 198, col. b. accusationem parliamenti, et jussit respondere. Qui dixit, " Res- [Sept. 21st.] pondere non expedit, quia scio quod ordinastis mortem meam prop- ter bona mea." Et notificaverunt sibi pœnam tacentis; et dixit dux, " Quia parliamentum te accusavit, meruisti decapitari sine responsione secundum legem tuam." Cui comes respondens dixit, " Ista feci propter circumstantias quæ tunc erant; et si errores fuerunt habeo indulgentiam regis."

VI.

[Page 11, line 10.]

Similiter dux Gloucestriæ adjudicatus fuit exhæredationi con- Folio 199. simili, et post mortem; quia, ut dixerunt, facta ejus ita notoria [Sept. 24th.] fuerant, et veniens responderat per scripturam.

Cernens et rex quod ipsi ejecerunt Archiepiscopum Eborum, et

A.D. 1397.
[Sept. 20th.*]

quod pacem non haberet cum Archiepiscopo Cantuariensi, fecit parliamentum accusare Cantuariensem Archiepiscopum. Et cum incepisset prolocutor proponere contra Archiepiscopum dixit rex, " Non proponas contra cognatum meum. Recede frater securus."

VII.

[Page 11, line 26.]

Folio 199.

Archiepiscopus dixit se recedere nolle, hîc se fuisse natum, et hîc se velle mori. Rex cum duce Lancastriæ intravit ad eum in cameram, cum aliis comitibus, in quâ testis sedebat. Et dixit sibi rex, " Ne tristeris, nec recedere recuses, quia te assecuro quod post breve tempus revocaberis, et nullus erit Archiepiscopus Cantuariensis nisi tu, quamdiu nos duo vixerimus." Cui dixit Archiepiscopus, " Ante recessum meum aliqua vobis dicam :" et protraxit sermonem de luxuriâ quæ regnabatur in personis eorum, et in curiis avaritia atque superbia, quibus inficiunt totum regnum. Et in die sibi assignatâ in vigiliâ sancti Michaelis in portu Doveriæ recessit.

VIII.

[Page 12, line 1.]

Folio 199,
col. b.

A.D. 1398.

Eodem anno rex scripsit a[d] papam, ut quendam laicum literatum Rogerum Walden in Archiepiscopatum Cantuariensem promoveret; asserens, ut quidam dicebant, Thomam esse mortuum.

A.D. 1398.
[Jan. 31st.]

Fecitque parliamentum hoc compromittere in xij personas, quæ continuando parliamentum ubicunque et quocunque regi placeret statuta sibi placita secum ordinarent.

Quibus omnibus peractis, in partes occidentales est reversus

* The Commons prayed for judgment against the Archbishop on this day, but sentence was not given till the 25th. (Rot. Parl. iii. 351.)

Nuncius festinanter rediens de curiâ Romanâ portavit bullas: et A.D. 1398.
rex fecit Rogerum consecrari. Et cito post, idem Rogerus cele-
bravit ingressum suum Cantuariæ sumptuosè. Et post hæc, rex
in diebus solemnibus, &c.

IX.

[Page 18, at the end of Richard II.]

Rex Ricardus in divitiis suis prædecessores suos studuit excedere, A.D 1399.
et ad Solomonis glcriam pervenire. Cæpitque plus illis infra Folio 200 b.
regnum post annum xjᵘᵐ formidari, quodvis prole careret et animo
bellicoso. In thesauris et jocalibus, in vestibus et ornamentis regalibus in quibus vehementer excessit, in splendore mensæ, in palatiis
quæ ædificavit, nullus in regibus eo gloriosior diebus suis. Et in
maximâ altitudine suæ gloriæ, subitò appensus et inventus minus
habens deponitur potens de sede; et statua percussa miserabiliter
est contrita; arborque procera in medio terræ omnibus opulentiis
privata, Vigili jubente Cœlesti, succiditur; et in carcere proprio,
videlicet, Pontis Fracti, fit habitatio ejus.

X.

[Page 20, line 5.]

Rex tenuit Natale Domini apud Windesorium, et quidam A.D. 1400.
armiger de Circestriâ, in armis multum exercitatus, secundùm Folio 200 b.
consuetudinem suam misit unum de suâ familiâ ad curiam regis,
ut sibi referret gesta forciâ hastiludensium. Archiepiscopus autem
Cantuariensis post Circumcisionem Domini movit a Cantuariâ usque
Windesorium, ut esset cum rege in die Epiphaniæ. Quidam de
familiâ regis interea jacebat unâ nocte, &c.

XI.

[Page 21, line 24.]

Alii insurrectores, clerici et laici, inter quos Rogerus Walden et episcopus Carleoli, Londoniis inventi, coram justiciariis statuuntur; et solus Rogerus Waldenus excusatur. Laici trahuntur et suspenduntur, clerici trahuntur et decollantur. Episcopus Merks incarceratur et episcopatu privatur; postea tamen rex gratiosè egit cum eo, visâ conversatione ejus.

Ricardus, olim rex, in carcere hæc audiens cæpit omnino de auxilio desperare; et confessus est eos, de consilio suo dato in castro de Conway, ista fecisse: et, ut dicebatur, pro tristitiâ comedere nolens moriebatur; corpusque ejus delatum est sanctum Paulum Londoniis, et facies sua ostensa est populo; et celebratis ibidem exequiis ejus per regem, apud Langley sepultus est.

Isabella secunda uxor regis Richardi, dote suâ nudata, multis cum muneribus dotata, ab Angliâ in Franciam pulsa est. Qua repatriante, Gallici treugas prius initas solverunt.

Tunc rex misit Londoniensibus ut aurum sibi mutuarent: ipsi autem ad eum accesserunt, quærentes an ipsa missio de voluntate suâ processit, referentes quomodo ipse promisit se ab hujusmodi mutuis et tallagiis abstinere. Qui eis respondens, dixit se omnino egere, et pecuniam ab eis tunc habere oportere. Hæc omnia facta sunt anno primo Regis hujus, et anno xxij° Ricardi, et anno Domini 1399°

XII.

[Page 22, line 31.]

Anno Domini 1401, Wallici contra regem Henricum 4^tum rebellant, et bona Anglicorum undique diripiunt; rex autem transiit in Walliam borialem et insulam de Anglesey, ubi fratres Minores de conventu Lamasiæ, et Wallici cum aliis, regi resistebant; et ideo A.D. 1401. exercitus regis fratres occidebant et captivabant, ac conventum spoliabant

Et Audoeno non comparente, revertitur rex.

Et Dominus le Gray manucepit tuitionem patriæ. Rex vero tradidit magistro ordinis fratres captivatos, et jussit omnia restitui conventui, et voluit quod conventus ille inhabitaretur ab Anglicis fratribus.

Hoc anno quidam frater Minor de Northfolchiâ in suo sermone Folio 201 b. recommendavit regem Ricardum, dicens quod viveret: et ille de carcere regis traditur magistro ordinis corrigendus.

Audoenus de Glendor dominum le Gray in bello cepit. [1402.]

Et eodem anno capitulum generale fratrum Minorum celebratur Leycestriæ in festo Assumptionis, in quo prohibitum est sub pœnâ perpetui carceris, ne aliquis fratrum loquatur verbum quod possit sonare in præjudicium regis. Et quod quilibet præsidens haberet potestatem totalem incarcerandi, qui ausus esset in hoc culpari.

XIII.

[Page 24, line 6.]

" Sibi plus teneor." Et rex ait, " Pugnares tu pro eo?" Res- A.D. 1402. pondit frater, " Ita verè." Et rex, " Cum quo?" Respondit frater, Folio 201 b. " Cum eo quod haberem, fortè cum baculo." Et rex conclusit, " Ergo tu velles quod ego esse mortuus, et omnes domini de regno meo complures." Respondet frater, " Non." Et rex, " Quid faceres mecum, si super me haberes victoriam?" Cui frater, " Facerem vos ducem Lancastriæ." Tunc rex ait, " Tu non es amicus meus: per hoc caput meum tu perdes caput tuum." Et statutus est frater coram justiciario apud Westmonasterium, cum quodam seculari sacerdoti conspiratore, apud quem literæ con-

A.D. 1402. spiratoriæ inventæ sunt. Et justiciarius dixit, "Frater, tu exultasti quòd audivisti regem Ricardum vivere, et divulgasti hoc in populo." Frater respondit, "Non divulgavi verbum." Et justiciarius, auditâ duodenâ, tulit sententiam, dicens, "Tu traheris per medium Londoniarum super claiam usque ad Tyburne, et ibidem suspendaris, ibique decollaberis, et caput tuum ponetur super pontem Londoniensem." Quod et de utroque factum est, atque per viam preco clamabat casum eorum.

XIV.
[Page 26, line 26.]

Hoc autem anno, duo alii fratres de conventu Leycestriæ capti fuerunt in partibus Lichfeldiæ per familiam principis, et ibidem tracti et suspensi sunt et decollati. Caput magistri delatum est Oxoniam in vigiliâ sancti Johannis Baptistæ; et coram processione venientis clamabat preco, "Iste magister, frater Minor de conventu Leicestrensi, in hypocrisi et adulatione et falsâ vitâ prædicavit multoties, dicens quod rex Ricardus vivit, et excitavit populum ut quærerent eum in Scotiâ." Et caput ejus ibi super palum positum est.

Hoc anno, rex Scotiæ misit literas regi Franciæ, dicens quod quidam venit in Scotiam, et duo Jacobitæ dixerunt ipsum fuisse regem Ricardum, sed [et?] rumor ille magìs augebatur, sicque dicebatur quod fuisse in Scotiâ.

[June.] Hoc insuper anno Audoenus de Glendor cepit Edmundum de Mortuo Mari, multis Anglicis de marchiâ Walliæ interfectis: et rex
[Aug. 27th.] congregato exercitu transiit in Walliam, ubi prohibentibus maximis tempestatibus in Septembri tonitruorum, imbrium et grandinis, equitare non potuerunt; et multi de exercitu frigore mortui sunt.

Ibi frater iste qui fratres suos regi acensavit captus est a Wallico et, quia fatebatur se esse de familiâ regis qui accusabat fratres, a A.D. 1402. Wallico occisus est.

Hoc autem anno, rege existente in Walliâ, Scoti irruperunt in Folio 202 b. Angliam: sed comes Northumbriæ et filius ejus Henricus Percy, valens miles, pugnabant cum eis, et ceperunt comites* eorum, [Sept. 14th.] et x. M¹ interfecerunt de Scotis.

Item, hoc anno, rex desponsavit relictam Johannis de Monte A.D. 1402. Forti, ducissam Britanniæ, filiam regis Navarræ; et eam coronari [Feb. 7th] fecit.

Hoc anno dominus le Gray, grandi redemptione solutâ, liberatus [November.] est.

Post festum sancti Michaelis factum est parliamentum Londoniis, et decima cleri et xv. populi exactæ sunt, dicente rege se nil habere. [Sept. 30th.] Communitas quæsivit ubi fuit thesaurus Ricardi regis. Tandem responsum fuit, quod comes Northumbriæ, qui regem introduxit, et alii illum habuerunt. Rogavit et communitas regem, quod, quia multa sibi tribuunt et ipse nil habet, sinat officiales suos super hoc examinari, sed non assensit.

Hoc anno, dux Aurelianensis, vir valde superbus et malus, misit [Oct. 2nd.] regi Angliæ literas provocans ipsum ad duellum. Rex respondit quod non pugnaret cum minore se, nec cum consanguineo pugnare [Dec. 5th.] licet. Dux dixit, " Dignitatem quam injustè invasisti, in te non A.D. 1403. veneror; et ita decenter mecum pugnare potes, sicut occidistis [March 26th.*] regem cognatum tuum:" et multa alia convicia scripsit regi.

XV.

[Page 29, line 18.]   A.D. 1404.

Hoc anno (1403) clerus Angliæ concessit regi petenti medietatem Folio 203, col. b. unius decimæ. Post festum sancti Hillarii inceptum est parlia- [Jan. 14th.]

* Battle of Homildon Hill, Sept. 14th.   + Carte, ii. 656.

mentum, et duravit usque ad Pascha; quia rex exigebat magnum tallagium, dicens se habere bellum cum Wallicis, Scotis, Hibernicis, et Gallicis in Vasconiâ; insuper custodia Calesiæ magna fuit, et maris Anglicani. Communitas respondit dicens, quod " ista non inquietant Angliam multùm, et si inquietarent, adhuc rex habet omnes proventus coronæ [et] ducatus Lancastriæ: at theolonia notabiliter excessivè elevata pro rege Richardo, ita ut proventus theoloniorum, lanarum et aliarum mercium excedant proventus coronæ. Habuit similiter wardas quasi omnium comitum, baronum et nobilium Angliæ; quæ theolonia et wardæ olim erant concessæ regi in subsidium communitatis pro guerris, ut a tallagiis exoneretur regnum." Rex autem dixit, " se nolle perdere terras patrum snorum in diebus suis, et ideo omnino tallagium habere oportuit." Tunc communitas petiit a rege, ut " si tallagium habere omnino velit, quod theolonia minuerentur." Rex respondit, quod "theolonia habere vellet sicut habuerunt sui prædecessores." Et cum mansissent Londoniis in gravibus expensis usque ad Pascha talia disputando, tandem exegit ab eis, quod pro omni parte terræ in Angliâ valente annuatim xx$s$., solverentur xii$d$.; exceptis terris quas ecclesiastici habuerunt ante annum octavum Edwardi Primi, filii Henrici; in quo ordinatum fuit, quod ecclesiastici in possessionibus non crescerent. Ipsi tandem attediati de morâ hoc concesserunt sub hâc cum (sic) conditione, quod eligerent certas personas qui tallagium reciperent et pro guerris tum expenderent, et inde computum parliamento darent; et rex auctoritatem recipiendi et ex-

pendendi per chartam suam eis daret. Rex videbatur assentire, ac electæ sunt personæ, et charta scripta sed non sigillata, et solutum est parliamentum.

XVI.

[Page 30, line 11.]

Adhuc rumor de vitâ regis Ricardi invaluit in Angliâ, et A.D. 1404.
quod ipse moraretur in Scotiâ in castro ducis Roseyæ, quod Albion Folio 203 b, col. b.
dicitur.

Quidam vir venit ad comitissam Oxoniæ, et affirmavit regem
Ricardum vivere, quæ ex hoc gaudens arrestata fuit et posita
in Turri Londoniensi, quæ insuper post grandem redemptionem
liberata est.

Similiter abbates sanctæ Osithæ et Colcestriæ accusati, pro pecu-
niis gratiam regis habere meruerunt.

Hoc anno Bonefacius papa moritur, et eligitur Innocentius, jurans
quod laboraret ad unionem ecclesiæ.

Quo insuper anno statutum parliamentum apud Coventriam [Oct. 6th.]
statim post festum sancti Michaelis. Et rex mandavit quod nullus
juris peritus ad illuc veniret, et notificavit vicecomitibus quos
milites et communitatum procuratores voluit illuc mitti. Et ibi
exegit duas decimas cleri, et duas quintas decimas laicorum.

XVII.

[Page 31, line 32.]

—— Item, quod juris periti ad parliamenta veniant, et suâ A.D.1405.
sapientiâ consulant: quod milites comitatuum et burgenses civita- Folio 204 b.
tum mittendi ad parliamenta per comitatus et civitates eligantur,
et non per regem assignentur: et quod parliamentum statuatur
Londoniis, qui locus est magis purus, et ubi hæc melius corrigi
possunt; quæ si correcta sunt, habemus firmam spem quod Wallia
erit subjecta Angliæ, sicut fuit temporibus Edwardi et Ricardi.
Hæc in Anglico scripta, &c.

[Page 32, line 25.]

A.D. 1405.
Folio 204 b,
col. b.

Archiepiscopus Cantuariensis, his auditis, venit cum festinatione ad regem. Et quidam miles aulicus regis videns eum dixit regi, " Si iste Archiepiscopus Eborum veniet, omnes nos a vobis recedemus." Et Archiepiscopus in præsentiâ cujusdam notarii dixit regi, " Domine, ego sum pater vester spiritualis," &c.

[Page 33, line 4.]

Rex vero intravit aulam Archiepiscopi ad prandendum, et habuit secum Archiepiscopum Cantuariensem, et totam familiam suam, et dum pranderent adjudicati sunt Archiepiscopus Eborum, dominus Mowbray et quidam miles prædictus; et extra civitatem decollantur

[June 8th.]

in festo sancti Wilhelmi.

XVIII.

[Page 33, line 17.]

A.D. 1405.
[July]
Folio 205.

Comes Northumbriæ et dominus Bardolf, de castro Berwici, recesserunt in Scotiam. Rex autem venit ad Berwicum, et expugnando castrum, multos lapides jactari fecit cum bombardis ad muros castri: sed frangebantur lapides per murorum duritiam. Tandem accidit, quod lapis quidam percussus sit ferramentum cancellatum cujusdam fenestræ in quodam tenui muro, et homines ibidem ascendentes occidit. Et ex tunc omnes inclusi amiserunt corda, et vecordes effecti exierunt, gratiam regis implorantes; quos rex jussit decollari.

Et reversus transiit in Walliam australem, et castrum de Coyfy diu a Wallicis obsessum liberavit. Et in redeundo cariagium suum et jocalia sua Wallenses spoliabant.

Papa autem, auditâ morte archiepiscopi, &c.

[Line 26.]

" Vide si tunica hæc filii tui sit an non:" et quievit materia.

Hoc anno factum est parliamentum post dominicam primam xl^æ, A.D. 1406. et duravit usque ad Natale Domini. Clerus autem in convocatione [March 1st.] concessit regi unam xx^{am} et vj*s*. viij*d*. a quolibet annuario sacerdote; sed laici nil solvere volebantur (*sic*), nec (*sic*) eis daretur computus de receptis sicut prius ordinatum fuit et per regem promissum. Rex breviter respondebat, quod " reges non solebant computum dare." * Officiales dixerunt, quod " nullus eorum scivit computum reddere." Ordinati ad recipiendum collectam anni præcedentis dixerunt " se auctoritatem recipiendi non habere, nec aliquid acceperunt;" et sic negotium remansit imperfectum hoc anno.

XIX.

[Page 36, line 22.]

Anno Domini 1407, et anno regis Henrici 4^{ti} 7°, dux Aurelia- A.D. 1407. nensis, multùm odiosus in Franciâ, propter turbam cum quâ sæpe Folio 205, col. b. equitabat, interfici non potuit; ideo in civitate Paris, ubi cum paucis ambulabat tanquam securus, occiditur—hoc modo. Unus inimicus suus cereo incendit quandam domum, et socii sui occidunt ducem et abierunt festinanter, clamantes " Ad ignem! ite ad ignem!" Familia autem ducis clamabat " Proditio! proditio!" Sed populus [Nov. 23rd.] transiit ad ignem. Rex autem Franciæ turbatus est et omne concilium suum cum illo, inquirentes quis hoc fecit. Dux Burgundiæ dixit, " Juretis mihi quod tenebitis consilium per 3 dies, et dicam vobis quis hoc fecit." Et juraverunt; et ipse confessus est de scientiâ suâ hoc factum fuisse. Tunc excluserunt eum a concilio. Ipse vero transiit in Flandriam et Alemanniam colligens exercitum copiosum, invocavitque auxilium regis Angliæ. Rex autem pro illo murdro contempsit eum. Rex vero Franciæ misit pro duce. Dux respondit quod non veniret, nec approbaret mortem

* Bishop Wilkins has quoted the above paragraph. (Concil. iii. 282.)

A.D. 1407.

hominis morte dignissimam: quia fuit homo luxuriosissimus, jactans se violasse uxores multorum dominorum et nobilium Franciæ, reginam, et totam prolem regiam suam esse affirmavit. Et minabatur consiliariis regis, si contrarium consulerent, quod morerentur.

XX.

[Page 34, line 7.]

A.D. 1407.
Folio 205 b.

Rex itaque per magnum tempus non solveret soldariis, custodibus Calesiæ, sua vadia; quare ipsi detinuerunt lanas mercatorum quæ fuerunt ibidem, veruntamen mercatores conquesti sunt regi, et rex petiit ut mutuarent sibi pecunias; mercatores autem se excusabant. " Vos habetis aurum," dixit rex, " et ego volo habere aurum—ubi est?" Tandem, post longam moram, mercatores concesserunt sibi aurum eâ conditione, quod cancellarius Archiepiscopus Cantuariensis et dux Eboracensis manucaperent pro resolutione: quod et factum est.

A.D. 1408.

Tunc proceres Scotorum deduxerunt comitem Northumbriæ et dominum Bardolf et abbatem de Hayles usque ad aquam Twede, dicentes eis, "Jam procedatis! vos habetis Angliam vobiscum." Qui venerunt cum parvâ comitivâ usque ad Tadcastre. Et vice-

[Feb. 18th.]

comes Eborum venit cum exercitu, et trucidavit eos:* capita eorum posita super pontem Londoniensem.

* At the battle of Bramham Moor, Feb. 18th.

NOTES.

Page 1, line 10. *the erl of Dene.*—The son of the earl of Denia, who had been taken captive at Navaretta. The earl had been adjudged prisoner of the two esquires, Hawley and Shakell, by the Black Prince and sir John Chandos, their master; and had been permitted to return to Spain, upon leaving his son as his security. The earl died, and the son remained the prisoner of the two esquires. His release was probably commanded by the king, to answer some ends towards Lancaster's acquisition of Castille (see Wals. 1574, p. 216; Speed, 731; Tyrrell, iii. 840); but as little was offered for the young earl, and the esquires had expected the full ransom since the preceding August, 1377 (Rymer, vii. 171), they would not produce him. Hawley and Shakell were sent to the Tower, and from thence petitioned parliament for a commission to inquire into their rights. (Rot. Parl. iii. 50.) They managed to escape, and fled to Westminster sanctuary. Sir Alan de Buxhull, constable of the Tower, sir Ralph Ferrers—and some say lord Latimer (Stowe)—were sent to remove them by force, and Hawley was slain in the church. The case was taken up in parliament; the convent of Westminster petitioned for protection of its privileges (iii. 37); and the archbishop demanded redress. All concerned in the murder were excommunicated: and the bishop of London on several successive Sundays continued to pronounce the curse from St. Paul's. (Wals., Rot. Parl.) The murder was committed on the 11th August, 1378. Hawley is buried in the Abbey. (Seymour's Survey, ii. 516; Stowe, Annals, 282.)

Page 2, line 1. *dredyng.*—No notice is taken of this form beyond the present: it is so common in the same connection, that probably the writer intended it for the past tense.

Line 22. *how saint Peter halowed it, as folowethe* . . . .—See Appendix, Supplementary Add. I. The chronicle "brought forth" seems to have been that of Ailred of Rievalle. The history of the consecration, as given in the Eulogium, has been printed in the Appendix as it was contained in the original text, though it differs but little from that of Ailred printed in the Decem Scriptores, col. 385-6.

Line 28. *unkid.*—(Sax. uncuᵹ). Unknown, inexperienced, and so to be dreaded, marvellous. The word still lives in these senses in the Oxfordshire dialect.

Page 3, line 5. *Reme, and paide for hir xxij. m^l marc.*—See Appendix, p. 121. The princess Anne, afterwards "the good queen Anne," was daughter of the late emperor Charles IV. and sister of the emperor Wynceslaus, king of Bohemia. Wynceslaus was to receive from Richard 10,000 marks, and to bear no share in the expenses attending the journey to England. Richard was to have received a large sum with the duke of Milan's daughter. (Tyrrell, iii. 871.)

Line 6. *Ther was offrid vnto him the erlis douȝter of Flaunders.*
Richard had already been engaged in two marriage negociations: first for Catherine, daughter of Barnabas duke of Milan, in 1379 (Rymer, vii. 213); afterwards for Catherine, daughter of the late emperor Louis, in 1380 (id. 257). But the text is wrong. Margaret, daughter of Louis count of Flanders, and widow of Philip duke of Burgundy, who died in 1361, had married Philip of Burgundy, son of king John of France, in 1369: the marriage contract bears date April 12. (Corps Diplomatique du Droit des Gens, ii. 72.) In Rymer are several documents relating to a proposed alliance between Edmund Langley, *uncle of the king,* and Margaret of Flanders, ranging from Feb. 8, 1362, to Oct. 24, 1365. (Rymer, 1830, iii. 636, 744, 750, 758, 761, 777.) Louis himself was anxious for the marriage, but Charles V. of France and his own mother, Margaret of Artois (Mezeray, 4to. ii. 581), dissuaded him, and he obtained an acquittal of his engagement in 1368. (Froissart, i. cclviii.) Philip had been created duke of Burgundy by his father, king John, to whom the dukedom had passed upon the death of the former duke Philip, on Sept. 6, 1363;

and in right of his wife obtained the *counties* of Flanders, Artois, and Burgundy.

Line 9. *The vij. yeer of king Richard.*—This confederation of the French and Scots was in 1385, 8 Ric. II., not as in the text. The document in Rymer (vii. 434), July 26, 1384, proves that the Scots were then included in the armistice which had been made with France in January. Upon the expiration of the truce, May 1, 1385 (Rymer, vii. 418), the duke of Vienne sailed with 300 ships to Scotland, to assist in a descent upon England, while French fleets were to attack her coasts on the east and west. (Knyghton, 2675 ; Wals. 342 ; Evesham, 61.) Richard, from Reading, June 4, ordered his troops to be assembled at Newcastle-on-Tyne by July 14, when he intended to lead in person. (Rymer, vii. 473-4, 476.) He was at Leicester on July 7, and marched northwards with an army unequalled in magnitude. The Scots fled at his approach. He burnt the abbey of Melrose and city of Edinburgh; and then, contrary to the advice of Lancaster, led his army back, in the early part of September, to find that the Scots had penetrated to Carlisle, and carried off more plunder than he had from their capital. Froissart says that Richard destroyed Perth, Aberdeen, and Dundee, and plundered the whole country; other historians give a more humble account. While this was happening, disturbances from the Gantois detained the French fleet at Sluys. (Walsingham, Knyghton, Stowe, Speed, Froissart, ii. clxv–vii.)

Line 23. *The viij. yeer of king Richard.*—This year Edmund Langley was retained to serve in the Scottish wars (Dugd. Bar. ii. 155), and was created duke of York for his various services, Aug. 6, 1385, 9 Ric. II. His Portuguese expedition followed upon the treaty with England against John of Castille, on the part of England, May 20, 1380; of Portugal, July 5. (Rymer, vii. 253, 262.) On the same day (July 5) Ferdinand of Portugal undertook John of Ghent's quarrel against Castille, which he claimed in right of his wife, and promised to marry his daughter Beatrice to the son of the earl of Cambridge, upon the appearance of the earl with 1000 spears and 1000 archers. The earl was sent with exactly half that number about May, 1381 (Rymer, vii. 305); and Lancaster was to join with a large force after he had settled some disturbances in Scotland. In

CAMD. SOC. U

January 1382 he petitioned parliament for 60,000*l.* pay for 2000 heavy armed and 2000 archers, for half a year (Rot. Parl. iii 114), without effect; and Ferdinand, in consequence of his non-appearance, made peace with Castille. The earl of Cambridge then returned, about October 1382 (Froissart), carrying with him his son John, although betrothed to Beatrice. In October the following year Ferdinand died, and John his natural brother was proclaimed king, in April, 1385, to oppose the claims of John of Castille, who had married Beatrice, Ferdinand's illegitimate daughter (formerly betrothed to John of Cambridge). The cause of Portugal was embraced by English auxiliaries, who with permission joined his standard. (Rymer, vii. 450, 453, 455, 462, 472.) And in August, by their help, an important victory was obtained over the Castillians and French at Aljubarota. (Froissart.) Perhaps this is the foundation for the account in the text. Finding himself too weak to prolong the contest, John king of Portugal sent ambassadors to England, who arrived in the autumn of the same year, 1385.

Last line. *The king of Ermonie.*—Late in the year 1385, Leo king of Armenia visited the English court. He came as a peace-maker between France and England. (See in Rymer, vii. 491, document dated Jan. 22, 1386, 9 R. II.) But his chief object was to implore assistance in an attempt to regain his kingdom. Richard entertained him at Eltham, and would have assisted him in every way; but the council negatived the idea of sending troops so far from home, and advised the king to make a present of money. (MS. Rawl. 173.) Richard therefore settled on Leo 1,000*l.* per ann. on Feb. 3, 1386, to be received by equal portions at the Exchequer until he was reinstated in his dominions. (Exchequer Issue Roll, 15 R. II. Dec. 12th; Rymer, vii. 494.) He presented him also with 1,000*l.* in a ship of gold. (Evesham, 71.) Froissart says, Leo refused the rich presents pressed upon him, reserving only a gold ring. In the summer or autumn of the same year he offered to return, but the nobles declined the honour of a second visit. (Wals. 354; Evesh. 76.) Yet the king and his council seem to have wished it, and we find letters of safe conduct granted to Leo March 18th, to last till Aug. 1st; and May 12th till Christmas 1386. (Rymer, vii. 502, 503.) And again, Dec. 11th, 1392 (736.) The king's chamberlain, however, made periodical visits to the English exchequer. (See Rymer vii. 549, 706, 767.)

Page 4, line 8. *the erlle of Oxenforde.*—Robert de Vére, created
marquis of Dublin, with the dominion and revenues of Ireland for life, in
the parliament which commenced Oct. 20, 1395, 9 R. II. (Rot. Parl. iii.
209.) This was the first time the title of marquis was conferred, and
gave great offence on account of the precedence before the other nobles
which it gave this worthless favourite. (Wals. 320; Dugdale, Bar. i.
194; Stowe, 299.) De Vere was further advanced to the title of duke of
Ireland.

Line 16. *in the pleyn parlement.*—That is, "en le pleyn parlement,"
" in pleno parliamento."

Line 18. *the which erl ... was slayn in Yrlond.*—Roger Mortimer earl
of March was earl of Ulster and lord lieutenant of Ireland. In Pell Issue
Roll, Easter, 16 R. II. is a compensation paid to the earl for lands devas-
tated by the Irish. He was slain July 20th, 1398, 22 R. II. He was
declared heir-apparent in the parl. 9 R. II. (See Dugdale, Bar. i. 150;
Fabyan, 9 R. II.; Leland, Coll. ii. 481.)

Line 19. *the wilde Yrishmenne.*—Richard, writing from Dublin to the
duke of York, custos of England, Feb. 1st, 1395, 18 R. II., says ... "en
nostre terre d'Irland sont trois maners des gentz, c'est as savoir, Irrois
savages, nez enemis, Irroix rebelx, et Engleis obeissantz." Proceedings
of Privy Council, i. 56.

Line 20. *be counsel of a burgeis of London.*—(See Appendix, p. 122.)
In the parliament at Westminster, Oct. 1st, 1386, 10 R. II., the Commons
impeached Michael de la Pole, the chancellor, and placed the legislative
power in the hands of fourteen commissioners selected by themselves, with
the king's sanction, for one year. (Knyghton, 2684, 2685; Rot. Parl. iii.
216-220; Stat. Realm, ii. 40-46.) The displeasure of Richard was not
shown openly; but in August the following year, 1387, he held two con-
ferences with certain judges at Shrewsbury, and at Nottingham on the
25th, on the subject of the legality of the late proceedings in parliament.
They declared that the commission was illegal, and that all engaged in it
deserved the punishment of traitors (Knyghton, 2694-2696; Rot. Parl.

iii. 233, 357, 358; Stat. Realm, ii. 102–104.) The two following months Richard travelled about the North of England secretly to procure troops to support his intended resumption of power—though the legal expiration of the commission was at hand—and an indictment of Gloucester and those of his party. Failing of much support he resolved, perhaps at the advice of sir Nicolas Brember, to try the affections of the men of London. (Knyghton, Tyrrell, Lingard.) Brember had been several times mayor, and was afterwards charged with causing the city guilds to take an oath to support the power of the favourites. (Rot. Parl. 234, 235.) On Sunday, Nov. 10th, the king made his entry into London, and was met by the mayor and aldermen in state; but Roger Fulthorpe, one of the justices he had consulted, had betrayed the proceedings at Nottingham to the earls of Kent and Northumberland, bidding them inform the chancellor and the king's council. (Rot. Parl. iii. 239, v. 393.) On the next morning, the king heard of the arrival of Gloucester, Arundel, and Warwick, with a large body of forces, at Haringay park, not far from the walls of London. There were some about the king who advised an appeal to arms, but the citizens would not be roused. The lords were joined on Thursday 14th, at Waltham Cross, by the earls of Derby and Nottingham, and these five appealed of treason the five favourites, before some of the parliamentary commissioners, the archbishop of Canterbury and bishop of Ely. On the Sunday they made their appeal before the king against Robert de Vere duke of Ireland, Alexander Neville archbishop of York, Michael de la Pole earl of Suffolk, Robert Tresilian false justice, and Nicholas Brember false knight. The king assured them a full hearing in the next parliament, which was fixed for Feb. 3rd, 1388. (Knyghton, Walsingham.)

Last line. *same place for to refourme pee; betuene thaym.*—The Eulogium from which our author here translated has confused the history. Upon the king's promise to give the appellants an opportunity to prosecute their charges in parliament the accused persons had fled—the archbishop into the North, Michael de la Pole shaved his head and crossed in disguise to Calais, and de Vere, " cum conniventiâ regis," (Wals., Rot. Parl. iii. 418, 1 Hen. IV.) raised forces in Cheshire. On his return he was met by the duke of Gloucester and the earl of Derby, and compelled to a battle at Radcote bridge, near Chipping Norton, Oxon, on Dec. 20th. He escaped with life by swimming across the Isis. The king and queen were spending Christmas in the Tower when Gloucester and Derby, on Dec. 26th, encamped their army, of about 40,000 men, within sight of its walls at Clerkenwell. The citizens doubted whether to obey the king or the lords. The lords seemed the more powerful party, and the mayor received them in a house close by the city gates, supplied them with all that was wanted, and distributed wine with beer and bread and cheese throughout the army: a favour which we are told was gratefully remembered. Strict watch was kept upon the Thames to prevent the king's escape, and the lords demanded an interview. He offered to receive them in the Tower, and to let them search it if they were suspicious. Gloucester then had an interview with the king; he complained of his treachery, and extorted a promise that he would meet them on the following day at Westminster. At that meeting Richard, "sore against his mind" (Stowe), gave permission for the arrest of those who were obnoxious to Gloucester's party, to be reserved for judgment at the ensuing parliament. (Walsingham, Evesham, Knyghton.) On Feb. 3rd, 1388, the "merciless parliament" assembled, and the charge of conspiracy against the parliamentary commission was prosecuted. Robert de Vere, M. de la Pole, and archbishop Neville, were out of the way; but Tresilian, who had taken sanctuary in Westminster, was dragged out and suffered death on the 19th, Brember on the 20th Feb., Sir Simon Burley on the 5th, and Beauchamp, Salisbury, and Berners, on the 12th May. A free pardon was granted to the appellants; and on Wednesday, June 3d, the 121st day of the parliament, the king renewed his coronation oath and the lords their homage. No statute of the present parliament was ever to be annulled, and the bishops pronounced an excommunication against all who should at any time break the oaths then made. (Rot. Parl., Stat. Realm.)

Page 5, line 26. *ser Simon of Beverley.*—An intollerable proud man, and great oppressor of the poor (Stowe): an accomplished scholar, tutor to Richard II. and afterwards his chamberlain; sent to Prague to negociate his marriage with Anne of Bohemia; constable of Dover Castle, warden of the cinque-ports, and a knight of the garter—"a gentle knight, and of strong good sense," says his friend Froissart, who was afflicted at sir Simon's death. (Froiss. iii. lxxx.)

- Page 6, line 16. *John Wiclif.*—According to Walsingham, he was seized with paralysis, as he was about to preach something heretical, on the day of St. Thomas of Canterbury, and lingered till St Silvester's, 1385. (Wals. 338; Upod. Neus. 142.) The correct date of his death seems to be Dec. 31st, 1384. (Stowe, 296; Wood, Antiq. 193.) He had been suffering from paralysis for two years. His doctrines were condemned, and his books, and bones, if they could be separated from those of the faithful, were ordered to be burnt by decree of the 8th session of the Council of Constance, May 4th, 1415. (Mansi, Concil. Collect. xxvii. 630, &c.; Foxe, i. 605.)

. Line 19. *The xij. yeer of king Richard.*—The English chroniclers agree in placing these jousts in this year. A cause may be found for them, in the celebration of the king's resumption of power, in May, 1389, 12 Ric. II. But Froissart places them in Michaelmas 1390, 14 Ric II ; and Stowe, on the 10th, 11th, and 12th Oct. 1390, which seems to be the favoured date.

Line 32. *through all Spayne,* &c.—See Appendix, p. 125. After the return of Richard and the duke of Lancaster from the expedition into Scotland, in Sept. 1385, the Portuguese ambassadors were received; and Lancaster obtained a liberal grant from parliament (Rot. Parl. iii. 204), which met Oct. 20th. Preparation was made for his departure early the next year, 1386. On March 15th and 26th, orders were issued, according to a destructive custom of the time, for seizing ships and mariners for the expedition. By April 20th the duke was at Plymouth, waiting for more ships and transports, when he received a letter from the council, stating, that, as the greater part of the navy of England would sail with him, it would be necessary for him to see to their return. (Rymer, vii. 501, 504, 509, 524.) Lancaster had taken leave of the king a little before Easter, (not, as Knyghton says, on Easter day, April 22nd,) when the king and queen presented the duchess and himself with regal crowns of gold. (Knyghton, 2676.) The expedition sailed from Plymouth on July 9th; it consisted of 20,000, and was amply blessed by pope Urban VI: who granted a pardon to all who should sail in it. (Wals.) Sir Thomas Percy, afterwards earl of Worcester, was the admiral, and John Holland earl of

Huntingdon the constable. (Froissart.) On the voyage the duke landed for two days to relieve the garrison of Brest, blockaded by the Bretons, and then sailed into Corunna on August 9th. The reduction of Gallicia followed. On the frontier of Portugal the duke was met by king John, when operations against Castille were agreed upon, and the marriage of John himself with Philippa the duke's daughter. This took place in the spring of the next year, 1387. The campaign was not prosperous. The climate disagreed with the English soldiers; the duke fell into ill health, and wrote strongly for reinforcements from England, which, we are told, he scarcely dared expect. (Froissart.) Policy then suggested a French alliance, through the marriage of his daughter Catherine with the duke of Touraine, the younger brother of Charles V. The duke of Berri also happened at this time to solicit his daughter's hand, and Lancaster took care that the news should reach king John of Castille, who, dreading a French alliance with Lancaster, offered his own son Henry, a boy of nine years of age, as a match for the duke's daughter. The articles which followed were advantageous to Lancaster; a vast sum of money was paid down by the king of Castille, and a large annuity was settled upon the duke and duchess during either of their lives. Constance duchess of Lancaster was to resign her claim to Castille in favour of her daughter; the king was to retain the crown during life; at his death, which followed shortly after, it was to descend to Henry and Catherine, and their descendants; and, failing their issue, to the children of Edmund Langley, who had married Isabella the younger daughter of Peter of Castille. (Knyghton, 2677; Evesham, 120; Walsingham; Froissart.)

Page 7, line 11. *And in that viage many a worthi man died upon the flixe.* (Rawl. 173, Rawl. 190, f. 144, b.) Descriptive of Lancaster's return.—Soon after the king's sudden resumption of power in May, 1389, 12 R. II. he wrote urgently to Lancaster requesting his immediate return from Guienne, where the duke had retired to recruit his health; his presence was needed in England to preserve a balance among factions. On Aug. 11th, 1389, an order was issued for seizing six ships and a barge in Dartmouth harbour, and rendering them fit for service, to bring back the duke from Bordeaux to England. (Rymer, vii. 641.) On the 30th October the king wrote to the duke desiring him to provide for the govern-

ment of Guienne, and to return. (648.) On the 28th Nov. letters patent
were prepared for him according to desire, to insure him against suspicion
on his road through France. (Acts of Council, i. 14.) On the 10th Dec.
1389, 13 Ric. II. letters were sent from Reading to the regent of Guienne,
acquainting him with the return of the duke of Lancaster. (i. 17.)

Line 12. *also relece the remenaunt of kyng Johannes raunsoun.*—See
Appendix.

Line 23. *Edmund hadde a crokid back and was a mysshape.*—See Appendix. This story is explained by Hardyng, in additions to his
Chronicle, which, according to Sir Henry Ellis, occur only in two MSS.;
one among the Harleian MSS. (661) in the British Museum, the other is
the splendid Selden MS. of Hardyng in the Bodleian Library, said to have
been a presentation copy to Edward IV. The explanation of Lancaster's
fraud occurs immediately after the letter of defiance from the Percies to
Henry IV. before the battle of Shrewsbury. These prose additions have
been printed in the " Hereditary Right to the Crown," pp. 81–86 (a translation only of the letter of defiance, which is in Latin), by Sir Henry
Ellis, in Archæologia, vol. xvi. pp. 140–144, and in his edition of Hardyng.
Hardyng must have added these passages not long before his death, in the
early part of Edward IV. to settle the Yorkist succession against those
who still adhered to the house of Lancaster. He had been from twelve
years of age brought up in the service of the Percies; at the battle of
Shrewsbury he was twenty-five years old; and he had often heard the
earl of Northumberland affirm that the duke of Lancaster was the author
of the report that Edmund, from whom he was descended, was the elder
son of Henry III. and set aside on account of his deformity. The duke
had forged a chronicle to prove his point, and " dide put [it] in divers
abbaies and in freres, as I herde the said earl ofte tymes saie and record
to divers persouns, forto be kepte for the enheritaunce of his sonne to the
croune, whiche title he put furste forth after he hade kynge Richarde in
the Toure; but that title the erle Percy put aside." In the speech which
bishop Merks is said to have delivered, in favour of Richard, at the election of Henry IV. allusion is made to this story as an exploded fable;
while Henry seemed to build his title partly upon it. Otterbourne men-

tions the search among the chroniclers at Henry's election, no doubt, to clear up the point, as Hardyng states; and it is rather remarkable that not an allusion to this story was made by the duke of York in declaring his title to the crown in 1460, 39 Hen. VI. (see page 100), though it is evident from Hardyng that many persons, even in the early part of Edward IV. believed Edmund to have been the elder son of Henry III. According to Lambard (Perambulation, 1656, p. 504), sir John Fortescue wrote a treatise, which he tells us he " once saw," defending the title of Lancaster as derived from Edmund. Selden, in the Preface to Fortescue's " De Laudibus " (Pref. lv.), has given a list of most of his works. His treatises on the titles of the houses of York and Lancaster, and genealogy of the house of Lancaster, were formerly in the Cottonian Library, but were destroyed in the fire of 1731.

Line 27. *the erlle of Penbroke.*—John Hastings. Stowe (305), from the Tower records, places his death at Christmas 1390, 14 Ric. II.; Dugdale the year preceding, making him seventeen years of age; according to whom also (Bar. i. 578) he carried the gold spurs at the coronation of Richard II. before he was five years old. There is an account of an allowance to the earl in Acts of Privy Council, i. 12.

Page 8, Line 6. *horsbred, horsloof.*—Pain pour chevaux. No doubt the coarsest kind of bread; but innkeepers were not allowed to make it at this time, but bakers only, by stat. i. cap. 8, 13 Ric. II. and afterwards 4 Hen. IV. cap. 25. Village innkeepers might make it, by 32 Hen. VIII. cap. 41, a permission taken away by 21 Jac. I. cap. 21, " No hostler or innholder shall . . . . make horsebread in his hostery nor without, but bakers shall make it, ... and the hostlers or innholders shall *sell* their horsebread, and their hay, oats, beans, peas, provender, and also all kind of victual both for man and beast, for reasonable gain." (Stat. Realm.) In the Assisa Panis et Cervisie, and Stat. de Pistoribus, of uncertain dates (Stat. Realm, i. 199, 200, 202), we read of wastel-bread, cocket-bread, treet or trite-bread, and common wheaten-bread. The legal profits of the bakers are made out clearly in these ancient documents, as settled by the king's bakers. The Stat. Pistor. orders that every baker shall have his own mark on the different kinds of his bread.

CAMD. SOC.   X

Line 6. *ostrie hous.*—Hostery; an inn.

Line 8. *why he dede so, and this.*—" Romayne turned ayene, and brake
the bakers hede.   And neighboures come out, and wolde have restid this
Romayne, and he brak from hem, and fledde unto his lordis place; and
the constable wolde have had him out, but the bisshoppes men shute faste
the ʒate," &c. (Rawl. 173; Rawl. 190, f. 144-5.)   From this, according
to the Brute, resulted riots, on account of which the city privileges were
withdrawn.   The king's resentment had been excited by the citizens refus-
ing to lend him 1000*l* ; and he took occasion, from some disturbance of
this kind, to visit the city with his indignation.   The courts of law had
been removed from Westminster to York on March 20, 1392, 15 Ric. II.
(Rymer, vii. 713.)   Upon the occurrence of this riot in Fleet-street, in
which much of the public money had been endangered by the attack on
the house of the bishop of Salisbury, John de Waltham, then treasurer of
England, John Hende the mayor, the sheriffs, and twenty-four aldermen
were cited to appear before the council at Nottingham on the 24th June,
16 Ric. II. (Knyghton, 2740.)   On the day following, sir Edward de
Dalingridge was appointed custos of London (Rymer, vii. 723), and the
city functionaries were thrown into prison. (736.)   They were brought
again before the council at Windsor, on July 22nd, when the liberties of
the city were seized into the king's hands, and sir Baldwine de Radyngton
was appointed to supersede Dalingridge. (731.)   The Londoners saw that
"the end of these things was a money matter" (Stowe, 307); and on
Sunday, August 18th, the chief inhabitants made a formal submission to
the king, and bound themselves to pay him 100,000*l.*, a debt which was
remitted at the prayer of queen Anne. (Rymer, vii. 736.)   But a present
of 10,000*l.* the king accepted, and promised to visit the city of London on
the 21st. This he did in company with the queen,[*] and at her intreaty
granted a pardon, dated Woodstock, Sept. 19th. (Rymer, vii. 735.)   The
courts were restored to London after Christmas, 1392, 16 Ric. II. and the

* A very interesting account of the royal procession through London, and of the
presents to the king and queen, written in Latin elegiacs by Richard Maidstone, has
been published by the Camden Society. " Richard Maidstone," says Mr. Wright, " was
in great repute at court," and contemporary with what he describes, since he died in
1396.

citizens were allowed to elect a new mayor on Jan. 5th. (Fabyan.) According to Stowe entire reconciliation was not made till Feb. 23rd.

Line 13. *the erlle of Arundelle.*—Richard Fitz-Alan, earl of Arundel and Surrey Two dates are given for his arrest: according to the Rolls of Parliament it was on July 8th (Rot. Parl. iii. 435), from which source we get the following particulars:—The arrest took place in the presence of the king, who promised the earl, under oath made before the archbishop of Canterbury and sir John Wiltshire, who were also present, that he should neither suffer in his person or property. This was before the arrest of Warwick, which took place on the 10th. Otterbourne, however (190), says that the duke of Gloucester and earl of Arundel were invited to the dinner at which the earl of Warwick was seized; the duke was ill and could not come; Arundel suspected treachery and refused; and upon this the king employed the archbishop (much as in the Eulogium) to bring him into his power. Walsingham (354), placing the arrest after that of Warwick, says that Arundel was brought into the king's power by treachery. He was immediately confined in the Tower, and then moved to Carisbrook Castle, in the Isle of Wight, where he remained till Wednesday, Sept. 19th, when he was brought up to the parliament.

Line 16. *the erlle of Warwic.*—Thomas Beauchamp: he was arrested on the 10th July. (Rot. Parl. iii. 436; Otterb. 190.) The rolls state, at the house of the bishop of Exeter, the chancellor, near Temple Bar; Otterbourne and Walsingham, Holinshed, Stowe, &c. say that it was on the day the king had invited him to dinner. Perhaps these statements are not contradictory. He was confined in the Tower first, and then sent to Tintagel castle, in Cornwall, and was brought up to the parliament on Friday, Sept. 21st.

Line 19. *the duke of Gloucestre.*—The arrest of Thomas of Woodstock followed immediately after the capture of Arundel and Warwick. There is a difficulty in accounting for the suddenness of these arrests. With regard to Gloucester, his opposition to the king had been reaching a climax for some time. He had opposed the king's own marriage and the peace with France; had refused to attend the parliament in which Lancaster's chil-

(dren by Katharine Swynford were legitimated, and one of them, John Beaufort, created earl of Somerset; had openly insulted the king, and was dreaded at court (see Froissart's account, iv. lxxxviii.); was said to have been engaged in a conspiracy to dethrone Richard, and place Roger Mortimer, earl of March, on the throne; had excited the Londoners against Richard, &c. The Chronique de la Traison et Mort de Ric. II. (Eng. Hist. Soc.) further relates a conspiracy to dethrone Richard, which began at the dinner-table of the abbot of St. Alban's, godfather to Gloucester, in the early part of July, when Gloucester and the prior of Westminster were dining with the abbot. The prior and the abbot told visions relating to the dethroning of Richard, which they had each had on the preceding night, and Gloucester invited them to meet him that day fortnight at Arundel Castle. The earl promised a welcome, and "on the 8th day before the month of August," July 24th, there met Gloucester, Arundel, Warwick, Derby, Nottingham, archbishop of Canterbury, abbot of St. Alban's, and the prior of Westminster. Richard was to be imprisoned with the dukes of Lancaster and York, and the lords of the council were to be drawn and hanged. All this was to happen in August; but the earl of Nottingham betrayed the conspiracy. The " Chronique " has been followed by Fabyan, Holinshed, Carte, but not by Stowe, who had it in his possession. Fabyan has altered the date of the confederacy at Arundel from the " 8th day before August " to August 8th. These dates are both wrong, as the arrests took place certainly as early as July 10th. Carte, apparently on his own authority, has altered the day to July 8th, which would suit tolerably well (ii. 621). If the author of the " Chronique" himself supplied many of the details, we may well believe that he had fact to build upon.* The great objection appears to be, as Lingard (iii. 359) observes, that no charge founded on any such conspiracy exists on the rolls. Gloucester was arrested by the king in person at Pleshy, given in charge to the earl marshal (earl of Nottingham, captain of Calais), and hurried off to Calais immediately. (Rot. Parl. 418; Froissart, iv. lxxxviii. &c.) These arrests of the three lords, a proclamation stated (July 15), were made with the advice of the earls of Rutland, Nottingham,

* We are indebted to the English Historical Society for this valuable and interesting chronicle: translated and edited, with copious notes, by Benjamin Williams, F.S.A.

Kent, Huntingdon, Salisbury, Somerset, lord Despencer, and William le Scrope, with the approval of the dukes of Lancaster and York and earl of Derby; they were caused by *new crimes* (Rymer, viii. 67), which should be declared in the ensuing parliament. In the 6th article of deposition, it was alleged against Richard, that, notwithstanding the proclamation, nothing had been brought against them besides the proceedings of the 10th and 11th Ric. II.

Line 23. *Frenssherenne 'forto helpe him.*—See Appendix, p. 130. The king had been said to have *intended* calling over the French to help him against his barons; this chronicle says they came!

Line 30. *under colour of borowyng.*—Compare letters of obligation, which were never fulfilled by the king, on account of loans made to him, dated Aug. 10th, 1397. (Rymer, viii. 9–12.) He seems to have borrowed chiefly from religious houses, though private gentlemen accommodated him with large loans. On Aug. 14th (p. 13), the king issued letters to the archbishops of Canterbury and York, directing them to summon a convocation of their clergy on Oct. 1st, to make the king a grant to meet his heavy expenses in defence of the realm. Walsingham (353) says, that rumours were afloat that Richard was to be elected emperor; this may have increased his extravagance.

Last line. *erl of Norynghame, and othir, appelid.*—The appeal of treason against Gloucester, Arundel, and Warwick was made by the eight lords mentioned above, in note, line 19, on the feast of St. Oswald the king, Aug. 8th, in the great hall of Nottingham Castle (Rot. Parl. iii. 374), when the king promised them a patient hearing in the parliament, which was to open on 17th September.

Page 9, line 5. *And the duke wroot. . . .*—See Appendix, p. 129, &c. The duke of Gloucester had been hurried off to Calais before the middle of July; and on Aug. 17th a commission was directed to sir William Rickhill, one of the judges of the common bench, to take his depositions in prison. (Rot. Parl. iii. 431; Rymer, viii. 13.) At midnight, Sept. 5th, the judge was awoke at Essingham, Kent, by Mulso, a king's messenger,

who brought a writ, ordering him to be at Dover the following evening, to
meet the earl marshal.   On Friday the earl passed over to Calais; Mulso
and Rickhill accompanied him in another ship, Rickhill knowing nothing
of what was to be his business.   However, at the hour of vespers that day
the earl delivered to him the king's commission for examining the duke of
Gloucester.   The judge objected that the duke was dead, as it was universally believed in England; but on the Saturday morning he was admitted
to Gloucester's presence, whom he found well, and in sound mind.   He
had the precaution to insist upon witnesses to all that passed, and advised
the duke to return his answer in writing, and to keep a copy.   The duke
delivered his answer after the dinner hour the same day, requesting Rickhill to return the next morning, in case he should have remembered anything more to add to his defence.   On Sunday morning admission to the
castle was refused, and the earl, to whom Rickhill had complained, inti-
mated to him that he would not be allowed to see the duke again.   On
Tuesday, Sept. 11th, Rickhill was ready to return to England, and before
sailing sent a message to the duke, explaining that he had endeavoured
to return to him, but had not been permitted: and on Sunday, 16th, the
day before parliament met, he presented to the king Gloucester's confession. (Rot. Parl. iii. 379, 430-432.)   The day of the unfortunate duke's
death we do not know, nor what instructions had been given to the earl
marshal, besides delivering the commission to Rickhill.   On some day
about this time he was smothered with a feather-bed, according to the
confession of John Hall, in Parl. 1 Hen. IV. who, for his share in the murder, was executed 17th Oct. 1399, 1 Hen. IV. (Rot. Parl. iii. 452, 453.)
However, on Sept. 21st, 1397, a warrant was sent to the earl marshal
captain of Calais for bringing Gloucester before parliament for his examination, and on the 24th came the earl's answer, reporting that Gloucester
was dead. (Rot. Parl. iii. 377, 378; Rymer, viii. 15, 17.)   On Oct. 6th,
1397, Richard directed prayers to be said for his uncle's soul, because he
had confessed before his death.   (Rymer, viii. 19; Rot. Parl. iii. 409.)

Line 10.   *a long and large hous of tymber in the paleis at Westmynstre.*
" In the year 1397, the great hall at Westminster, being out of reparations,
and therefore new builded by Richard II.: he, having occasion to hold a
parliament, caused a large house to be builded in the midst of the palace

court, betwixt the clock-tower and the gate of the old great hall. This house was very large and long, made of timber, covered with tiles, open on both sides and at both ends, that all men might see and hear what was both said and done. The king's archers, in number 4,000 Cheshire men, compassed the house about with their bows bent and arrows notched in their hands, always ready to shoot. They had bouch of court (to wit, meat and drink), and great wages of 6d. by the day. The old great hall being new builded, parliaments were again there kept as before, namely, one in the year 1399 for deposing Richard II." (Strype's Stowe's Survey, ii. bk. vi. 49.)

Line 17. *the whiche* . . . .—" Sone afterward turned the king to grete losse, shame, hindering, and his utterly undoyng and destruccione." (Rawl. 173.) The rapacity and violence of these Cheshire guards at this parliament were made the 5th article against Richard at his deposition. (Rot. Parl., Knyghton, Tyrrell, Rapin.)

Line 18. *so evir procurid.*—In this parliament, which commenced Sept. 17th, the parliamentary commission of fourteen, constituted in the 10 Ric. II. was declared illegal, and those concerned in it were pronounced traitors; the opinion of the judges at Nottingham on the commission was confirmed; the judgment against M. de la Pole reversed; the Acts of 10 and 11 Ric. II. annulled. (Rot. Parl., Stat. Realm.)

Line 21. *the chartris of pardoun, and* . . . . *the pardoun* . . . . *to the erlle of Arundelle.*—The general pardon extorted by the appellants was revoked (Rot. Parl. iii. 350), and a special pardon granted to the earl of Arundel, dated Windsor, April 30, 1394, 17 Ric. II. (351.)

Line 24. *Also atte supplicacion.*—The Commons petitioned for the royal pardon to be extended to the following members of the late commission:—Duke of York, bishop of Winchester, Richard Scrope, who were then alive; William archbishop of Canterbury, Alexander late archbishop of York, the bishop of Exeter, and Nicholas abbot of Waltham, who were dead. Also for a pardon to the earls of Derby and Nottingham, because they *had deserted* from the duke of Gloucester as soon as they became

aware of his treason, and came honourably to the king. (Rot. Parl.
iii. 353.) The chief articles exhibited against Gloucester and the others
were, the commission, the assembly at Haringay, death of Burley and
proceedings in the parliament of 11 Ric. II., and having at Huntingdon, the
Thursday after the feast of saint Nicolas, Dec. 12th, 1387, in the 11th
year, purposed the dethroning of the king.   Nottingham and Derby may
have come to the king with some tale of Gloucester's ambition; but when
Gloucester, in the parliament of Feb. 1388, 11 Ric. II. complained to the
king that he had been accused of aspiring to the throne, Richard said
he disbelieved it.

Page 10, line 23.   *Thanne on saint Matthewe₃ day* —Sept. 21st.   In the
" Antient Kalendars and Inventories of the Treasury of Exchequer " (Sir
F. Palgrave), iii. 303–7, is an inventory of goods and chattels belonging
to this earl delivered into the treasury by the sheriff of Shropshire.   Also
(p. 307) a privy seal directing treasurer and chamberlain to deliver the
armour of this earl, with the armour of the duke of Gloucester and earl of
Warwick, to the keeper of the king's armour in the Tower of London.

Last line.   *ser Richard erl of Warwick.*—Thomas Beauchamp (*not*
Richard).   The earl of Warwick's plea before the parliament, as given
p. 11, certainly seems to countenance the relation of the " Chronique de
la Traison " about the conspiracy at Arundel: the abbot of St. Alban's and
prior of Westminster, as has been already stated, were chief movers in
that conspiracy.

Page 11, line 10.   *Yle of Mann.*—The Pell Issue Roll of Exchequer
contains payment to William le Scrope earl of Wiltshire, treasurer of
England, for charges incurred in conducting Thomas late earl of Warwick
to the Isle of Man, and for his support there.   (Easter, 22 Ric. II.)

Line 19.   *he was exilid for euer.*—On the 20th September the Commons
petitioned that Thomas Arundel, archbishop of Canterbury, might be
brought to trial, since he had, while chancellor, advised the commission
(10 R. II.); had abetted the insurrection of Gloucester (11 R. II.); and the
death of Burley and other faithful subjects.   The archbishop would have

answered, but the king silenced him, desiring time to consider. On the
25th the Commons prayed for judgment, when the king replied that the
archbishop had put himself under his grace. His judgment, therefore, was
exile, and confiscation of his temporalties. He was to leave England from
Dover within six weeks from St. Michael's Eve. (Rot. Parl. iii. 351; Stowe,
316.) Richard's conduct to the archbishop formed the thirty-third and
last article at his deposition He is charged on all sides with treachery to
Arundel: there it is said that, after the archbishop's impeachment by sir
John Bussy, he was persuaded by the king to reserve his defence; that for
five days the king deceived him, begging him not to come to the parliament, but to remain at home, assuring him that he should receive no
injury; that in these circumstances, during his absence, the archbishop
had been exiled, and his goods confiscated; that the jewels of his chapel
had been appropriated by the king, who had possession of them, as was
pretended, to prevent their being seized; that the king had promised that
if *obliged* to go into exile he should be recalled at Easter, and that he
should not lose his archbishoprick. (Knyghton, Rot. Parl.) Stowe says
(316) that the king sent the bishop of Carlisle to forbid Arundel coming
to parliament. Arrangements were made for seizing the property of the
archbishop, Gloucester, Arundel, and Warwick, also for arresting their
horses. (Issue Roll, Mich. 21 Ric. II.)

Line 32. *Thanne the archbisshoppe took his leve.*—For his farewell, see
Appendix, p. 132.

Line 12. *Coumprensitte into xij diuers persone3 continuyng the said
parlement.*—The "great parliament" was adjourned on Sept. 29th, on
which day the creation of peers had taken place. It met again at Shrewsbury, Jan. 28th, 1398, 21 Ric. II., and was dissolved on Jan. 31st, on which
day the authority of parliament was given to 18 commissioners for answer-
ing petitions still undetermined; 12 peers or 6 of them, 6 commoners or
3 of them. The attempt to repeal any of the statutes made in this parliament was pronounced treason, and the king granted a general pardon in
consideration of a subsidy for life. (Rot. Parl. Stat. Realm, ii. 95-107,
110.) The commission thus constituted proceeded, with the connivance
of Richard, to further business derogatory to the power of parliament. The

CAMD. SOC. Y

8th article of deposition charges Richard with this, and with having blotted and altered the rolls of parliament to countenance this dangerous precedent. (Knyghton, Rot. Parl.)

Line 28. *drede of men of Londoun and of xvij. shiris.*—Vast sums of money were extorted from these counties, on account of their having been inclined to rise with Gloucester and Arundel. The king threatened to treat them as an enemy's country, unless the lords temporal and the clergy and people of those counties bought his " good grace." The sums of redemption were called "Le pleasaunce." (Wals. 357; Upod. Neus. 553; Otterb. 199.)

Page 13, line 10. *the duke of Lancastre tolde it to the king.*—On Wednesday, Jan. 30th, the duke of Hereford exhibited to the king, in the parliament at Shrewsbury, a schedule containing an account of a conversation which had passed between the duke of Norfolk and himself in December last; written out in obedience to the king's command, when he had previously accused Norfolk before the king at Haywood. The parliamentary commissioners just constituted were referred to, and the dukes were ordered to appear before the king at Oswestry on Feb. 23; they were then put off till April 28th, and, as no clearer evidence of treason on either side appeared likely to be discovered, it was resolved, as agreed in such a case on March 19th, that they should have the trial by combat at Coventry Sept. 16th. Such is the account on the Rolls. (iii. 382, 383.) On the Issue Roll are payments to messengers and couriers for making proclamation for bishops, barons, knights, and esquires to assemble in all haste at Coventry to witness the duel. (Easter, 21 Ric. II.)

Line 23. *made him swere that he sholde not speke with maister Thomas Arundelle.*—Both dukes were forbidden to communicate with each other, or with archbishop Arundel. (Rot. Parl. iii. 383.) Letters of passage were made out for them on Oct. 3d (Rymer), and they were to be out of the kingdom before the octaves of St. Edward the Confessor. (Rot. Parl. iii. 383.)

Line 29. *blanc chartris.*—These extraordinary powers were extorted from the city of London and the seventeen counties as a further act of oppression. (Wals. 357; Upod. 553; Otterb. 200.) They are called "Ragmans" on the rolls, and were annulled 1 Hen. IV. (Rot. Parl. iii. 426, 432.)

Page 14, line 14. *an egle of gold.*—The sacred oil so inclosed was given by the Virgin Mary to archbishop Becket to be kept while he was in exile, to comfort him with the knowledge that its virtues should dispose future kings of England to defend all the rights of the Church. After this it was lost for a time, and then discovered by miracle to a holy man, who gave it to the first duke of Lancaster; by him it was given to Edward the Black Prince, that he might be anointed with it on the death of his father Edward III. The prince deposited it in the Tower, where it remained forgotten or unheeded till Richard II. obtained possession of it. Richard carried it over to Ireland with him, with many of the crown jewels; and he was obliged to deliver it up to the archbishop of Canterbury, when just before his deposition he was a prisoner at Chester. This oil was used at the coronation of Henry IV. (Wals. 360, 361.)

Line 28. *Thanne made the king his testament.*—Richard's will is printed in Rymer, viii. 75-77, apparently from an imperfect copy. Another copy is printed in Nichols's Collection of Royal Wills (1780), 191-201, from the original in the Chapter-house, Westminster. It bears date April 16, 1399, 22 Ric. II. There are ample directions for the royal funeral, followed by certain bequests and legacies. The residue of his estate, after payment of just debts, was to go to his successor, provided he confirmed the proceedings of parliament in the 21st and 22d years of his reign; so anxious was Richard to render lasting these late acts. The will was opened, and the clause binding his successor to the late acts at Westminster, Shrewsbury, and Coventry, "full grievous to the realm," formed the 31st article against him at his deposition. (Knyghton, Rot. Parl., Rapin); and this notwithstanding a permission given by parliament, 16 R. II., to the king freely to make his will, with the assurance of a due execution of it. (Rot. Parl. iii. 301.) Richard had also procured a papal bull to perpetuate the acts of the 21st and 22d years, and had caused the clergy and people to take oaths to support them. (Lowth's Life of Wickham, 260, &c.)

Line 32. *he wente forth into Yrlond.*—Richard embarked on this fatal
journey on May 29th from Milford Haven, and landed at Waterford on the
31st. He was accompanied by the dukes of Aumarle, Exeter, and many
other nobles; the abbot of Westminster and several bishops and clergy;
and with a vast body of his Cheshire guards. When they were gone
England had time to think of her grievances.

Page 15, line 8. *and landid at Ravenesporne.*—On July 4th, when
Richard had been five weeks in Ireland. He was accompanied by archbishop Arundel, Thomas Fitz-Alan, who had been arrested with his
father the earl of Arundel, lord Cobham, and others. Upon landing he
was joined by the earl of Northumberland, with his son Hotspur, the earl
of Westmerland, &c.; he soon had an army of 60,000 men, and advancing to London was received with acclamation. He then marched to
Bristol, to follow Richard's partisans, who intended to escape into Ireland to join him. At Bristol the treasurer Scrope, and Bussy and Green,
members of the council, were beheaded on July 29th; Bagot had taken
a different line, and fled to Chester. From this place he escaped into
Ireland, and was the first to bring the news of the revolution to Richard.
(Tyrrell, iii. 997.) This was probably at the beginning of August or the
end of July. Stormy weather had prevented vessels passing over to Ireland before that " one ship " which brought the evil tidings. (Creton.)
Creton, however, says that the king remained more than eighteen days in
Ireland after he heard the news (75, &c.) : the " Chronique," that he
directly prepared himself to pass over to England. (180.)

Line 13. *The duke of York that was lieutenant of Engelond.*—Upon
hearing of Henry's landing the duke had ordered sheriffs of counties to
collect troops at St. Alban's, where 60,000 archers and many thousand
lancers were mustered, according to the author of the " Chronique." (184.)
Instead, however, of advancing to meet Henry he marched to Oxford, and
thence to Berkeley castle, Gloucestershire, which he reached about the
time that Henry, whose movements were rapid, entered Evesham, Worces-
tershire. Henry followed the duke, and they met in conference in the
church at Berkeley on Sunday, 27th July, where they came to an agreement with regard to what should follow in relation to Richard. They

then went down to Bristol, where the castle surrendered to the duke of York, and the executions above mentioned took place. York was left with forces at Bristol and Henry marched northward to Chester: no doubt that both entrances into England might be secured.

Line 26. *Whanne kyng Richard herde telle alle this.*—Richard arrived at Milford Haven on Aug. 13th . ("Cronique de la Traison," 194.) There accompanied him the dukes of Aumarle, Exeter, and Surrey, the earl of Worcester, with other lords, the bishops of London, Lincoln, and Carlisle. The earl of Salisbury had sailed before the king, and landed at Conway for the purpose of gathering troops in North Wales and Cheshire. Richard could travel fast as well as Henry of Lancaster; and, in the dress of a friar (Creton,) at midnight, immediately after his landing, he rode off from the army in company with Exeter, Surrey, and the earl of Gloucester, and others, to the number of fourteen, to join Salisbury at Conway. On arriving they found his army disbanded. Richard then sent Exeter and Surrey to Henry to demand his intentions, and to act as they could for the best. The king himself having first crossed to Beaumaris Castle went westward to Caernarvon. but without finding money or men, or indeed food. Otterbourne says the king fled from castle to castle, among those along the coast of North Wales. (207.) He then waited for the return of his messengers at Conway.

Line 30. *ser Thomas Percy, stiward of the kyngis hous.*—He had been created earl of Worcester, 21 Ric. II. Upon discovery of the king's flight from Milford Haven, the duke of Aumarle and earl of Worcester declared for Henry, and the army immediately broke up. It was at Milford, no doubt, the earl broke his staff of office. (Comp. Wals. 358.) Creton mentions sir Thomas Percy as coming to the king at the castle of Flint, in , company with Henry and archbishop Arundel; and Percy, *at that time,* wore the livery of duke Henry (the collar of Esses) and *not* the Hart. (Archæol. **xx**. 158.) The ceremony of breaking the staff would have been superfluous when he wore Henry's livery. It may be observed, that our English compiler has altered the locality here from *Conway* to *Flint;* the Eulogium has *Conway:* also, that he has added the king's exclamation.

Page 16, line 11. *the duke and maister Thomas Arundel.*—The Eulogium places this interview at Conway; the English compiler has altered it to Flint, more happily than in the last instance. Upon receiving Richard's messengers, Henry sent the earl of **Northumberland** from Chester to Conway to obtain possession of his person. The earl had with him 400 lances and 1000 archers; on his way he took possession of Flint and Rhuddlan̄castles, and halted his troops in a place concealed by the rocks on the road half-way between Rhuddlan and Conway. He then, with five attendants, rode on by the sea-side to Conway Castle. Admission was granted, as he appeared to be the bearer of the duke's answer to Richard's message. The articles proposed by Henry seemed favourable, and the king agreed to accompany the earl **to** Flint to a conference with the duke of Lancaster. Northumberland's stratagem succeeded, and on the evening of August 18th Richard found himself a prisoner in Flint castle.

Page 17, line 3. *saide he wolde resigne.*—The king's resignation was at Flint. Mr. Webb (note, Archæol. **xx.** 139) remarks, that there may have been a design in placing Richard's resignation at Conway (as Wals. Eulogium; Rot. Parl. 1 Hen. IV.), since *then* he was at liberty, which he was not from the moment he entered Flint castle. Though Richard became a prisoner half-way between Conway and Rhuddlan, his arrest is said to have taken place at Flint. (Rot. Parl. v. 463, &c.) Richard was taken to Chester. From thence a proclamation was made by the king, evidently under constraint, dated August 20th, Chester (Rymer, viii. 84), in favour of the duke of Lancaster. On the third day, Henry, with the royal captive, began his march to London. The first night they slept at Nantwich, the second at Newcastle-under-Lyne, the fourth at Lichfield, when the king nearly effected his escape. On the last of the month the king seems to have slept at Westminster; the next day he was removed **to** the securer confinement of the Tower. (See Stowe, 322, 323.)

Line 6. *And aftirward, in the vigile of saint Miyhelle.*—The rolls of parliament, however, place Richard's resignation, the promise of which he was said to have given at *Conway*, on Monday, Sept. 29th, in presence of the duke of Lancaster, lords de Roos, de Wiloghby, Bergavenny, &c. (iii. 416, 417.)

Line 26. *Aftir this the duke wente to Westmynstre.*—On Tuesday, the feast of St. Jerome, Sept. 30th, the parliament met in Richard's name. Richard's resignation, read in Latin and English, was accepted: thirty-three articles were exhibited against him, to show how he had broken his coronation oath. After this the sentence of deposition was pronounced by eight representatives of the different grades of the nation; by the bishop of St. Asaph for the archbishops and bishops; abbot of Glastonbury for abbots and priors, and the clergy generally; earl of Gloucester for dukes and earls; lord Berkeley for barons and bannerets; sir Thomas de Erpingham and Thomas Grey for the bachelors and commons; sir John Markham and William Thirnyng for the judges. (Rot. Parl. iii. 417, 422.)

Line 30. *he sate down in his fader sete.*—He took his seat as duke of Lancaster The " Eulogium " mentions the presence of the bishop of Carlisle, Thomas Merks, but says nothing of his speech in favour of Richard: " Ponebat se in sede patris sui juxta episcopum Carlioli." The " Chronique de la Traison " gives the bishop's protest; and, if it is the chief authority for it, we must be cautious, as Mr. Williams observes, in rejecting the testimony of a contemporary. Creton, however (Archæol. xx.), says that Richard's partisans dared not say a word in his favour.

Page 18, line 7. *dampned the said king Richard to perpetuelle prisoun.*— This is misplaced. In the parliament which commenced Oct. 6th, 1 Hen. IV. a question was asked by the archbishop of Canterbury, on the part of the king, on Thursday Oct. 23rd, what was to be done with Richard, " sauvant sa vie, quele le roi voet que luy soit sauvez en toutes maneres?" He was to be safely guarded, it was replied, in some secret place, where none of his old associates should have access to him. On the following Monday, Oct. 29th, Richard was sentenced to perpetual imprisonment, in manner prescribed. (Rot. Parl.)

Line 9. *how he descendid and cam doun lynealli of kyng Harri, the sone of kyng Johan.*—See note on page 7, line 23, at p. 152.

Line 13. *Thanne amoz the archbisshoppis of Cauntirbury and of York.*— After Henry's claim, the archbishops led him to the throne; Arundel

made a sermon, " Vis dominabitur," &c. in Latin, which is on the Rolls.
Henry made a protest against being considered merely a conqueror of the
throne; and the coronation day was fixed for Oct. 13, the Translation of
St. Edward Confessor.   On the day after these proceedings, Wednesday
Oct. 1st, a deputation went to Richard in the Tower, and justice Thirnyng, in a long speech, told him he was deposed.   Richard answered that
he no longer looked for allegiance, " but he sayde that after all this he
hopyd that his cosyn wolde be a goode lord to hym." (Rot. Parl. iii.
423, 424.)

Line 16.   *colacion.*—A discourse, sermon.   This colacion is in Knyghton, Rot. Parl., Fabyan, &c.

Page 19, line 21.   *made ser Roger Waldenne . . . . bisshop of London.*—
Walden had descended from his archbishopric on Henry's accession, and
on Oct. 30th the duke of York and earl of Northumberland prayed that
Arundel might be enabled to recover damages from him.   Walden was a
learned man.   He became secretary to Richard II., dean of York, treasurer of Calais, treasurer of England, archbishop of Canterbury, and
remained primate for two years: he was made bishop of London, after
being without a bishopric, on Dec. 10th, 1404 (not as in text).   He died
within a year of his appointment.   (Godwin's Catalogue of Bishops.)

Page 20, line 6.   *cam thider vnto him the duke of Aumarle.*—The date in
the text is too late.   On Jan. 5th, the sheriffs of London were enjoined to
seize the person of Thomas earl of Kent, John earl of Huntingdon, or any
of their adherents; on the 6th, letters were sent to Peter Courtney, captain
of Calais, empowering him to arrest any of the insurgents who might
attempt to land at Calais or on the coast of Picardy.   (Rymer, viii. 120.)
According to the interesting narrative of the " Chronique," Aumarle was
dining with his father, the duke of York, on Sunday Jan. 3rd, when he
received a letter from the conspirators, which the duke desired to see.   As
soon as he discovered the contents, York cried, " Saddle the horses directly.
Hey! thou traitor thief! thou hast been traitor to king Richard, and wilt
thou be false to thy cousin Henry?   Thou knowest I am thy pledge-
borrow, body for body.   By St. George! I had rather thou shouldst be

hung than I!" He rode off for Windsor with his son's letter; and the
son, seeing his only course, passed the duke, who was " heavy," on the
road, and arriving first disclosed the conspiracy. (Chronique, 233, &c.)
According to Creton, Aumarle voluntarily showed the letter to the duke
of York, who sent him on to the king. (Archæol. **xx.** 211.) The " Eulogium " gives *only* the story which follows in the text. Holinshed has
followed the " Chronique;" Stowe, Creton.*

Line 27. *the kyng . . . rood . . . . to Londoun.*—Immediately upon the
arrival of the duke of York with the letter confirming what the king had
heard from his son. On his way he was met by the mayor, hastening to
warn him that the lords had taken the field with 6,000 men. A proclamation was issued calling upon faithful subjects to join the king's standard,
and by the next morning, Jan. 5th, 16,000 men were paid and ready.
(Chronique.)

Page 21, line 3. *But as sone as the said lorde3,* &c.—On the evening of
Jan. 4th the insurgents, with 400 men, entered Windsor Castle, and,
finding the king had escaped, withdrew to Sunning, near Reading, where
they persuaded the queen that Richard had escaped from Pontefract. The
" Chronique " relates a skirmish between the king's troops and the insurgents at Maidenhead Bridge, with a threat of Henry to put Richard to
death if he found him among the rebels. However, on the night of
Jan. 6th they were at Cirencester, having passed through Wallingford,
Abingdon, Farringdon; they said by the way that Richard had escaped, and
had dressed up Maudelain to personify him. Creton says he was exactly
like king Richard. It surely must have been after the interview with the
queen: she would not have consented to such deception. At Cirencester
the lords were attacked by the mayor and townspeople, in obedience to
the king's writ just received: the " Chronique " says at the instance of an
archer of king Henry's—perhaps the royal messenger. Kent and Salisbury were beheaded; the earl of Huntingdon, lord Despencer, and Maude-

* Creton's narrative of the revolution by Henry of Lancaster and the deposition of
Richard, &c. has been translated, with plentiful notes and historical excursuses, by Rev.
John Webb, in Archæologia, **xx.** Creton was an ardent admirer of Richard; he tells us
he loved the king because he dearly loved the French.

CAMD. SOC.   Z

lain set fire to some houses in hope of diverting attention from themselves, and escaped. (Creton, Otterb., Stowe.)

Line 15. *At Oxenforde.*—These executions, with others to the number of twenty-six, took place at Oxford on Jan. 11th. (Stowe, 325.)

Line 17. *at Pritwelle, in Essex,* &c.—In Rymer (viii. 120) is an order to the constable of the Tower for confining John earl of Huntingdon: he does not, however, appear to have been received there, but to have been captured in his flight, at the house of " John Pritewelle of Prittlewell," in Essex, by order of the countess of Hereford, and to have been executed at Fleshy by her command. (Chronique de la Traison, 252, and App. A, 269.)

Line 22. *at Bristowe,* &c.—Lord Despencer had fled to Cardiff Castle, which was his property, and intended to escape beyond sea. He embarked in a vessel, but the sailors had been bribed, or were aware of the value that would be set upon him, and he was carried, in spite of entreaties, to Bristol, where he was immediately executed. (Evesham, 166, 167.)

Line 25. *Whanne kyng Richard herde alle this.*—See Suppl. Add. The " Eulogium " states that this insurrection was in obedience to Richard's commands given at Conway. At that time the king had no idea of being deposed, and it is scarcely likely that he would have planned a revolution on a probability. He had no opportunity at Flint. It was an advantage to the lords to be considered as acting for the king; and we must remember that they had all been degraded (Rot. Parl. iii. 452), had gained nothing, and lost much by Henry's accession. The use of Richard's name had enabled them to send to the king of France for assistance. (Rymer, viii. 165.)

Line 27. *for sorow and hunger he died in the castle of Pountfret.*—This English chronicle from the "Eulogium" is one more authority for the story of Richard's voluntary starvation. Walsingham (363), Evesham (169), Otterb. (228), Hist. Croyland Continuatio (Gale, i. 495), have given this version of his death. Creton, the former page of Richard, gives it as the

general report, but believes that he is still alive. (Archæol. xx. 219.)
Yet a few passages on he proves that he was by no means certain of it.
It is to be regretted that this chronicle throws no new light upon the controversy respecting the fate of Richard; but it shows very clearly the
general uncertainty and excitement which prevailed on the subject. (See
pp. 23–26, &c.; Appendix, 135, 136.)

Last line. *buried at Langley.*—Stowe, following Walsingham no doubt,
places Richard's death on Feb. 14th. It may have been a few days later.
(See Acts of Council, 1 H. IV. 1400, and sir H. Nicolas's remarks.) The
body of Richard—or, as Creton thought, of Maudelain, Richard's chaplain—
had been exhibited at St. Paul's on March 12th. (Chronique, 261.)
The funeral services were performed at St. Paul's in the presence of the
king and people, and the body was then carried to Langley to be buried in
the church of the Preaching Friars. There the office was performed by
the bishop of Chester, the abbot of St. Alban's, and the abbot of Waltham,
"sine magnatum præsentiâ, sine populari turbâ, nec erat qui eos invitaret ad
prandium post laborem (!)" Wals. (364), Otterb. (229).

Page 22, line 2. *ser Johan Maudeleyn.*—Maudelain, Richard's chaplain, certainly suffered death before the end of January, probably before
the month was drawing to a close.

Line 5. *none ascapid, saue onli ser Roger Waldenne.*—Walden and
Thomas Merks, bishop of Carlisle, were committed to the Tower on Jan.
10 (Rymer, viii. 121): but Walden was soon liberated, with the abbot of
Westminster, as they could satisfactorily refute the charges of being concerned in the conspiracy. (Otterb. 228.) Merks, upon Henry's accession, had been committed a prisoner to the abbey of St. Alban's, and was
pardoned upon being deprived of his bishopric in November, by being
translated to the isle of Samos (Godwin). After the Kingston insurrection
he remained incarcerated until Jan. 26th, 1401, when he was committed to
the Marshalsea; but, upon strength of a pardon granted him Nov. 28, 1400
(Rymer, viii. 165), was soon set at liberty. He retired to his own monastery
of Westminster (Evesh.), and in 1404 was presented by the abbot and
convent to the rectory of Todenham, Gloucestershire. (Carte, ii. 648.)

Line 6. *quene Ysabelle.*—Immediately upon Henry's accession ambassadors had arrived from France, in Oct. 1399, demanding the restoration of Isabella with her jewels, according to the marriage treaty. Henry endeavoured to negotiate a marriage between Isabella and the prince of Wales, or between any other of his children and Charles's children. After many delays Isabella arrived at Boulogne, Aug. 1st, 1401. (Rymer; Acts of Council.) Her dowry was not considered due, since she was under 12 years of age; but the council decided that her jewels should go with her. Many had been distributed among the royal children. (Acts of Council, 134; Sir H. Nicolas's Preface.) Some of her valuables were kept back, since in a treaty between Charles VI. and Henry V. the latter was to pay a sum of money in lieu of the jewels detained. (Rapin, i. 523.) The passage of the royal suite to Boulogne and back cost 79*l.* (Issue Roll, Easter, 3 Hen. IV.)

Line 11. *erl of Dunbar.*—George Dunbar, earl of March, in consequence of a private feud with Robert III. In Rymer is the indenture of alliance, dated July 25th, 1400. The castle and lordship of Somerton, Lincolnshire, were to be the earl's; also the manor of Clippeston, Sherwood Forest, for life. (viii. 153, 154.)

Line 14. *Oweyn off Glendore.*—Born May 28th, 1354, or, as some say, 1349. Holinshed relates the story of blood in his father's stables on the night of his birth, which is in this chronicle told of Edmund Mortimer. (See Speed.) He entered the Inns of Court and became a barrister. Afterwards he entered the service of the earl of Arundel, and then of Richard II. After his revolt he pretended to regal dignity, and made an alliance with the king of France. Glyndwr and lord Grey had had a law-suit about a certain common in the time of Richard II., which lord Grey lost; but upon the accession of Henry, trusting to his power at court, he seized the common; hence the quarrel. (See Thomas's Memoir of Glyndwr.)

Line 21. *emperour of Constantinople.*—Manuel Palæologus crossed from France in December, 1400. He was endeavouring to raise the Western powers against Bajazet emperor of the Turks. He had before sent ambassadors to the courts of Europe, and Richard II. had made him a grant of

£2000. (Issue Roll, Easter, 21 Ric. II.) Henry IV. was just to him if not generous, and paid what might have been considered as due from Richard. (Mich. 2 Hen. IV.) The emperor was poor, and satisfied with one boat on his way back to Calais, and Henry paid the hire, which was ten marks. (Easter, 3 Hen. IV.) During his stay in England the emperor had mass celebrated daily in his own house after the Greek ritual. (Eulogium.)

Line 26. *the Wals&menne began to rebelle.*—The national antipathy was strong. When the bishop of St. Asaph intreated the parliament (1 Hen. IV.) not altogether to despise Glyndwr, the answer he received, according to the " Eulogium," was " se de scurris nudipedibus non curare;" in our English text, " they saide they set nou3t be him." Glyndwr had the right on his side, but could find no redress from Henry's parliament. The laws of the early part of this reign were not conciliatory towards the Welsh. By stat. 2 Hen. IV. Jan. 1401, no person born in Wales of Welsh parentage could purchase land or tenement in or near the cities in the Marches of Wales: he could not henceforth receive the freedom of any city or borough. All Welsh citizens were to produce security for their conduct: they were not to be admitted to any municipal office, nor to wear armour in their town or borough. (Stat. Realm, ii. 124.) No Welshman might purchase land in England, &c. (129.) By stat. 4 Hen. IV., Sept. 30, 1402, English- men could not be tried by a Welsh jury in Wales; minstrels, rhymers, wasters, and *other vagabonds*, were condemned; meetings were not allowed; no Welshman might carry arms: Welshmen were not to have castles; the fortresses were to be manned by English; even Englishmen *married* to Welshwomen were prohibited from bearing office in Wales or the Marches· (140, 141) Thomas (Memoir of Glyndwr) archly quotes this law as a proof that the dreadful stories told by Otterbourne, and other English writers, of the atrocities of the Welsh WOMEN must be calumnies.

Page 23, line 3. *lord Grey wedde on of his doughtris.*—According to Dugdale this Reginald lord Grey married, 1. Margaret d. of William lord Roos; 2. Joanna d. and heir of William lord Astley. (Bar. i. 717.) Where also see his ransom. (Rymer, viii. 279; Otterb. 238.) According to the Welsh writers he married Glyndwr's daughter Jane. (Thomas's Me- moirs of Glyndwr, 51.) So also Carte. (ii. 654.) He was taken prisoner early in 1402. This chronicle is an independent authority for his having married Glyndwr's daughter. The "Eulogium" is silent on the point.

Page 24, line 31. *lewde.*—Unlearned, ignorant.

Line 31. *the maister.*—This Master of Divinity confessed that he had been a rash interpreter of prophecy, and to that he attributed all his misfortunes. (Eulogium.) He meant, no doubt, the prophecy of Merlin.

Line 25. *saw.*—Relate, say.

Line 32. *seche him in Scotland.*—The account Henry IV. wished to be believed of the pretended Richard in Scotland is evident from stat. 5 Hen. IV. cap. 15, in which there are excluded from a general pardon " William Serle, Thomas Warde de Trumpyngton qui se pretende et feigne d'estre Roy Richard, et Amye Donet." (Stat. Realm, ii. 148.) Part of the earl of Cambridge's conspiracy in the 3 Hen. V. was said to have been the purposing to bring forward Thomas de Trumpyngton, an idiot, to personify Richard II. (Rot. Parl. iv. 65.) According to the Scotch chronicler, Bower, the continuer of Fordun, Richard escaped from Pontefract, and was recognised in the kitchen of Donald lord of the Isles by one who had formerly been his jester. Donald presented him to Robert III., who maintained him in seclusion. After Robert's death, the duke of Albany, the regent, became his patron. At last he died himself, in the castle of Stirling, and was buried in the church there. (Bower, in Fordun, 1068, 1133.) He wrote after 1441. (Lingard.) Wyntown, who wrote about 1420, cannot explain how Richard escaped from Pontefract, but says he was recognised by an Irish lady who had seen him in Ireland, in spite of his altered appearance, &c. (388, 389.) He mentions his living under the knowledge of the duke of Albany, but *no one was certain* whether he had been the king or no. Mr. Fraser Tytler's hypothesis of Richard's escape to Scotland is discussed by Mr. Williams in his Introduction to the Chronique, p. lii. &c.

Page 26, line 1. *seche king Richard in Walis.*—So uncertain were the reports about him. Reports of Richard being alive in Wales must tend

to weaken the credit which has been given to those of his having escaped
to Scotland, which the Scotch historians favoured. Richard was said to be
at Chester at the head of an army just before the open rebellion of the
Percies.

Line 30. *Edmund Mortymer . . . . . wedded on of Owenez douztris.*—
Edmund Mortimer's marriage with Glyndwr's daughter does not appear
by any means certain from the Welsh historians (see Thomas's Memoir of
Glyndwr, 52; also Carte, ii. 658), yet English writers make no doubt of
it. Great confusion exists between this Edmund Mortimer, prisoner in
Wales, and his nephew, Edmund earl of March, son and heir of Roger,
who was killed in Ireland, 1398, 22 Ric. II. Edmund earl of March and
his brother Roger were confined in Windsor Castle on Henry's accession.
On Feb. 14, 1405, lady Despencer, widow of lord Despencer, late earl of
Gloucester, procured their liberation by means of false keys, and hurried
them off to join Glyndwr, but they were quickly retaken, and remained
captives. Edmund Mortimer, uncle to Edmund earl of March, was taken
prisoner by Owen, June 1402, perhaps married his daughter, and espoused
his cause about the end of the same year. Henry would not allow him
to be ransomed; lord Grey's imprisonment he bore less quietly.

Page 29 line 7 and note.—The origin of the date in the "Chronicle"
appears to be the following verses quoted in the "Eulogium:"—"De quo
quidem conflictu quidam metricè sic scripsit:

> " Anno milleno, quater et centesimo, bino,
> Bellum Salopie fuit in Mag. nocte Marie."

Hardyng was in the battle, and gives the true date. The real cause of
the rebellion of the Percies is no doubt correctly given by our author
(page 27, line 12). In their defiance of Henry (Hardyng, Hall, Grafton,
Hered. Right) they proclaim their intention of restoring the throne to
the right line—to the earl of March; also that their former support of
Henry was in consequence of his oath to them at Doncaster, that he only
intended to recover his rights, nothing in prejudice of Richard II.; that,
nevertheless, he had starved him to death, keeping him fifteen days and
nights without food; that he had refused to allow the ransom of Edmund

Mortimer. In spite of this declaration of Richard's death, they had taken
advantage of the popular belief to raise the larger forces in Cheshire (page
28), and their use of the badge of the hart shows that they wished to
appear engaged in a disinterested quarrel. In the "Acts of Privy Council"
are some very interesting letters from the Percies, dating from April 10,
1401, to June 26, 1403, less than four weeks before the rebellion. In
these letters they demand payment for their guardianship of the east and
west marches—the king underrates the importance of the marches—should
anything happen, which God forbid, it would not be their fault—their
personal property was spent in paying the king's debt, and they could not
bear the continual demands the soldiers were making upon them: the last
letter is a strong *demand* for payment from the earl. The "Issue Roll"
contains the payment of a few small sums to the earl and Hotspur during
this time. The rebellion came very suddenly upon the king. A letter
to the council from Higham Ferrers (co. Northamp.), July 10th, shows that
he was ignorant of any threatened rebellion—he was going "vers le parties
d'Escoce . . . . . pour ye donner aide et confort a noz trescheres et foialx
cousins le conte de Northumb. et Henry son filz . . . . contre les Escotz
noz enemys." From Burton-on-Trent he writes, July 17th, that he has
just heard that Henry Percy calls him nothing but "Henry of Lancaster,"
and has made proclamation in Cheshire that Richard is alive. Four days
more and the battle was ended. Henry's frequent promises, without any
chance of fulfilment, exasperated the Percies.

Line 15. *so he cam to the parlement.*—To throw suspicion from himself,
the earl had agreed in August, at Pontefract, to surrender his castles to
the king. (Nicolas's Privy Council, i. 211.) He submitted himself to
the king at York: and on Wednesday, February 5th, urged that submission before parl. 5 Hen. IV. 1404, and again on Feb. 7th; when the lords
gave judgment that he had only been guilty of a trespass, and therefore
must submit to a fine. He then exonerated the duke of York, archbishop
of Canterbury, and other suspected persons, from being concerned in the
rebellion. (Rot. Parl. iii. 524.)

Line 29. *dame Blaunche.*—To Master John Chaundeler, clerk, appointed treasurer to Blanch. In money paid to him by Richard Clifford,

clerk, junior, for 10 cloths of gold and other merchandise purchased of
Richard Willington, citizen and merchant of London, 215*l.* 13*s.* 4*d.*; and
by Wm. Cromer, clothier, of the said city, 380*l.* for apparel and parapher-
nalia of the said Blanche, in her voyage to Cologne to be married to the
son of the king of the Romans.   By writ, &c. 595*l.* 13*s.* 4*d.*   (Devon's
Issue Roll, Easter, 3 Hen. IV.)   On May 15 the king wrote to the council
from Berkhamstead, complaining that the money assigned for the expenses
to be incurred on his daughter's passage had been paid in another di-
rection; he begs it may be refunded, for he can stand no expenses himself.   (Acts of Council.)   Nor were preparations for his own marriage
very liberal   On Dec. 9, 1402, Henry Beaufort, bishop of Lincoln, who,
with the escort appointed to meet Joanna of Navarre, was waiting in Plymouth harbour, wrote to the king from thence, complaining of the non-
payment of the wages of the mariners and soldiers.   (Acts of Council, i.
189.)

Line 31.   *Richard Clifford.*—At this time bishop of Worcester: translated to London Oct. 13, 1407.   In 1414 he was at the Council of Constance, when he preached in Latin before the emperor.   He was among
the thirty persons added to the electing body of cardinals on this occasion, and nominated cardinal Colonna for the papacy, who was elected
under the title of Martin V.   Clifford died Aug. 20, 1421.   (Gibson's
Catalogue, 200.)

Page 30, line 1.   *dukeȝ son of Beyre.*—Lewis, surnamed Barbatus, son
and heir of Rupert or Robert, emperor of Germany, count palatine of the
Rhine, and duke of Bavaria. ˋ

Line 6.   *yle of Cagȝnt.*—Cadsand, Holland.   *Carrakeȝ,* carrack, a large
merchant vessel.   *Jeneȝ,* Genoa.
Line 18.   *the Camer beside Wynchilse.*—Camber, now called Rye, harbour.   The sea formerly washed below the foot of Camber Castle, now a mile
or more inland.   The outline of this coast is much altered.   From stat. 2 and
3 Ed. VI. cap. 30, 1543, we find that the old harbour could contain 200
or 400 sail of ships, . . . and being there, might not only issue out at
all times to encounter their enemies, but also in times of stormy winds

might have had rescue and good harbour, to the great safeguard of the king's ships and merchants passing to and fro upon the narrow seas ; yet now, not only the said harbour and road called the Camber, but also all the " inne creekes nere unto Rye and Wynchelsey," partly by occasion of casting ballast into the same harbour and creeks, and partly "bycause dyvers mershes inned take in no water to scower the channell, but lett oute the freshe water at guttes, so that the channell there is so choked, swared, and fyllyd uppe," that not more than thirty or forty vessels can lie there without danger. (Stat. Realm, iv. 72.) In spite of precaution the harbour became choked, and a new one was made in 1726, which also became useless. The new harbour is nearly on the site of the old. (Haydn's Dic.)

Line 9. *canted.*—Sold by auction.

Line 12. *Johan Serle.*—*William,* not *John,* Serle; he was present at the murder of Gloucester (Rot. Parl. iii. 453); and was excepted out of a general pardon, Jan. 5, Hen. IV. 1404 (544).

Line 29. *like to king Richard, but it was not he.*—Cum adhuc non quievit rumor ille de vitâ ejus, semper Scoti illum rumorem auxerunt. (Eulogium.)

Page 31, line 11. *the cause of the said risyng.*—Probably much as given here: lord Mowbray had been deprived of his hereditary office of earl marshal, and the earl of Northumberland of the guardianship of the Marches: the earl of Westmerland had stepped into both. Henry IV. was at Worcester when suspicion was first aroused by a letter from the council. They wrote that they had heard from John of Lancaster, the king's son, that lord Bardolf, who had been ordered to join the king in the Welsh marches, had taken himself off to the North. They had despatched chief justice Gascoigne and lord Roos to the North to frustrate any evil that might arise. And, as they knew the king was poor, they sent him 1000 marks. (Acts of Council.) On the 28th May the king acquainted them from Derby of the truth of the insurrection, and bids them hasten to Pontefract with all the followers they can collect. On

July 2nd the king wrote, relating his success, from Warkworth Castle, which, formerly belonging to the earl of Northumberland, had surrendered to him the day before. He was about to attack Alnwick. (Acts of Council.)

Page 33, line 6. *beheddid withoute the cite of York.*—See Appendix. Clement Maydestone gives a different account of the archbishop's execution. (See the Abps. Articles, &c., and Martyrdom, Anglia Sacra, ii. 369-372; Cotton. MS. Vesp. E vii. f. 94-101; Foxe's Acts and Monuments.) The concluding words of the archbishop given in the text are not in the "Eulogium."

Line 17. *many grete miracles.*—Usque hodie mirabiliter operatur. (Eulogium; see Anglia Sacra, ii. 371-2.) The last sentence of the " Eulogium " gives an account of the success of a prayer to St. Richard (Scrope), in stopping a fire which had broken out in a belfry near York.

Line 27. *the pope answerde.*—It is to be feared that our English compiler was himself the author of this answer. It is not in the " Eulogium." Whether the *king* was given to witticisms we need not inquire.

Page 34, line 3. *dame Luce . . . weddid . . . ser Edmund erl of Kent.*— " With moche solempnyte and moche worship, for kyng Harry was ther hymselfe, and ȝave her at the chirche dore. And when mes was doone the kyng hymselfe ladde that lady home to the bisshoppes place of Wynchestre, and ther was a wonder grete fest to al maner of peple that thedre wolde come." (MS. Rawl. 190, f. 152.) Jan. 24. (Fabyan, sub ann.)

Line 6. *ser Robert Knollis.*—*Robert*, not *Ricardus*: famous under Edward III., especially at the battle of Poictiers. He accompanied the Black Prince into Spain, 41 Ed. III. in aid of Don Pedro; in 44 Ed. III. was general of forces then sent into France; 1 Ric. II. governor of Brest Castle; 3 Ric. II. aided the duke of Britany against the French; 4 Ric. II. suppressed Jack Straw's insurrection; 8 Ric. II. defeated a conspiracy for murdering sir Nicholas Brember, mayor; seneschal of Guienne early in

Hen. IV.; founded a college, &c. at Pontefract; built bridge at Rochester; founded an hostelry for English strangers at Rome; enlarged house of the Carmelites, White Friars, London, where he was buried with Constance his wife. He died Aug. 15. (Dugdale, B. ii. 412; Stowe, 334-5; Carte, 571, &c.) The example of Robert Knollis was commended by Caxton, at the end of his " Ordre of Chivalry," to the imitation of the knights of his day; instead of "going to the baynes and playing at dice." (See Dibdin's Typograph. Antiq. 225-228.)

Line 8. *ser Thomas Rempstoun.*—He was Constable of the Tower, Admiral of the West, and Knight of the Garter; drowned by an accident at London Bridge, 7 Hen. IV. (Fabyan; Rawl. 190.) Stowe mentions a Sir Thomas Rampton as vice-chamberlain to Henry IV.; and sailing in company with him from Queenborough, Sheppey, into Essex, to avoid passing through London, where pestilence raged, he was taken prisoner by the French, in the summer of 1406.

Line 11. *dame Philippe the yonger, douʒtir of king Harri.*—She was married to Eric, associated with his great-aunt Margaret in the throne of Norway, Denmark, and Sweden. Sole monarch in 1412. Fabyan places her departure from England in May. The marriage was celebrated at Lunden, according to Pontanus, as late. as Oct. 25 the same year, 1406 (Rapin, 498): but on July 28th Richard Clifford, junior, clerk of the wardrobe to the lady Philippa, the king's daughter, queen of Sweden, Denmark, and Norway, was paid 248*l.* 10*s.* 6*d.* for pearls and cloth of gold purchased at the time of the marriage. (Issue Roll, Easter, 7 Hen. IV.) The marriage may have been splendid, but the Danish historians must be wrong in supposing Philippa brought Eric a large fortune. (See Univ. Hist. xxxii. 299.)

Line 13. *Edmund Courteneye.*—*Richard*, not *Edmund.* He was chancellor of Oxford, not bishop till 1413. (Gibson.)

Line 17. *the Walssh clerc.*—Nov. 8 Hen. IV., Fabyan. But in Issue Roll, Mich. 3 Hen. IV., March 14th, 3*l.* 6*s.* 8*d.* were paid to the earl of Westmerland, marshal of England (so made 1 Hen. IV.), for appointing lists at Smithfield for a duel between Yevan appe Griffithe Lloyt, appellant, and Perceval Soudan, knt., defendant, respecting certain articles of treason.

Line 30. *quarel.*—An arrow with a square head, (*quarellus, quadrillus,* from *quadrum.*) *Briae.*—St. Brieux.

Page 35, line 2 and note.—Robert Hallam, bishop of Salisbury, Henry Chicheley, then bishop of St. David's, and Thomas Chillingdon, prior of Christ Church, Canterbury, were sent by the convocation at London to the council of Pisa. Hallam was chancellor of Oxford in 1403; was made cardinal June 1411. He died while at the council of Constance, Sept. 4, 1417. (See the Archæologia, vol. xxx. 430–437.) The council of Pisa lasted from March 25 to August 7, 1409. It excommunicated the rival popes Gregory XII. and Benedict XIII., and elected Peter de Candia, cardinal of Milan, as pope, at 70 years of age, by the name of Alexander V., June 26th. (Onuphrius in Platina.)

Page 37, line 4. *his other son John, duke of Bedford.*—A mistake: the creation is rightly placed in *margin, p.* 40, in the 2 Hen. V., and by the same hand. His creation bears date from May 6, 1414, 2 Hen. V. Until then he was styled John de Lancaster. (Dugd. Bar. ii. 200.)

Line 6. *the duke of Awmarle he made duke of York.*—The dukedom of Aumarle was never restored to the earl of Rutland; and he had succeeded his father as duke of York Aug. 1, 1402. He is called duke of York by our author before this, under 1405. *See page 34.*

Line 9. *Hoggis.* Le Hogue.

Line 10. *the lorde Hambe.*—*Hamby,* Rawl. 173; *Aumbes,* Rawl. 190; *Hambo,* Polychron., &c. The lorde de *Hambre* was employed by the king and Burgundians against the Armagnacs (Monstrel. i. lxxxv.): and the lord de *Rambures,* master of the cross-bows, was sent to stop the ravages of the English reinforced garrison of Calais (Mons. i. xcvii.) this year, 1412. Perhaps one of these is intended.

Line 16. *ser Johan Beaufort, erl of Dorset.*—A mistake: *John* Beaufort,
eldest son of John of Ghent by Katharine Swynford, was created earl of
Somerset 20 Ric. II., and *marquis* of Dorset, and marquis of Somerset,
21 Ric. II.: he was captain of Calais, and died on Palm Sunday, March 16,
1410, 11 Hen. IV. *Thomas* Beaufort, youngest son of John of Ghent, was
chancellor of England 11 Hen. IV., and in 13 Hen IV. (as in the text) was
advanced to the title of earl of Dorset: and in 4 Hen. V. created duke of
Exeter for life. (Dugd. Bar. ii. 121-125.)

Line 30. *entrete him to resigne the croune to prince Harri*—This the
king refused, and although "horribiliter aspersus leprâ, statim equitavit
per magnam partem Angliæ, non obstante leprâ supradictâ." (Eulogium.)
Compare the interview between the king and prince. (Stowe, 339-341;
also Shakspere, Henry IV. Part II. Act 4, Scenes 10 and 11.)

Page 38, line 4. *yburied in Crichirche of Cauntirbury.*—Henry IV. died
on Monday, March 20th, 1413, in the fourteenth year of his reign. (Sir
H. Nicolas's Chronology; Stowe, &c.) His body was conveyed by water to
Feversham, and from thence by land to Canterbury, "with moche torche-
lighte," where he was buried in the cathedral. (Rawl. 190, &c.) Clement
Maydestone gives a strange story, which he heard a person tell his father
Thomas Maydestone, that as the body of king Henry was being carried
by water to Feversham a storm arose, and the body was thrown into the
sea by this stranger and two others, and the waves subsided upon the body
being thrown out. The storm scattered the eight boats containing members of the nobility which followed in procession, and these men carried
the splendid coffin on to Canterbury where it was buried Hence the
monks say, " The *sepulchre* of Henry IV. is with us, but his *body* is not."
(Anglia Sacra, ii. 372.)

Page 39, line 7. *translatid his body fro Langley vnto Westmynstre.*—We
slander the noble character of Henry V. if we do not take this as a proof
that he believed in the *death* of Richard. Henry feared no enemy, and
had released the earl of March, who had been prisoner all his father's
reign. Issue Roll, Mich. 1 Hen. V., Feb. 20, contains payment for a

" horsbere," a coffin, and other necessary things for the removal of the
body of Richard late king of England, 4*l.*

Line 15. *Fikettis'feld.*—" In quendam campum, vocatum Fykettefelde
non procul a Westmonasterio." (Elmham, 31.) In Issue Roll, Mich.
1 Hen. V., are payments for the arrest of Lollards: especially to one constable for seizing Lollard books in the house of a *parchment-maker;*
another for searching the house of William, the *parchment-maker*, in Smithfield, where sir John Oldcastle dwelt.

Line 21. *parlement at Westmynstre.*—This parliament commenced
Nov. 19th, at Westminster: there had been a parliament before this year
at Leicester, April 30.

Page 40, line 22. *Kitcaux.*—The old district of Caux lay on the right
bank of the Seine, and took its name from the ancient Caletes. It
included that triangle of country formed with the British Channel and
the Seine, by drawing a straight line from St. Valery on the coast to
Meulan on the Seine. " There is a point which advances into the sea,
called the Cape of Caux." (Brice's Geog. Dic.) Stowe fixes the landing
at " Kedicaux, in Normandie, which is betwixt Hereflete (Harfleur) and
Humflete (Honfleur); scarcely three leagues (so Elmham) from Hereflete."
Kitcaux is universally named as the place in the " Brute " Chronicles.

Line 25. *commaundid his gonners to bete down the wallis.*—" And there
he plaid at tenys * with them that were in the towne . . . . and alas that
eny soche ballis (*i.e.* gon-stonys) were made, and cursid the tyme that
ever they were begon!" (Rawl. 190, f. 156 b. &c.; Chronicles of King
Henry V., Claudius A. viii. &c.) Guns had been in partial use from
about 13 Ed. III. (Bree's Cursory Sketch, i. 136); yet, according to Speed,
they were first used in England at the siege of Berwick Castle by

* Alluding to the present of tennis-balls said to have been sent by the Dauphin to
Henry. " Somewhat in scorne he sent to the kyng a tonful of tenys ballis, for to play him
withal and his lordis, and said that hit become hym better than to mayntayne ony werr."
(Rawl. 190, &c.; see Poem on the Siege of Harflet and Battle of Agyncourt, Hearne's
Elmham, 359.)

Henry IV., 1405 (p. 775), where the discharge of one large piece of
ordnance caused the surrender of the fortress. (Also Stowe, 333; see
Appendix, p. 140.)

Page 41, line 3. *watir of Swerdis.*—So Ashmole, 791, &c. "The river
of Ternoise, called the river of *Swords*." (Tyler's Henry V. ii. 163.)

Line 23. *euery Englishe manne knelid doun, and put a litille porcion of
erthe in his mouthe.*—"In remembrance that they were mortal, and made of
earth, as also in remembrance of the Holy Communion." (Stowe, 349.)

Page 42, line 7. *erl of Narbonne.*—"The earl of Naverne." (Claudius, A. viii. &c.) "The count de *Nevers*, brother to the duke of Burgundy." (Monstr.) A few months after this, count de *Narbonne*, as admiral
of the French fleet, attempted to recapture Harfleur: he was killed at the
battle of Verneuil, 1424.

Line 18. *ioie and worshippe.*—He "landed at Dover, in Kent, with
alle his prisoners in saftee, thankede be Jhesu: and so come to Caunterbury, and so rood forth thoruȝ Kent the nexte wey to Eltham, and there
he restede him, til he wolde come to Londoun. And thanne the mayr of
Londoun, aud the aldermen, shereffes, with alle the worthi comeners and
craftes, comen to the Blakeheth, weel and worthily arayed, to welcome
oure kynge with divers melodies; and thanked Almyȝti God of his gracious
victorie that He had shewed for hym. And so the kyng and his prisoners
passede forth bi hem, til he come to seynt Thomas Waterynge. And
then ther mette with him alle religious with processione, and welcomede
hym. And so the kyng come ridyng with his prisoners thoruȝ the citee of
Londoun; where that ther was shewede many a fayr syȝt at alle the
coundites, and at the Crosse yn Chepe, as yn hevenly araye of aungelle,
archaungelle, patriarkes, prophetis, and vergines, with divers melodies,
sensying and syngyng to welcome oure king: and alle the coundites
rennyng wyn. And the kyng passed forth unto seynt Powles; and there
mette with hym xiiij. bisshoppes cenersede and mytrede with sensers to
welcome the kyng, and songen for his gracious victorie, 'Te Deum
Laudamus.'" (Rawl. 196; Claudius, A. viii. &c.)

Line 19. *Sigismund, the emperour.*—The " Acts of Council," 4 Hen. V., give the arrangements for his reception. A muster of troops was to receive him at Calais, and the " clerk of the navy " was to have ships in readiness to convey the emperor and suite into England. At Dover, the duke of Gloucester, earl of Salisbury, &c. were to receive him; at Rochester, the constable and marshal of England, &c.; at Dartford, the duke of Clarence, earls of March, Huntingdon, &c. The mayor, aldermen, and notables of London were to welcome him at Blackheath; and the king himself midway between Deptford and Southwark, or at St. Thomas Watering. " Ther they kissed togedras and brasede eche other: and thanne the kyng toke the emperour bi the hande, and so they come ridyng throu; the citee of London vnto seynt Poules; and ther they lighte and offrede, and alle the bisshoppes stoden cenersed with censeres in here handes censwinge. And thanne they toke here hors and riden to Westmynstre." (Rawl. 196, 216; Ashmole, 793, &c.)

Page 44, line 1. *the king brou;te him to Caleis.* — The Issue Roll, Easter, 4 Hen. V., contains payments for guns, gunpowder, &c. for the king's voyage: payments for Sigismund and the duke of Holland, with their retinues, at Westminster; and for the emperor's household removing from Westminster to Leeds Castle while visiting England. All knights, esquires, valets, and others of the king's retinue were to be at Dover by August 18, to accompany the king, with their best equipments, to Calais, upon causes concerning the whole commonalty, July 23. " To our lord the king in his chamber:—In money paid for carriage of tents ornamented with gold and cloth of arras, with hangings and sides of arras, and other appurtenances, for the king and emperor to dwell in at Calais during their stay, 20l. July 29." (Devon's Issue Roll.)

Line 7. *Counselle of Constaunce.*—The council lasted from Nov. 16, 1414, to April 22, 1418. In the 41st session (Nov. 11, 1417), cardinal Colonna was elected pope as Martin V. in room of the three rivals, Benedict XIII. and Gregory XII. (before deposed by Pisa) and John XXIII. successor to Alexander V. who had been appointed by the council of Pisa. The *five nations*—Italy, Germany, France, Spain, and England, assisted, each by six representatives, in the election of Colonna. Before this council, the *name* of a "nation," and the other privilege in the text, " had been delayed and letted from England by men of other nations for envy." (Stowe, 352.)

Page 45, line 16.   *Louers.*—Louviers.

Line 31.   *Baious.*—Bayeux.

Page 46, line 3.   *Valeys Newelyn.*—Mentioned as one place; so in the chronicles generally.   *Valeys*, Falaise?   *Newelyn*, " Castrum de *Neweley* Anglicorum industriâ subjugatur." (Elmham, 116.)

Line 12.   *Cessy*, Seez.   *Launson*, Alençon.   *Belham*, Bellesme.

Line 14.   *Pount large.*—Pont de l'Arche.

Page 47, line 20.   *Roon.*—This famous siege has been celebrated in a long old English poem, occurring in three manuscripts of the Brute; namely, MSS. Harl. 753 and 2256, and one at Holkham (No. 670). It has been printed in the " Archæologia," xxii. 350-398, by sir Frederick Madden, 1829.

Line 6.   *the dolfyneȝ ambassiatours.*—The king had meditated an alliance with the dauphin, against the duke of Burgundy.   Ambassadors were appointed to treat, Oct. 26, 1418, 6 Hen. V. (See a document relative to the alliance, Acts of Council, ii. 350-358.)

Page 49, last line.   *Bokende Villers.*—From Pontoise the king " sent the duke of Clarence with a chosen power of men to Paris, to view the situation and strength thereof; before which city when he had tarried certain days, and had seen all that him likid, and that none of the Frenchmen would issue out of the city to fight with him, he returned to the king and ascertained him of all that he had seen.   On the 18th August king Henry with his host departed from Pontoise; and because the *castle of Bokinvillers* had done certain inhuman cruelties to the king's land . . . . he assalted the same castle." (Stowe, 358.) The castle surrendered from dread of Henry's name. (Titus Livius, 77 ; see also Elmham, 233.)

Page 51, line 32. *duke of Clarence was slayn.*—At the battle of Beaujé, March 22nd, 1421. (Monstrelet.)

Page 52, line 2. *crouned at Westmynstre.*—Fabyan has preserved a full account of the marvellous banquet of fish on this occasion. There is also a tolerably full account of it in Rawl. 173; different from Fabyan's, but agreeing with him nearly in the description of the dishes, though not giving Fabyan's explanation of the "sotilties."

Line 3. *At midsomer.*—By letters patent from Dover, June 10, 1421, 9 Hen. V. the king appointed the duke of Bedford, as before, lieutenant of England, and was himself at Rouen on the 17th of that month. (Rymer, x. 129, 131.)

Line 13. *buried at Westmynstre.*—See the account of the funeral procession from the Bois de Vincennes to Westminster, in Stowe, 362-3. The king's body, embalmed and closed in lead, was laid in a "chariot drawn by four great horses: and above the dead corpse they laid a figure made of boiled hides or leather, representing his person as nigh as could be devised, painted curiously to the similitude of a living creature; upon whose head was set an imperial diadem of gold and precious stones, on his body a purple robe furred with ermine, and in his right hand he held a sceptre royal, and in his left hand a ball of gold, with a cross fixed thereon." The Issue Roll, Easter, 10 Henry V. contains the following entries: "Sept. 26. To John Ardern, for 26 tons of Caen stone for the tomb of king Henry V., in the church of Westminster, who is there buried, 12*l.* To Simon Prentct, wax-chandler of London, for divers hearses provided by him at Dover, Canterbury, Hosprynge, Rochester, Dertford, St. Paul's London, and Westminster, for the funeral of the king Henry V. so brought from France into England, 300*l.* 12*s.* 6*d.* To John Ardern, clerk of the king's works, for making the tomb of king Henry V. erected in the church of the blessed Peter, Westminster, who is there buried, 23*l.* 6*s.* 8*d.*" (Devon's Issue Roll.) A silver gilt effigy was placed upon the tomb by order of the queen. The head, which was of massive silver, was broken off in the time of Henry VIII. and the silver plates were also stripped from the body. (Stowe.)

Page 54, line 21. *the duke of Gloucestre...protectoure.*—It had been
provided on Dec. 5, 1422, that the duke of Bedford should be protector of
England and chief councillor whenever he might be in England; but that
in his absence the duke of Gloucester should be protector. (Rymer, x.
261.) On this occasion of the young king's going into France Gloucester
had been formally declared lieutenant of England, April 23, 1430.
(Rymer, x. 458.)

Line 22. *Jacke Sharpe, &c.*—Probably a Lollard insurrection. Priests'
heads were to be as cheap as sheeps'. (Fabyan; Stowe.) Payments were
ordered to be made to the duke of Gloucester, lieutenant, for inquiring into
certain disturbances and punishing Lollards and other heretics in the
midland counties on May 11 (1431), June 12, July 16. (Acts of Council,
iv. 88, 89, 91.) On the next day (July 17) 500 marks were paid to the
duke. (Issue Roll, Easter, 9 Hen. VI.) The Issue Roll (Mich. 10 Hen. VI.)
contains payment to the duke of Gloucester for executing Sharp and sup-
pressing his rebellion. Sharp is there called "the most horrible heretic
and impious traitor to God and the lord the king." Also 20*l.* were paid
to the informer against "William Perkyns, who calling himself Jack
Sharp was making a disturbance at a certain place in Oxford." (Feb. 16,
10 Hen. VI.)

Line 28. *the lord Fitz Watier...was...drounde.*—Nov. 25th, 1432.
(Stowe.) Dugdale (i. 223) does not mention the circumstance: according to whom his will was proved Nov. 10, 1432. This lord Fitz Walter
had been a valiant knight under Henry V. In the 9 Henry V. he was
taken prisoner at the battle of Beaujé, when the duke of Clarence was
killed. He had been joined with the earl of Mortayne in the command of
troops then sent into France.

Line 30. *Dope.*—Dieppe.

Page 55, line 5 —*saint Kateryne; day vnto Sheoftide.*—St. Katharine's
day was Nov. 25. "The 25th Nov. to 10th Feb." (Fabyan; Holinshed·
Stowe.) Feast of St. Andrew's, Nov. 30th to Feb. 14th. (W. Worcester.)
Sheoftide must be for *Shrovetide.* Shrove-Sunday, 1434, was Feb. 7th.

Page 56, line 12. *a prest called ser Richard Wyche.*—"Vicar of Hermets-worth in Essex or Middlesex [Harmondsworth in the latter county], sometime vicar of Dertford in Kent, who had before abjured, was burnt on the Tower hill the 17th June." (Stowe, 378.) Stowe has taken his account of the "ashes" of Rychard Wyche from our author. "Richard Wiche, priest, mentioned both in Robert Fabian, and also in another old English chronicle borowed of one Perminger. What his opinions were they doe not expresse." (Foxe's Acts and Monuments, 676.)

Page 57, line 3. *the iiij. ordris of freris.*—They are thus mentioned in cap. 17, stat. 4 Hen. IV., which provides that infants under fourteen years of age shall not be received into any of the four orders of friars without the consent of their parents or guardians: Friars Minors, Augustines, Preachers, and Carmelites. The provincials or principals of the four orders were to make oath to observe the statute. (Stat. Realm, ii, 138.)

Line 5. *maister Roger Boltyngbroke*, to page 60, line 25, *livid not long aftir.* —Stowe has taken his account of Bolingbroke and dame Eleanor Cobham chiefly from this passage. Compare the later writer W. Worcester's account of Bolingbroke, Eleanor Cobham, and the Witch of Eye. (460, 461.) It will be observed that Stowe has altered the date of the year in the text: yet he still says that July 25th was Sunday. The dates on pages 59, 60, are correct for 1441.

Line 28. *sownyng.*—Signifying, sounding.

Line 30. *fledde be nyҙte in to the sayntewary.*—On July 19th, "vigilia sanctæ Margaretæ" (W. Worcester), but 27th in this Chronicle. High treason was not debarred from the privilege of sanctuary until 26 Hen. VIII. cap. 13. This defect in the law a papal bull taught Henry VIII. in part to remedy, and he might appoint keepers to such persons to prevent their escape. (Seymour's Survey, ii. 592.) An inference from the text would be that the sanctuary was the common resort of persons suspected to be treasonous. Even sacrilege, which was considered a greater crime, we find *prohibited* from sanctuary by the 32 Hen. VIII., although it had been forbidden shelter by the laws of Edward I. (Fleta, i. 69): a proof that sacrilegious persons were protected, and that the privilege of sanctuary was much abused. From 32 Hen. VIII., when eight sanctuaries only were retained, and great offences were debarred from them, until 21 James I., when all were abolished, they became the resort of debtors; and in Elizabeth's reign an oath and order of admission were introduced to place some little obstacle in the way of those who sought shelter simply to defraud their creditors. (Stat. Realm; Strype's Stowe; Seymour.)

Page 58, line 12. *of heresy.*—This seems to show that Lollardry was one of the charges. The treason was endeavouring to compass the king's death, by making an image of him in wax, and gradually consuming it, &c. (See Fabyan.)

Line 16. *she was committed to the warde of sir John Stiward, &c.*— There are several payments on the Issue Roll, Mich. 22 Hen. VI., relative to her custody. She had been deprived of her dowry. (Rot. Parl. v. 135.) She was sent to Chester Castle (Issue Roll, Feb. Mich. 20 Hen. VI.;) thence removed to Kenilworth Castle, Oct. 26, 1443, 22 Hen. VI. (Rymer, xi. 45.)

Line 25. *to enquire of al maner tresons, &c.*—" To divers doctors, notaries, and clerks, lately by the king's command laboriously employed respecting a superstitious sect of necromancers and persons charged with witchcraft and incantations. In money paid them by the hand of master Adam Moleyns, in discharge of 20*l*. which the said lord the king commanded to be distributed among them, to have by way of reward 20*l*" Issue Roll, Mich. 20 Hen. VI. (Devon's Issue Roll.)

Page 60, line 7. *wherynne she was al her lif after, &c.*—" May 15th. To Ralph lord de Sudeley, constable of the king's castle of Kenilworth, to whom the lord the king, on Dec. 5th last past, committed the custody of Eleanor Cobham, for whose security and safe custody the said lord de Sudeley continually had twelve persons in attendance, viz. one priest, three gentlemen, one maid, five valets, and two boys: which said Ralph received . . . . daily for himself 6*s*. 8*d*. per day; for the said priest, two gentlemen, and one gentleman, each of them 8*d*. per day; and for the said maid and each of the said valets 6*d*. per day; and for each of the said boys 4*d*. per day. And, moreover, the said Eleanor received for her daily support 100 marks yearly. . . . . By writ, &c. 33*l*. 6*s*. 8*d*." (Devon's Issue Roll, Easter, 22 Hen. VI.) From Kenilworth Castle she was removed by an order of council to sir John Stanley, to be imprisoned in the Isle of Man. (Acts of Council, vi. 51, July, 24 Hen. VI. 1446.) Afterwards she was brought back to London. (Issue Roll, Easter, 25 Hen. V. July.)

Line 13. *Roger Bolyngbroke*, &c.—Feb. 24th, Barthol. Halley, one of the valets of the crown, received 10*l*. in discharge of 20*l*. for expenses attending the custody of Roger Bukbroke, upon whom the laws were executed—hire of horses, boats, bed, food, drink, &c. as well for himself as for the said Roger and two attendants during eight weeks six days. (Devon's Issue Roll, Mich. 20 Hen. VI.) This man was also called Onley. (Hardyng; Lambard.)

Page 61, line 6. *And the Sunday next before Witsuntide the xxiiij. day of May.*—There is a confusion in the Chronicle here between the proposition which the earl of Suffolk made at the treaty of Tours for a marriage between Henry VI. and Margaret of Anjou (Monstrelet, Stowe, Rapin, Carte, &c.), and the proxy-marriage which took place between Margaret and the earl of Suffolk for Henry VI., not earlier than, and no doubt in, November. (Stowe, Rapin, Carte.) I am indebted to Mr. Durrant Cooper for the following particulars, communicated to me through the kindness of Mr. Nichols —From the Issue Rolls of Exchequer it appears that in negociating the treaty of Tours for a truce (which was agreed to on the 25th May, and ratified 27th June), sir Thomas Hoo, one of the commissioners with the earl of Suffolk, whose history Mr. Durrant Cooper has been investigating, embarked on the 22nd April, and was paid 20*s*. per day from that day till 27th June, when he had returned. (Issue Roll, Easter Term, Sept. 30th, 23 Hen. VI., and 20th July, same term and year, and 16th July, Easter, 22 Hen. VI.) [According to our chronicler the commissioners started about the end of February or beginning of March.] On the 6th July three messengers were appointed from Henry to Margaret: Robert lord Roos, sir Thomas Hoo, and Garter King at Arms. On the 23rd July Hoo drew 91*l*., and also (Issue Roll, Easter, 22 Hen. VI.)

26*l*. 13*s*. 4*d*. on account of his expenses, and started only on the 26th August, landing again in England, in company with the queen and others, on 11th April, 1445, being absent half a year and fifty-one days. The earl and countess of Suffolk did not start from England till 5th November, 1444, and were absent 157 days. (Issue Roll, Easter, 23 Hen. VI. 20th July.) These facts satisfactorily show that the proxy-marriage cannot have taken place much before the middle of November. The only matter in the Issue Rolls, Mr. Durrant Cooper observes, which in any way appears to confirm the chronicler's date for the marriage, is an entry on July 23rd, Easter, 22 Hen. VI:—" To Robert baron Roos, Thomas Hoo knt., and Garter King at Arms, whom the king sent to France towards ' his most dear consort,' by the hands of Stephen Kyrkeby his chaplain, &c. 26*l*. 13*s*. 4*d*." In Devon's Issue Roll are payments to the earl and countess of Suffolk on their journey and residence between Nov. 1444 and April 1445, but he does not print the entry of the 20th July, Easter, 23 Hen. VI., which distinctly states the employment of the earl and countess to have been from the 5th Nov. 1444, and the whole sum paid to them to be 1408*l*. for the 157 days.

Line 12. *but what treson grew vnder tho trewe3.*—At Suffolk's proposition for the marriage of Margaret of Anjou with Henry, during the treaty of Tours, he agreed to the surrender of Anjou and Maine to Réné, king of Sicily, Margaret's father. (Stowe, Rapin; see also further on, p. 68.)

Line 18. *condue* (so written twice).—Conduct.

Line 19. *markeys of Suffolk.*—The earl was advanced to the title of marquis of Suffolk, Sept. 14, 1444; 23 Hen. VI. (Dugdale, ii. 188.)

Line 21. *Humfrey erl of Stafford maad duke of Bukynghame.*—Sept. 14, 23 Hen. VI. 1444. (Dugdale, i. 165.)

Line 25. *Henry erl of Warwic maad duke of Warwic.*—April, 1444, 22 Hen. VI., with precedence of the duke of Buckingham, and place next to the duke of York. The Act of the *next* year (23 Hen. VI.) settled the disputes which had immediately arisen between the two dukes; and from the

2nd Dec. ensuing (1444) they were to take precedency by turns year by year; Warwick to have the first turn. (See Dugdale, i. 248.)

Line 26. *the lord Beaumond maad vicount Beaumond.*—The first person who bore the title of viscount: so created with precedency over all barons, and twenty marks yearly fee out of the county of Lincoln, Feb. 2, 18 Hen. VI. 1440. And in the 23 Hen VI. (the year under consideration) he had grant to himself and heirs male of precedency over all viscounts thenceforth to be created, and also over the heirs of earls; and to rank in all parliaments and meetings next to earls. (Dugd. Bar. ii. 54.

Page 62, line 3. *crowned at Westmynstre.*—The Issue Roll, Easter, 23 Hen. VI. contains several payments relative to the coronation. One to minstrels of the queen's father, king of Sicily. "June 18. To 5 minstrels of the king of Sicily, who lately came to England to witness the state and grand solemnity on the day of the queen's coronation, and to make a report thereof abroad, to each of them 10*l.* of the king's gift, by way of reward, 50*l.*" Again, to 2 minstrels of the duke of Milan on the same errand, 5 marks to each, 6*l* 13*s.* 4*d.* To John de Surencourt, an esquire of the king of Sicily, and steward of the queen's household abroad, who came previously to the queen's reception to witness the solemnity of her coronation and to report the same, 33*l.* 6*s.* 8*d.* To "John d'Escoce, an esquire of the king of Sicily, who, as a true subject of the queen's father, left his own occupation abroad, and came in the queen's retinue to witness the solemnity of the day of her coronation; in money, &c. by writ, &c. 66*l.* 13*s.* 4*d.*" (Devon's Issue Roll.)

Page 62, line 12. *the parlement at saint Edmundis Bury.*—This parliament was first summoned for Westminster, but as its object was the condemnation of Gloucester (a favourite in London), the place of meeting was altered to Bury St. Edmund's. (Carte, ii. 727.) Upon the duke's arrest, immediately after his arrival at Bury, reports were sent abroad that he had purposed the death of the king, and liberation of his duchess Eleanor Cobham from Kenilworth Castle. On these charges his retainers were afterwards tried and condemned. But the charge in the text, that he was engaged in a conspiracy with the Welsh, seems

likely to have been brought against him, for the statute passed at this
same parliament revives and confirms all the rigorous laws made
against the Welsh; indeed nothing else was done in it (Stat. Realm,
ii. 344.)

Line 19. *ordeyned that euery lorde sholde come . . . . withe strengthe.*—
So with the memorable parliament, 21 Ric. II. The Suffolk militia were
ordered out in full force, to the number of 40,000 (Appendix, p. 116), to
guard all the roads round Bury: the distances they came prove the
stringency of the muster.

Page 63, line 7. *he deide for sorou.*—Stowe has borrowed our author's
words. The date for this event is given Feb. 28th (see Carte, Lingard);
24th (Fabyan, Holinshed, Stowe): but Richard Fox's circumstantial
narrative almost *fixes* it on Thursday 23rd (Appendix, p. 117.) According to our chronicler the duke was murdered (see next page, l. 22):
although in this passage he speaks cautiously. His knowledge of a "prive
conclusioun," on the part of the government, "the whiche as yit is not
come to the knowlege of the commune peple," is rather remarkable. The
Yorkists almost always declared the duke was murdered. (See the Articles, p. 88.) Whethamstede (365, &c.) abbot of St. Alban's, says he
died a natural death: Richard Fox, in the Appendix (117), implies the
same. These two monks of St. Alban's must be considered as high authorities. Fox wrote but a few months after the duke's death, and probably
assisted at his funeral. His death is told naturally. Fox calls him " the
good duke," and is not likely to have kept back from his monastery,
through fear, any particulars of the death of their common patron. The
duke granted the priory of St. Nicholas, Pembroke, to the abbot and convent of St. Alban's, (see the charters in Whethamstede, Aug. 21 Hen. VI.,
311–316,) to pray perpetually for his soul. (Rot. Parl. v. 253, 307.) It
seems he had first (April, 21 Hen. VI.) intended it for the chapter of Salisbury. (Acts of Council, v. 266.) The fullest particulars of the duke's
funeral are given in the Appendix, and it is thought that the following
document may be considered interesting enough to appear in this place.
It is from Claudius A. viii. f. 195.

" In this cedule be conteyned the charges and observances appointed by the noble prince Humfrey, late duke of Gloucestre, to be perpetuelly boren by thabbot and conuent of the monasterie of seint Albone.

"First, the abbot and conuent of the seid monasterie haue payd for makynge of the tumbe and place of sepulture of the seid duke withinne the seid monasterie abcue the summe of . . . cccc.xxx.iij *li*. vj *s*. viij *d*.

"Item, to ij. monkes prestes dayly seiynge messe at the auter of sepulture of the seid prince, euerich of them takynge by j. day, vj *d*. Summe therof by j. hole yere is . . . . xviij *li*. v *s*.

"Item, to thabbot ther yerly the day of anniuersary of the seide prince attendynge his exequyes ther . . . . xl *s*.

'Item, to the priour ther yerly the same day in like wyse attendynge . . . . **xx** *s*.

"Item, to xl. monkes prestes yerly, to euerych of them the same day vj *s*. viij *d*. Summe therof . . . . xiij *li*. vj *s*. viij *d*.

"Item, to viij. monkes not prestes yerly the seid day, to eueryche of them iij *s*. iiij *d*. Summe therof . . . . xxvj *s*. viij *d*.

"Item, to ij. ankresses, j. at sent Petures chirche, another at sent Michael's, the seid day yerly, to eueryche xx *d*. Summe . . iij *s*. iiij *d*.

"Item, in monie to be destribut to pore peple ther the seid day yerly . . . . xl *s*.

"Item, to xiij. pore men berynge torches the seid day aboute the seid sepulture . . . . ij *s*. ij *d*.

Item, for wex brennynge dayly at his messes and his seid anniuersary, and of torches yerly . . . . vj *li*. xiij *s*. iiij *d*.

"Item, to the kechen of the conuent ther yerly in releef of the gret decay of the liuelode of the seid monasterie in the marches of Scotlond, whiche before tyme hathe be appointed to the seide kechyne . ix *li*."

Page 64, line 2. *maister Adam Moleyns.*—This bishop, in conjunction with sir Robert Roos, as king's commissioner, delivered up Maine to Charles VII., March, 1448; and, according to W. Worcester, was murdered for his share in that unpopular business. It was also said that the duke of York had a hard in his death. (Stowe, Gibson.) He was succeeded by the celebrated Reginald Pecock.

Line 10. *William Ascoghe.*—Stowe has taken his account of the murder of Ascoth from this manuscript. According to Thomas Gascoigne he was made king's confessor, being the first bishop that held that office. He had also been clerk of the king's council. (See Godwin's Cat. of Bishops.)

Page 64, line 23. *And this same yeer, in the moneth of May*, to page 68, line 9, *harm to meny persone*;.—Stowe's account of Cade's insurrection, *partly* from our author, is very interesting and full. In the "Issue Roll" are several payments relative to the capture of John Mortimer, alias Jack Cade: and there is a compensation to the duke of York for jewels stolen from him by this rebel—a first-sight argument, at least, that the duke had not secretly urged on his rebellion. The Issue Rolls prove the serious nature of the insurrection. The following entry occurs: Easter, May 17, 31 Hen. VI. "To Lancaster king of arms, who . . . . with great speed rode from Leicester to London, Daventry, and divers places, in which journey he injured two horses worth 8*l.* and moreover paid for the hire of other horses 40*s.*; by which riding he was a loser, &c. 26*l.* 13*s.* 4*d.*" However, the date of the entry shows no hurry was made to remunerate him. The Acts of Council, vi. 96-99, 101, July 12 to Aug. 25, 28 Hen. VI. contains several orders for seizing property stolen by the Captain of Kent, gold, silver, cloth of arras, &c.; payments for his arrest, &c. Also an order to treasurer and chamberlain of exchequer to deliver to master Andrew Holes, keeper of the privy seal, who was about to undertake a journey for the king, and was "destitut of hors, six horses lately belonging to that traitour calling himself captain of Kent, by way of lone" On the insurrection see sir H. Nicolas's Preface to vol. vi. Acts of Council, xxvii. xxviii.

Line 24. *a ribaude.*—A ruffian. (French, *ribaud*, deriv. *hrid*, pugna, *balldr*, audax. Todd from Ihre.) The derivation gives the history of the word. Originally, in a *good* sense, it was applied to stout, brave, tried soldiers; the word degenerated and became the description of rapacious, lawless fellows, bandits, libertines, &c. Perhaps was never used in a good sense in England, but, with *ribaudry*, had a low, licentious meaning. (See Dict. de Furetiere, Richelet.)

Page 66, line 15. *Kyllyngworth.*—Kenilworth.

Line 26. *brigaundyne5.*—A coat of mail; a scale armour, very light and pliable. (See Halliwell's Archaic Dict.) But here it seems to mean *greaves; " a pair of"* greaves. The *coat* was of blue velvet.

Line 27. *a gilt salat.*—Salad, a helmet.

Line 31. *the lord Say.*—A literary character, if there is any foundation for Shakspere's anachronism, so cleverly introduced. (Compare Henry VI. pt. ii. act 4 scene 8.) If this is the case, it will account for Gibbon's satisfaction in proving his descent from this lord Saye. (See Memoir, Miscell. Works, 4to, 1769, i. 6.) Lord Saye had been made sheriff of Kent, 15 Hen. VI.

Last line, note.—So also Fabyan: " Thanne vpon the morne, beyng the iij. day of Julye and Fridaye, the saide captaine entred against the cytie."

Page 68, line 15. *menu5id.*—Diminished.

Line 26. *at instaunce and petition of the said Commune5.*—On Feb. 7th, 1450, 28 Hen. VI. nine articles were exhibited by the Commons against Suffolk. He was charged with having attempted to dethrone the king— having procured the liberation of the duke of Orleans—having, " while oon of youre ambassiatours to youre saide adversarie Charles callyng hymself kyng of Fraunce, above his instruction and power to hym by you committed, promysed to Reyner kyng of Cicile and Charles d'Aungers his brother, youre grete ennemyes, the delyveraunce of Maunce and Mayne, without the assent or knowyng of other youre ambassiatours:" the loss of these provinces occasioned the loss of Normandy—he had betrayed his country to the French, &c. (Rot. Parl. v. 177–179.) The duke was at this time in the Tower, where he had been committed Jan. 28. (Id. 177.)

Page 70, line 15. *the erle of Shrouesbury was slayne,* &c.—At the siege of Chatillon near Bordeaux; lord Lisle, the earl's eldest son, and sir Edward Hull were also killed, and lord Molins taken prisoner. (Stowe, 397; Dugd. i. 330.) Sir Robert Hungerford, in right of his wife, became lord Molins, 19 Hen. VI., and succeeded his father as lord Hungerford, 37 Hen. VI. (Dugd. ii. 207.)

Line 31. *the erle of Douglas of Scotlonde.*—The murder of William earl of Douglas was the conclusion of a conference with the king at Stirling Castle, Feb. 22, 1452; but did not put an end to the contests between the government and the Douglasses. James, brother of the murdered earl, openly denounced the king, and a battle was fought May 18, 1452, in which the king's troops were victorious. Sir James Hamilton of Cadyow was sent by Douglas to beg assistance from England; but, as the earl could obtain nothing but promises and advice from thence, he was compelled with the troops he had to meet the king near Abercorn; and the desertion of Hamilton and most of his troops obliged the earl, with his family, to seek refuge in England. Douglas made a last attempt, in conjunction with the earl of Northumberland, guardian of the marches, to regain power in Scotland, and found himself defeated by his old ally Hamilton of Cadyow. (Drummond, Hist. Scot. 1655, 54–66.) In Rymer is a safe-conduct for members of the earl's family for two years, to pass over to Calais and return, dated July 16, 1454, 32 Hen. VI. Issue Roll, Easter, 33 Hen. VI. contains the following entry of payment to Douglas for his services:—" To James earl Douglas, to whom the present lord the king, with the advice of his council, on the 4th August [1455], in the 33rd year, granted 500*l.* yearly for the services performed by the said earl to the said lord the king, &c. until the said earl should have recovered or be restored to his inheritance, or to the great property taken from him by the person who calls himself king of Scotland, 100*l.*" (Devon's Issue Roll; see also Rymer, xi. 367.) He never was summoned to parliament.

Page 71, line 24. *gadered priuyly a power of peple, &c.*—From this history it would appear that the king had no idea of the proximity of the Yorkists. The duke must have forced his marches excessively, as his army was collected from the Welsh Marches, and the king, upon hearing of the muster of forces there, had gathered troops and left London. Henry was hastening to Leicester to hold a council, probably on the best way of opposing the duke, and also that the struggle might be away from London, where the Yorkist cause was favoured. The king's first stage was to Watford; the next morning he arrived at St. Alban's, and was surprised by the Yorkists. (Compare Stowe, 398; see also Polydore Vergil, edit. Camd. Soc. p. 95.)

Line 27. *sente to the kyng.*—This demand of the duke of York, with the king's answer, and the duke's address to his troops, are preserved in Stowe. (398, 399.) Somerset is not *expressly* named in the demand, " *deliver such as we will accuse.*"

Page 74, line 30. *in the morow.*—In the morning. The exploit mentioned in the text is perhaps a new fact with regard to Sir Thomas Kyriel.

Page 75, line 2. *dyed the erlle of Deuynshire in the abbey of Abyndoun poysened.* He died upon the feast of St. Blase the Bishop, Feb. 3, according to Dugdale, who neither mentions the place of his death nor his supposed poisoning.

Line 5. *Reynold Pocock.*—Stowe has copied nearly word for word this account of Pecock, adding a list of his works. Reginald Pecock was born in 1390; became Fellow of Oriel College, Oxford, Oct. 30, 1417. He was patronised on account of his learning and worth by Humphrey duke of Gloucester, who called him up to the court. After some few minor promotions, and some years' study of the controversy between the Church and the Lollards, he was promoted to the bishopric of St. Asaph in 1444, and translated to Chichester March 23, 1449. He was deprived in 1457 (as in the text), and sent to the abbey of Thorney, Cambridgeshire, where he was to be confined. He was never to leave his cell; to have one serious person to attend upon him; no books but a mass-book, psalter, a legend, and bible; no paper, pens or ink, &c. From this rigorous confinement he was released by death, probably in 1460. (See Lewis's Life of Pecock).

Page 77, line 26. *laude.*—Laudum. (Wals.) An award, judgment.

Line 29. *amorteysed.*—Amortir. To alienate property in mortmain, *i.e.* to any corporation or fraternity, and its successors. (Cunningham, Law Dic.)

Page 78, line 13. *for certeyne causes and articles.*—See Stowe, 397. Edmund duke of Somerset was imprisoned twice by the influence of the Yorkist party in 1451 and 1453, before the duke of York was made Protector, which was on April 3, 1454. The latter and longer confinement of Somerset was terminated by the king's recovery and resumption of power; and the royal mandate for his liberation from the Tower is dated Feb. 5, 1455. (Rymer, xi. 361.) He was actually liberated, by his own confession, Feb. 7 (362); and from this document we arrive at the approximate date of his confinement (Nov. 1453). He was imprisoned "one hole yere, ten woks, and more." The duke fell at St. Alban's, May 22, 1455.

Line 26. *The xxxvij. yeer.*—This section is copied in Stowe, 404.

Page 79, line 17. *quynȝymes.*—Decima quinta. (So *quatrymeȝ*, p. 48, line 2, decima quarta.) A tax of the fifteenth part of the property of a town or city, &c. (See Cunningham, Law Dic.)

Line 28. *avoutry* —Adultery.

Line 29. *allyed vnto her*, to page 8, line 4, *purpos aboute.*—Copied in Stowe, 404.

Page 80, line 5. *The xxxvij. yere of kyng Harry*, to last line, *tenoure ys thus* —Evidently used, and the language partly adopted, by Stowe, 405.

Page 81, line 1. *Most Crystyne kyng*, to page 83, line 14, *abood there.*— Copied in Stowe 405, 406.

Page 83, line 15. *Thanne was a parlement holden at Couentre*, to page 91, line 23, *influence of bodyes transitory.*—Our author continues to be the basis of Stowe, 406–408. The language is frequently used: the articles sent by the Yorkists to the archbishop of Canterbury and the Commons are given at length; and the first two lines of the ballad set upon the gates of Canterbury are quoted.

Line 16. *they that were chosenne knyghtes of the shyres . . . were enemyes to the forseyde lordes.*—This was the charge brought against this par liament, when its acts were annulled by that of the ensuing year, and it was pronounced a " develish " parliament. (See Stowe, 412.)

Page 91, line 23, marg. *Balat set upponne the yates of Caunterbury.* This curious and interesting ballad would seem to show that the writer of the Chronicle was acquainted with Canterbury: he may have copied this Yorkist effusion from the city gates.

Page 92, line 15. *arn.*—Are in.

Line 22. *flemed.*—Banished, put to flight.

Page 93, Lne 5. *alle to.*—All-to, altogether, entirely (See Judges ix. 53.)

Page 94, line 8. *Thanne the noble erles,* to line 29, *nede were.*—Stowe (408) has much abridged this section. He has omitted mention of the herald from the earls to the Londoners; of the advice of the Lancastrian party among the citizens; and the delegation of twelve aldermen to convey to the Yorkists permission to enter the city.

Page 95, line 1. *Thanne was a conuocacione of the clergy,* to page 97, line 2, *in the Yeeld.*—Abridged in Stowe (408–409).

Line 22. *lorde Audeley.*—John Touchet: he adhered first to the Lan castrian interest, but after his captivity in Calais (see page 84) he became a stanch Yorkist. (See Dugdale, Bar. ii. 29.)

Last line. *lord Kendale a Gascoyne.*—John de Foix, a Gascon by birth, earl of Kendal, viscount Chatillon, and lord de Greilly. He was the son of the famous Gaston de Foix captal de Buch, and was made a knight of the Garter, with his father, by Henry VI.

Page 97, line 3. *The archebyshope of Caunterbury,* to line 8, *departed awey.*—Omitted by Stowe.

CAMD. SOC. 2 D

Line 8. *The bysshop of Herford, a Whyte Frere*, to page 98, line 11, *loged in the bysshop's paleys.*—Followed by Stowe, who copies the address of the earls.

Line 18. *vawewarde.*—Vanward, the forepart.

Page 98, line 13. *Nat longe before this batayle*, to line 18, *robbery.*—Omitted by Stowe.

Line 14. *Furthermore the Saturday*, to page 106, line 16, *protectoure of Englond.*—See Stowe, 409–411. The articles between the king and the duke of York, which are derived from the Rolls of Parliament, are copied from our author, with the exception of the word " lawfully," which Stowe has commented upon in the margin. Sir John Fortescue, in his " Defence of the House of Lancaster against that of York," maintained the illegitimacy of Philippa; but, in his " Defence of the House of York," which he wrote upon his pardon by Edward IV., he refuted his own arguments. Fortescue was chancellor to Henry VI., and accompanied queen Margaret and the prince of Wales in their exile, during which time he wrote his celebrated work, " De Laudibus Legum Angliæ." (See his Introduction to De Laud.) See extracts from Fortescue's " Defensio Juris Domus Lancastriæ," in ".Hereditary Right to the Crown," 234, &c. and App. I. &c.; Lingard, iv. 197. Fortescue's MSS., as has been observed, were lost in the fire of 1731, so destructive to the Cottonian Library.

Page 99, line 30. *kyng Harry the vj^{the} that now ys in to thys tyme.*—A proof that this manuscript was written at least before the *death* of Henry VI., in May 1471: but the most natural inference would be that Henry was *king* while the author was writing these words.

Page 101, line 1. *the yere of oure Lorde M^{l}.cc.*—So written: it should be M^{l}.cc.xlv.

Page 106, line 9. *royalx.*—Rolls.

Line 16. *protectoure of Englond.*—For the third time. On All Saints' day, Nov. 1st, the king, wearing the crown, went in state to St. Paul's, in company with the duke of York, to return thanks for the amicable arrangement between the two factions; and on the Saturday following, Nov. 8th, the duke of York was proclaimed by sound of the trumpet Protector of England. (Hall, Grafton, Pol. Vergil, Stowe, Carte, &c.) The duke had before acted for the king in parliament, by appointment, Feb. 13, 1454 (Rot. Parl. v. 239; Rym. xi. 344); made protector, April 3, 1454 (Rot. Parl. v. 243; Rym. xi. 346); protectorate ended in Feb. 1455. Protector the second time, Nov. 19, 1455 (Rot. Parl. v. 453; Rym. xi. 369; released from that office, Feb. 25, 1456 (Rot. Parl. v. 321; Rym. xi. 373). The duke was killed at the battle of Wakefield, Dec. 31, 1460.

Line 24. *lord Nevyle, brother to the erle of Westmorland.*—Stowe has taken his account of the treachery of lord Neville from this author. John lord Neville was grandson of Ralph first earl of Westmerland, and brother of Ralph then earl. He was killed at the battle of Towton, March 29, 1461, 1 Ed. IV.; and was included in the Bill of Attainder passed in the parliament which commenced Nov. 4 the same year. (Rot. Parl. v. 477, 480.)

Page 107, line 4. *lorde Haryngtone.*—William Bonville: he was grandson to William lord Bonville, who, within two months after this, was executed, after the second battle of St. Alban's. (Dugd. B. ii. 236.)

Line 15. *to reyse peple for to chastyse the peple and rebelles of the North.* There can be little doubt that the document referred to in the foot-note was for this purpose. Edward duke of York was raising forces in the Welsh marches when his father fell at Wakefield. He was at Gloucester when he heard of the duke's death, and then moved to Shrewsbury. On Feb. 2nd, or according to our author Feb. 3rd, he fought the battle of Mortimer's Cross; the next thing we know about him is his entry into London on Feb. 28th. (See page 110, and Stowe, 414.) Margaret had not taken advantage of her victory at Wakefield on Dec. 31, and probably she did not commence her march towards the capital until the beginning of February. It must have been upon hearing of this fresh danger in the

North that this mandate to the duke of York was issued on Feb. 12. The commission directed him to collect all true subjects in Bristol, in the counties of Stafford, Salop, Hereford, Gloucester, Worcester, Somerset, and Dorset, and lead them against *the rebels* in different counties. So the men may have been bound to serve, but there can be no doubt *where* those counties were situated, nor from *what quarter* danger then threatened. The stronghold of the Lancastrians was the North; and from thence Margaret was on her way to London. Though in these times marches were often very rapid, we also find that news could travel very slowly; and the Yorkists, in whose custody the king was, and who used his name to legalise their proceedings, may not have heard * of the approach of Margaret's army before Thursday, Feb. 12, when they thus sent for help, and left London for St. Alban's. This Chronicle describes the royal party as *surprised* by the Lancastrians. (Compare also the account of the *first* battle of St. Alban's, page 71, where the Lancastrians were surprised by the Yorkists.)

Line 16. *And they of the Northe heryng this*, &c.—Margaret commenced her march southward, according to our chronicler, in consequence of the commissions against her issued to sheriffs, &c. Stowe describes her army as composed of " Scots, Welshmen, and other strangers, beside the Northern men." It is to be observed that the march is described as rapid: " they came doune *sodeynly* to the towne of Dunstaple," though they stopped for plunder on the way. Stowe says that Grantham, Stamford, Peterborough, Huntingdon, Royston, Melborne (co. Cambr.), and all the towns, abbeys, and priories as far as Dunstable were pillaged by Margaret's army. (Stowe, 413.) The second battle of St. Alban's was on Shrove Tuesday, Feb. 17th.

Line 24. *the lorde Bonevyle and other*, to the end, page 110.—Stowe has occasionally used the language of the Chronicle, showing that he still followed it.

---

* We find a descent was *expected* as early as Jan. 28th, when the king issued letters to several noblemen, knights, sheriffs, &c. to flock to his standard with forces. (See Acts of Council, vi. 307-310, and our chronicler's statement.)

Page 108, line 20. *The lorde Bonevyle . . . . wolde haue withdrawe him.*
—This cotemporary writer *does* mention the protection promised by the
king to lord Bonville (compare Lingard's note, iv. 133); and, as the Act
of Attainder, 1 Edw. IV. (not printed in the Statutes of the Realm, but
occurring in Rot Parl. v. 476–482) asserts the same, we may consider it
as true. The king was but an instrument. The act says, " Sufferyng
wilfully thoo worthy and good knyghtes, William lord Bonvile and sir
Thomas Kiryell, for the prowesse of knyhthode approved in their persones
called to the order of the Garter, and William Gower squyer, the berer of
oon of his baners, whom to he made feith and assurans, under kynges word
procedyng from his mouth, to kepe and defende theym there from all
hurte," &c. (Rot. Parl. v. 477.) Lord Bonville had been appointed one
of the curators of Henry, with the duke of Norfolk, earls of Salisbury,
Warwick, &c.

Line 26. *ser Thomas Kyryelle.*—Sir Thomas Kyriel of Kent, a celebrated knight in the French wars. In Jan. 1429 he obtained with 400
men a victory over the French under the count de Clermont near Beau-
vais; in 1430 he was taken prisoner by the French, while fighting under
the duke of Burgundy near Guerbigny; in 1431 he was governor of
Beauvoisis castle; put down rebellion in the district of Caux, upon the
death of the duke of Bedford, in 1436; during Lent, 1450, he landed at
Cherbourg with 3,000 English, and took Valonges, &c.; April 12, he
advanced towards Bayeux and Caen, and on the 18th was defeated and
made prisoner by the count de Clermont; on Aug. 28, 1457, he drove the
French from Sandwich; was made a knight of the Garter on Feb. 8, 1461,
with the earl of Warwick and lord Bonville; beheaded Feb. 18, by order
of queen Margaret.

Line 27. *Ser John Nevyle, kyng Harryes chamberlayne.*—Since the
battle of Northampton, in July 1460, the king had been in the hands of the
Yorkists, and new officers no doubt had been appointed. This John Neville,
second son of the earl of Salisbury, was advanced to the title of marquis
Montague, 1 Ed. IV.; and was killed at the battle of Barnet, April 14, 1471.

Line 31. *manas.*—Manace, menace, threat.

Page 109, line 7. *the duchesse of Buckyngham, with other wytty men with her.*—After the queen's victory at St. Alban's, she sent to the mayor of London, desiring him to send Lenten fare for the army. He obeyed; but the citizens stopped the carts he had caused to be laden at Cripplegate, drove back some of the queen's soldiers, who were plundering the suburb, and killed three of them: " Whereupon the maior sent the recorder to Barnet, to the king's councell, there to excuse the matter; and the *duchess of Bedford*, the lady Scales, with divers fathers of the spirituallity, went to the queen to asswage her displeasure conceived against the city. The queene, therefore, at their humble request, by advice of her councell, appointed certaine lords and knights, with 400 tall persons, to ride to the citie, and there to view and see the demeanor of the people; and divers aldermen were appointed to meete them at Barnet, and to convey them to London." (Stowe, 414.) However, tidings of the approach of the young duke of York made the queen think it desirable to retire into the North without applying this test of affection. (See also Grafton, Holinshed.) The *duchess of Buckingham*, whose husband had died July 10, 1460, was probably of the party sent to intercede with the queen, if not the chief of them; it is likely that she possessed great influence with the queen as *godmother to the prince of Wales*. (See page 70.) The duke of Buckingham (grandson of preceding duke) was a child, and remained under the guardianship of Edward IV. (Dugd. B. ii. 167.)

Page 111, line 6. *he hulde a parlement in Irelonde.*—-Dublin, Monday, April 19th. See a letter from the king to the duke of York Custos of England and the Privy Council, dated Dublin, Feb. 1, 1395, 18 Ric. II. (Acts of Council, i. 55.)

Line 12. *sette a parlement at Londone.*—Wednesday, "in quindenâ Sancti Hilarii," Jan. 27, at Westminster. (Rot. Parl. iii. 329.) The duke of Gloucester left Ireland to represent the king's needs after the Epiphany, Jan. 6th. (Knyghton, 2742.) The duke of York had been made Custos of England, Sept. 29, 1394. (Rymer, vii. 789.)

Last line. *maystur John Wyccleef.*—Wiclif died Dec. 31, 1384.

Page 112, line 2. *sire Rycharde Sturry*, &c.—Compare Walsingham, 351.

Line 5. *xij chapytours of eresy.*—Foxe, " Acts and Monuments," edit. 1576, 490–492, gives these Conclusions, with a reference at the end to Wiclif's writings.

Line 23. *vers . . . sette vpon Powles dores.*—These verses are to be found in Foxe (Acts and Mon.), Stowe (Annals); they occur also in Cotton. MS. Vesp. D. IX. f. 51, headed " Versus Lollardorum contra prelatos ecclesiæ ad excitandum dominos temporales contra eos." In line 3 (in text) *Gieʒite Semoni nati. Gieʒite*, i.e. children of Gehazi. Mr. Macray has referred me to the form of that name in the Vulgate, *Giezi* (see 2 Kings, iv. v. *passim.*). In line 4, *Nontiui*, a corruption; Vesp. D. IX. and Foxe, read *Nomine*. In line 5, *populus*, populis. In line 6, *gladiis*, gladios. Foxe gives the following translation:—

> The English nation doth lament
> of Sodomites their sinne
> Which Paule doth playnly signifie,
> by idoles to begyn.
> But Giersites full ingrate
> from sinfull Symon sprong,
> This to defend, though priests in name,
> make bulwarkes great and strong.
> Ye princes, therefore, which to rule
> the people God hath placed,
> With justice' sword why see ye not
> This euill great defaced ?

Vesp. D. IX. gives the following answer:—" Versus cujusdam catholici contra eosdem Lollardorum."

> Gens Lollardorum gens est vilis Sodomorum,
> Errores eorum sunt in mundo causa dolorum.
> Hii sunt ingrati, maledici, Demone nati,
> Quos vos Prelati, sitis dampnare parati.
> Qui pugiles estis fidei, populisque preestis,
> Non horum gestis ignes prohibere potestis.

The same volume contains a long poem against the Lollards (f. 165-

168 b.) beginning, " Presta Jhesu quod postulo, Fac quod in tuo populo
Nulla labes resideat," &c.   At the beginning and end occurs the sentence,
" Dissipa gentes quæ bella volunt Domine Jhesu."

Page 113, line 18.   *And in this same ʒere, there apered in Fraunce,* to the
end, page 115.—Richard Fox has taken this from Walsingham, 351–353.

Line 19.   *Landavencis.*—Landunensis (Wals.).   *Laudunum?* Laon ;
twenty miles N.W. of Rheims; an ancient episcopal see suffragan to that
archbishopric.

Line 22.   *a barbour, called a Moret.*—Morectus ille Barbarus.   He was
general of the Turks at the siege of Constantinople, according to Walsingham.   Bajazet I. sultan of the Turks in 1395, invested Constantinople by
sea and land.   In consequence of this siege Manuel Palæologus, the Greek
emperor, sent ambassadors to, and then visited the courts of Europe to
implore help.   (See note, page 22, line 21.)   Mr. Nichols thinks that
under the spelling *a Moret* is disguised the name *Amurath,* and that *a
barbour* means a native of Barbary, or one so considered.   Though *Amurath* occurred to me, I thus followed the MS. because Richard Fox here
translates from Walsingham.   Knollys's " Hist. of Turks," p. 205, mentions
Temurtases as Bajazet's " great lieutenant in Europe," and as advising the
siege.   *Murtasis* occurs in the Short Chron. at the end of Ducas, " Hist.
Byzant." 196.

Page 114, line 7.   *hure.*—Their.

Line 13.   *sire John duke of Lancastre.*—The dukedom of Guienne had
been conferred upon Lancaster for life, March 2, 1390, 13 Ric. II. (Rot.
Parl. Rymer); but he did not leave England to take possession till late in
September, 1394.   He was recalled in the autumn of 1395, 19 Ric. II.
on account of the unpopularity of his appointment in Guienne.   Richard
Fox, in the text, gives Walsingham's account.   But see Appendix 128,
and Froissart, iv. cap. lxv.

Page 116, line 15. *Lanam.*—Lyneham, ten miles north of Devizes, Wilts.

Page 117, line 19. *Arteys*—So written twice. Arthur Tursey, esquire. (See Stowe, 386.)

Page 118, line 1. *Greye Freres of Babbewede.*—The Grey Friars settled at Bury St. Edmund's about 1257, and fixed themselves in the northwest part of the town, notwithstanding the opposition of the Benedictine monks of the place. In 1363, however, these Grey Friars were removed to a site beyond the north gate, called *Babwell*, where they remained till the Dissolution. (See Tanner's Notitia.)

Line 8. *Berkewey.*—Barkway, Hertfordshire.

Line 20. *hensemen.*—Henchmen, horsemen.

Page 119, line 1. *Sed Abbas*, &c.—See note, page 2, line 22.

Page 121, line 18. *qui nunc comitatum habet.*—The MS. ends in 1413. Philip of Burgundy died in the beginning of 1404, and Margaret his duchess on the Friday before Mid-Lent Sunday the same year. John duke of Burgundy succeeded to the counties of Flanders and Artois. (Monstrel. I. cap. xviii. xxi.)

Line 22. *Rupellâ.*—Rochelle.

Page 123, line 3. *minimum garcionem coquinæ tuæ.*—Perhaps a favourite expression of Richard's. According to Walsingham, he exclaimed to Gloucester and the others at this meeting, " Profecto de vobis omnibus non plus in hâc parte reputo, quam de *coquinæ meæ infimo garcione.*" Knyghton records the same expression used by the king before the deputation of the Commons, who waited upon him at Eltham in the autumn of 1386, to request the dismissal of M. de la Pole.

Page 125, line 18 *duodena miserorum.*—On page 26 we have an instance of a jury swayed by terror.

Page 126, line 23. *Ambianis.*—Amiens.

Page 128, line 24, *Shene.*—Sheen, near Richmond.

Page 130, line 12. *Marchio Dubluniæ.*— For the eight appellants, see note to page 8, line 19, at p. 157. There was no *marquis of Dublin* at this time; the title existed little more than two years.

Page 133, line 6.   *studuit . . . ad Solomonis gloriam pervenire.*—" Solomoni magno in expensis æquiparabatur. (Fordun, 1068.)

Page 135, line 1.   *Lamasiæ.*—Llanvais, or Llamausy, near Beaumaris. This house of Franciscans, or Friars Minor, was founded before 1240. See Tanner's Not., Stevens's Mon.; where also see this form of the word.

Page 136, line 5.   *claiam.*—Cleia, cleta, clades, a hurdle.

Line 19. *Jacobitæ.*—Dominicans, called also Black Friars, or Preaching Friars.

Line 23. *de Mortuo Mari.*—Mortimer.

Last line. *Frater iste qui fratres suos regi accusavit.*—This was the friar of Leicester (see page 24, line 14), who had accused ten of his brethren of exciting the people against Henry IV. The Welsh were devoted adherents of Richard, as an enemy to whom this friar met his fate.

Page 137, line 7.   *de Monte Forti.*—Joanna of Navarre had married John de Montfort, duke of Britany, Sept. 11, 1386; and was a widow and guardian of her son the young duke, on Nov. 1, 1399.

Line 20.   *provocans ipsum ad duellum.*—(See Monstrelet, I. cap. ix.)

Page 139, line 2. *in castro ducis Roseyæ.*—Richard, or rather perhaps the reputed Richard King of England, appears to have been detained first under the custody of Robert III.; after a short time he was delivered to sir David Fleming, lord of Cumbernauld ; upon the death of Robert III. in 1406, the duke of Albany the regent obtained possession of his person, and from that time till his death Richard was a prisoner in Stirling Castle. (See Tytler's Scotland, iii. p. 331.)

Line 12. *parliamentum apud Coventriam.*—Walsingham (369-370) speaks of an unusual tax extorted at this parliament, the accounts of which were ordered to be burnt, that no memorial of it might remain.

Page 140, line 11. *Comes Northumbriæ*, &c.—This section is thus introduced in the "Eulogium," interrupting the narrative relating to the archbishop of York's death.

Line 20. *Coyfy.*—So written; it should be, as Mr. Nichols has informed me, *Coyty*, in Glamorganshire, where there was a castle, the ruins of which remain.

Page 141, line 15. *eereo incendit quandam domum*, &c.—Compare the account of the murder of the duke of Orleans. (Monstrelet, I. cap. **xxxvi.**)

INDEX.

80; letter to the king, 81-85; at Calais, 83 ;
attainted in parliament, 84 ; articles sent to
archbp. and commons by, &c. 86-90; lands at
Sandwich with March and Warwick, 94 ;
governor of London, 95; takes up position
with Yorkists at Wakefield and Sandal, 106;
prisoner at battle of Wakefield, ransomed, beheaded by the people, 107

Salisbury, Alice, countess of, 84

—— sir John, capitally sentenced, 5

Sandal castle, Yorkshire, 106

• Sandwich, pillaged by the French, 74; duke of
Exeter sails from ; exploits of Warwick's
soldiers at, 85, 86; Yorkist earls land at,
94

Saundridge, Herts, king's position there, 107

Saye and Sele, lord, James Fiennes, enmity to
Gloucester, 62, 63 ; committed to the Tower,
65 ; executed by Cade's insurgents, 66, 67,
197

—— William, son of last, at battle of Northampton, 95

Scales, lord, Thomas, defeats Cade's insurgents
on London Bridge, 67; commissioned against
Yorkists of Newbury, 90; besieged in the
Tower of London, 95 ; how he met with his
death, 98

Scotland, king of, James I. besieges Roxburgh
castle ; murdered by duke of Athol, 56

—— James II. murders earl Douglas, 71; killed
by bursting of a gun, 99

Scrope. See Wilts, earl of—York, archbp. of

—— of Masham, lord, Henry, conspiracy and
execution, 40

—— of Bolton? lord, John, with Yorkists at
Northampton, 95

Seez (text Cessy), 46

Sely, sir Bennet, beheaded at Oxford, 21

Senlis, taken, 51

Sens, archbp. of, killed at Agyncourt, 42

Serle, William (text John), his fraud—execution, 30, 178

Shakell, Richard, 1

Sharp, Jack, executed, 54, 188

Sheen, near Richmond, queen Anne dies at, 128

Shelley, sir John, executed, 22

Shrewsbury, battle of—cause of it—altercation
between king and Hotspur, 27, 28, 175, 176;
earl of Worcester beheaded there, 29

—— earl of, John Talbot, surrender of Rouen
to the French, 63 ; slain at siege of Chatillon,
near Bordeaux, 70, 197

—— John, second son of last, killed at Northampton, 97

Sluis, harbour of, 3

Smithfield, 6, 31, 36, 59

Somerset, earl of, John Beaufort, made marq. of
Dorset, 12, 182; conducts his niece to Cologne,
29; challenged to joust, 35 ; dies, 37

—— duke of, John Beaufort, second son of last,
created—dies, 60

—— Edmund, brother of last, arrests duke of
Gloucester, 63, 117; surrenders Rouen, 63 ;
mismanagement in Normandy, 68 ; godfather
to prince of Wales, 70; people's hatred of, 71;
protector — committed to the Tower, 78 ;
leader of Lancastrians at battle of St. Alban's,
71, 199, 200 ; killed, 72

—— Henry, son of last, earl of Mortayne (q. v.),
reconciliation of Yorkists and Lancastrians,
77, 78 ; captain of Calais, 79 ; forced to retire
to Guisnes, 84 ; attempt to bring him back to
England, 85 ; returns, 99 ; battle of Wakefield,
&c. 106, 107 ; money promised to by Londoners, 109

Southampton, conspiracy against Hen. V. there,
40; forces meet at, 44; God's house, 61; earl
of Wilts. plan for escaping the country, 90

Southwark, 34, 42; bishop of Winton's house,
54; the Hart in, 66, 67

Southwell, Thomas, canon of St. Stephen's, Wes-
ton, 57; indicted of treason, 58; dies in the
Tower, 59

Sowdan, sir Percival, 34

Spain (Castille), John king of, vanquished by
Portuguese and English, 3; marries (his son

---

* Descended from the ancient barons de Vesci, and summoned to parliament as lord de Vessy, 24 Jan. 27 Hen. VI. 1449, with limitation of that honour to the heirs male of his body ; being (says sir H. Nicolas Synopsis, 86) the first and only instance of a barony by writ so limited. He died in 1468, when the barony became extinct.

---

† The land of the Western *meres*, not *moors*.

ERRATA.

Page 21, line 19, *for* " and vuto Plasshe," *read* " and led vnto Plasshe."

,, 70, line 16, *after* " saide erle," place the semicolon from preceding line.

,, 124, line 12. *for* " Radcolbrigge," *read* " Radcotbrigge."

,, 134, line 10, *for* " sanctum Paulum," *read* " ad sanctum Paulum."

,, 136, line 6, *for* " suspendaris," *read* " suspenderis."

,, ,, last line, *for* " acensavit," *read* " accusavit."

,, 141, line 3, *for* " xx^{am}," *read* " x^{am}."

London : Printed by J. B. Nichols and Sons, 25, Parliament Street.